THE WATERLOO ARCHIVE

THE WATERLOO ARCHIVE

Previously unpublished or rare journals and letters regarding the Waterloo campaign and the subsequent occupation of France

Volume V
German Sources

Edited by Gareth Glover

Foreword by
Prince Michael of Saxe-Weimar-Eisenach

Frontline Books, London

To Dad
My Eternal Inspiration
Sorely Missed

The Waterloo Archive: Volume V

This edition published in 2013 by Frontline Books,
an imprint of
Pen & Sword Books Limited, 47 Church Street,
Barnsley, S. Yorkshire, S70 2AS
www.frontline-books.com
email info@frontline-books.com

ISBN: 978-1-84832-684-2

A CIP data record for this title is available from the British Library.

For more information on our books, please visit
www.frontline-books.com, email info@frontline-books.com
or write to us at the above address.

Typeset by Palindrome in Stempel Garamond 10½/12 pt

Printed and bound in India by Replika Press PVT Ltd

CONTENTS

ILLUSTRATIONS

Colour Plates

FOREWORD

Considerations

The key to history lies not in history itself but in each individual.
THÉODORE JOUFFROY

Raise high the black flags, my children. No prisoners. No pity. I will shoot any man I see with pity in him.
FIELD MARSHAL GEBHARD VON BLÜCHER AT WATERLOO, ADDRESSING HIS TROOPS

Having been asked, as a direct descendant of Prince Bernhard of Saxe-Weimar, to support volume V of the Waterloo archive, the above quotes came to my mind: they best depict what I felt, when I read the first volume of the Waterloo archive.

Many intelligent analyses were made on the battle of Waterloo, many considerations on its impact on the political development in Europe, on literature, on the arts and on daily life in the nineteenth century. Never ever has the voice of the simple soldiers who took part in this unbelievably cruel event, which changed the face of our continent, mattered. Never ever were those, who took part in the campaign, called into the witness stand of history.

The credit belongs to Gareth Glover that the voices of soldiers and officers of all fighting nations at Waterloo, documented through their very personal and private letters (mostly to their families), can now, for the first time, be heard by the public. The human facets – the suffering, the heroism, the pity and the furore – all this has been the missing link when trying to understand this historical event, the battle of Waterloo.

Prince Bernhard believed in his mission: the rescue of Europe from the devilish and ingenious parvenu Bonaparte. His 2nd Brigade of the 2nd Dutch Division was the first of the Duke of Wellington's forces to arrive at the crossroads of Quatre Bras. Prince Bernhard's brigade held those crossroads, preventing Marshal Michel Ney with the left wing of the French Armée du Nord from taking them before the Duke of Wellington arrived. The successful holding action by the two brigades (the 1st Brigade joined the 2nd later) of the Dutch 2nd Division was one of the most important actions by any of the coalition brigades in the whole of the Waterloo campaign. At the Battle of Waterloo Prince Bernhard commanded the allied forces holding the farms of Papelotte, Frichermont and la Hay, locations of high strategic importance, because from there Prince Bernhard could hinder the French from outflanking Wellington before the Prussians arrived.

Michael, Prince of Saxe-Weimar-Eisenach
Duke of Saxony

ACKNOWLEDGEMENTS

A project of this complexity cannot be accomplished without the willing support of many others. First I must, of course, thank Martin Mittelmacher, who patiently and lovingly translated all of the copious material in the two German volumes, for which he has earned not only my heartfelt thanks but also my total respect for his incredible knowledge of the German troops at Waterloo. Particular thanks must also be offered in this volume to Michael-Andreas Tänzer, who very kindly copied to me a large number of very rare German publications for Martin to translate. My grateful thanks must also extend to the staff of the British Library, who have been incessantly bombarded by me for copies of various publications, and for their granting so freely permission to publish translations of the same. I must also thank Stefan Felleckner, archivist for the County of Gifhorn, for permission to publish the letters of Private Schacht and Lieutenant Hemmelmann of the Gifhorn battalion, originally published in *Erinnerungen an Waterloo: Weg und Schicksal des Landwehrbataillons Gifhorn,* published by Gunter Weinhold in 1985, and to Volkner Schwichtenberg, Managing Director of the Mönch Group, for kindly granting permission to publish translations of excerpts from Joachim Kannicht's book *Und alles wegen Napoleon: Aus dem Kriegstagebuch des Georg von Coulon, Major der Königlichen Legion, und die Briefe seiner Frau Henriette 1806–1815*, published by Bernard & Graefe in 1986. Also to Guntram Muller-Schellenberg, for his permission to publish the extracts of Private Leonhard of the Nassau contingent, which he originally jointly published with the late Peter Wacker in *Das herzoglich-nassauische Militar 1813–1866* (Schellenberg'sche Verlagsbuchhandlung, Taunusstein,1983). But more than anyone else, I must thank my wife, Mary, and children Sarah and Michael for their forbearance and encouragement, as always my work is dedicated to them.

I must also thank Philip Haythornthwaite for his expert help and suggestions regarding this text.

Gareth Glover

INTRODUCTION

Readers of the previous four volumes of the *Waterloo Archive* will already be aware of the reasons why I have embarked upon this crusade to bring into the public domain such a mass of new material relating to the Waterloo campaign and the subsequent occupation of France by the allied forces from 1815–18; however, a short recap for new readers will not go amiss.

A huge amount of material has been written regarding the Waterloo campaign, perhaps more than on any other campaign before or since, so what can possibly be new, and is there anything more to learn? Having spent years surveying the existing material published over the last nearly 200 years, the answer will perhaps be surprising to many: a resounding 'yes'.

In the previous volumes I have explored the archives of Britain and those of our ex-colonial* brothers where much material including art works which have never previously been published were discovered, including some astonishing finds of truly historical significance and I will return to this treasure trove in the final volume, VI, in due course.

But what of volume V? This time I return to the German troops,† who actually formed the majority of the forces present at the Battle of Waterloo including the troops of Nassau, a small German state, some of whose troops actually served in the Dutch army at the battle. Some record of the actions of the troops of the King's German Legion, which was considered as an integral part of the British army and thus partly officered by British citizens, has therefore been published in English, but to a very limited degree. However, this tiny portion of German material has been virtually all that has been available to students of this campaign who did not possess a high level of German language skills until very recently and it is therefore not very surprising that early British histories of the battle have largely sidelined the achievements of the German troops and this stance has been regurgitated by most that have followed. This situation did not

* Canada and Australia proving especially fruitful.

† For the previous material see *Waterloo Archive*, vol. II.

change at all until the 1990s, when Peter Hofschroer[*] published his two-volume version of the campaign from the German perspective, which included numerous snippets of various German documents published for the first time in English to support his view of the campaign; but even this is not satisfactory, as it left much more still to be translated and published and did not provide the whole documents to allow further interpretation. There is, therefore, still a great need to provide an English version of much of the original German source material to aid historians redress this imbalance.

Such a task is truly daunting, not just because of the scale of the task, but also the inordinate amount of time needed by a translator with the appropriate level of language skills and grasp of military history and terminology to produce a coherent, meaningful translation. I made a small venture into this area when I published *Letters from the Battle of Waterloo* in 2004,[†] when publishing the remaining Siborne letters, having cause to obtain translations of the numerous German letters in the files. I experimented with various means but all had their problems; professional translators proved extortionately expensive; charitable organisations which one still felt honour-bound to recompense, or friends and acquaintances who required no fee but forced me to accept interminable delays, were all unsatisfactory. I was thus, perhaps understandably, not very keen to venture into translation work again.

That is, until I had the luck to begin a correspondence with Martin Mittelacher, who is of German extraction, living in retirement in the United States of America and an expert on the Waterloo campaign. He had previously liaised with Peter Hofschroer on his translation work, which also gave me great confidence in his abilities. Having had the audacity to ask him if he would consider translating the vast amount of German material that I was able to obtain from obscure sources and explaining the project, I was overjoyed to hear of his acceptance. Since then Martin has worked tirelessly and diligently to translate all of this material and our combined expertise has been utilised to edit the material and provide learned footnotes.

Much of volume II was derived from *La Belle Alliance: Reports and Information on the Participation of German Troops of Wellington's Army in the Action at Quatre Bras and in the Battle of La Belle Alliance* by Dr Julius von Pflugk-Harttung, Privy Archive Councillor at the State Archive in Berlin, published in German in 1915. This book is a veritable gold mine

---

* *The Waterloo Campaign*, 2 volumes, London, Greenhill Books 1998–9.

† *Letters from the Battle of Waterloo*, London, Greenhill Books, 2004. In this work the 200-odd letters in the Siborne files, not printed by Herbert Siborne, were finally published.

of primary source material from German units. It is truly amazing, and it has been a great loss to many historians that it has never previously been published to any great extent in the English language. Some further material from this source is now printed in volume V, but does not this time form the majority of the book. Again, it is not intended to merely form a translation of Pflugk-Harttung's book and is not published here in exactly the same format. Pflugk-Harttung broke up the reports into sections of his work covering Quatre Bras, the Retreat and the Battle of Waterloo (Belle Alliance). To enable cross-referencing, I have joined these various portions back together to form one coherent report, but have clearly annotated each with the numbers of the letters they come from in his work.

The material has been set out in a very similar format to Siborne's *Waterloo Letters* and the editor's *Letters from the Battle of Waterloo,* for ease of use and all cross references are annotated in the notes virtually making all of these works one huge reference source on the Waterloo campaign.

But as well as Pflugk-Harttung there are many German memoirs of the Waterloo campaign which have been published in Germany over the last two centuries, but they are very rare even in the original German and have never been published in English before, and therefore have never been quoted in English histories of this campaign. The other joy that these memoirs bring is that, unlike the dry, staid and matter-of-fact reports that dominate Pflugk-Harttung's work, these German memoirs equal their British counterparts for grit, earthy humour and derring-do. Now it is truly possible to experience the life of a German soldier during the interminable marches both in blazing sun and in torrential rain, with little, if any, food and water, little rest and no dry clothes. Yet they were still able to perform with professionalism and unquestioned bravery for all those interminable hours of dreadful battle that they endured.

Some highlights from these personal memoirs of the battle published in this latest volume include those by various officers of the King's German Legion, including: Lieutenant Meier, 2nd Light Dragoons, KGL, who gives a fascinating account of the confusion in the final 'great advance' at Waterloo; Baron Estorff, who makes an interesting report on the extensive patrols made by the Bremen and Verden Hussars stationed at Halle* during the Battle of Waterloo; Henry Dehnel, 3rd Line Battalion, KGL, whose memoirs describe in graphic detail how he managed to endure the constant cavalry attacks upon the squares on the ridge that day; Ensign Uslar-Gleichen, 4th Line Battalion, KGL, who vividly describes the intense fighting in the orchard of Hougoumont; Lieutenant von

* Halle is a Walloon name; it is known as Hal in French.

Brandis, aide de camp to Colonel Ompteda, who was fully involved in the fatal advance in which Ompteda and his battalion were unnecessarily sacrificed and Lieutenant Biedermann, 2nd Light Battalion, KGL, who is another invaluable eyewitness to the heroic defence of La Haye Sainte.

But many other German contingents also fought that day and in this volume there are a number of accounts from officers with the Hanoverian Landwehr Battalions: Lieutenant Bülow of the Bremen Field Battalion and Lieutenant Hemmelmann and Private Schacht of the Gifhorn Landwehr give captivating glimpses of the militia units present, which also fought with bravery and tenacity in both the battles of Quatre Bras and Waterloo; Lieutenant von Horst of the Verden Landwehr gives a lively and interesting account of numerous incidents during his capture at Quatre Bras, his subsequent treatment by the French and his personal account of a fleeing Napoleon!

Then, of course, there were the Nassau troops; these troops are represented here by General Kruse's report giving much detail on the actions of the Nassau troops and further engaging material regarding disputed versions of events, such as Prince Bernard of Saxe-Weimar's letter claiming that the Nassau troops were routed in the Papelotte area and the subsequent vehement rebuttal by his own officers. But once again the memoirs of Private Henniger, 1st Nassau Regiment, prove even more compulsive, as he relates the destruction of part of his regiment by cuirassiers during an ill-advised charge on some French artillery. Captain Wirth's memoirs, of the 2nd Battalion, 2nd Nassau Regiment, form another very important witness to the defence of La Haye Sainte farm. But perhaps most significant of all is that of Sergeant Buchsieb, 1st Battalion, 2nd Nassau Infantry, who was fully involved in the defence of Hougoumont and who backs the theory that there were two nearly successful break-ins there. And finally, but not least, there is a truly spellbinding report by General Herzberg actions of the Brunswick contingent, which is incredibly informative and detailed on every aspect of the involvement of this corps during this campaign – even down to the colour of the horses of each senior officer!

A fascinating series of letters culminates this collection, which shows the investigations launched and the explanations given as to the whereabouts of a number of 'missing' Hanoverian regimental and Staff surgeons during the Battle of Waterloo and their subsequent courts martial.

Note

While seeking information on the various officers and men mentioned in these texts it soon became very apparent that there were no lists in

English of the officers of the Brunswick, Hanoverian and Nassau units at Waterloo. Therefore having been fortunate as to gain this invaluable material via the good offices of Ron McGuigan, who was able to supply me with the German sources, I now supply these lists for the first time in English as invaluable resource material.

These details are included in the six appendices to this volume, which will be invaluable to historians of these German troops. They are:

1 Evidence regarding Halkett's capture of General Cambronne
2 The exploits of KGL men at Waterloo who gained the Guelphic Order (additions to Beamish)
3 An officer list for the Brunswick Corps at Waterloo
4 A list of the KGL officers transferred to Hanoverian units in May 1815
5 A list of all officers in Hanoverian units at Waterloo
6 A list of all Nassau officers at Waterloo.

These German reports and memoirs are very often particularly frank and open with regard to the failings of the men concerned, honestly describing mistakes or errors of deployment that led to losses, and there is even naming and shaming both of officers and of men who failed to perform their duties, something that must have happened in every unit involved in such carnage – yet such honesty is virtually unknown within contemporary British accounts.

I am therefore very proud to present this second volume of German primary source material, only small parts of which have ever, to my knowledge, been published in the English language before, both for the use of eminent historians and as well as for those who are simply interested in gaining a greater understanding of that whirlwind campaign which occurred nearly 200 years ago.

Gareth Glover

THE STAFF

No. 1 From La Belle Alliance

Pflugk-Harttung's letter no. 121.
Report of the Duke of Wellington to the king of the Netherlands on the Belgian campaign. Special edition of the Niederländische Staats-Zeitung

S'Gravenhage, Friday, 23 June 1815

On this morning, Major van Hoof and Lieutenant Webster,* adjutants of the Prince of Orange, arrived at the Huis ten Bosch [Royal Palace] and had the honour to deliver to the king's hands the following report:

Waterloo, 19 June 1815†

Sire,
I have the honour to report to your majesty that Bonaparte, having collected the 1st, 2nd, 3rd, 4th, and 6th Corps of the French army, and the Imperial Guard and nearly all of the cavalry on the Sambre and between that river and the Meuse, advanced on the 15th and attacked the Prussian posts at Thuin and Lobbes on the Sambre at daylight in the morning.

I did not hear of these events till in the evening of the 15th; and I immediately ordered the troops to prepare to march, and afterwards to march to their left, as soon as I had intelligence from other quarters to prove that the enemy's movement upon Charleroi was the real attack. The enemy drove the Prussian posts from the Sambre on that day. General Ziethen, who commanded the corps which had been at Charleroi, retired upon Fleurus, and Marshal Prince Blücher concentrated the Prussian army upon Sombreffe, having occupied the villages of St Amand and Ligny in front of his position.

The enemy continued his march along the road from Charleroi towards Brussels and, on the same evening, the 15th, attacked a brigade

* Lieutenant Henry Webster, 9th Light Dragoons, Extra Aide de Camp to the Prince of Orange.

† Pflugk-Harttung's footnote: F. de Bas et T'Serclaes de Wommersom, *La Campagne de 1815 aux Pays-Bas*, III.

of Your Majesty's 2nd Division under the Prince of Weimar, posted at Frasnes, and forced it back to the farm house, on the same road, called les Quatre Bras. The Prince of Orange immediately reinforced this brigade with another of the same division under General Bijlandt, and, in the morning early, regained part of the ground which had been lost, so as to have command of the communication leading from Nivelles and Brussels to Marshal Blücher's position.

In the meantime, I had directed the whole army to march upon Quatre Bras; and the 5th British Division, under Lieutenant General Sir Thomas Picton, arrived at about half past two in the afternoon. It was followed by the light corps of troops under the Duke of Brunswick, and afterwards by the contingent of Nassau.

At this time the enemy commenced an attack upon Prince Blücher with his whole force, excepting the 1st and 2nd corps, and a corps of cavalry under General Kellermann, with which he attacked our post at Quatre Bras. The Prussian army maintained their position with their usual gallantry and perseverance against a great disparity in numbers, as their 4th corps, under General Bülow, had not joined; and as I was not able to assist them as I wished, as I was attacked myself, and the troops, the cavalry in particular, which had a long distance to march, had not arrived. We maintained our position and repulsed all the enemy's attempts to get possession of it. The enemy repeatedly attacked us with a large body of infantry and cavalry, supported by a numerous and powerful artillery; he made several charges with the cavalry upon our infantry, but all were repulsed in the steadiest manner. In this affair, HRH the Prince of Orange, the Duke of Brunswick, Lieutenant General Sir Thomas Picton, Major Generals Sir James Kempt and Sir Dennis Pack, who were engaged from the commencement of the enemy's attack, highly distinguished themselves; as also Lieutenant General Sir C. Baron Alten, Major General Sir C. Halkett, Lieutenant General Cooke, and Major Generals Maitland and Byng, as they successively arrived. The troops of the 5th division and those of the Brunswick corps were long and severely engaged and conducted themselves with the utmost gallantry. I must particularly mention the 28th, 42nd, 79th, and 92nd Regiments and the battalion [brigade] of Hanoverians. Our loss was great, and I have particularly to regret His Serene Highness the Duke of Brunswick, who fell fighting gallantly at the head of his troops.

Although Marshal Prince Blücher had maintained his position at Sombreffe, he still found himself much weakened by the severity of the contest in which he had been engaged, and, as the 4th corps had not arrived, he determined to fall back and to concentrate his army upon Wavre; and he marched in the night, after the action was over. This movement of the marshal rendered necessary a corresponding one upon my part; and I retired the next morning, the 17th, at 10 o'clock, from the farm of Quatre Bras upon Genappe and thence upon Waterloo.

The enemy made no effort to pursue Marshal Blücher. On the contrary: a patrol which I sent to Sombreffe in the morning found all quiet, and the enemy's videttes fell back as the patrol advanced. Neither did he attempt to molest our march to the rear, although made in the middle of the day, excepting by following, with a body of heavy cavalry brought from his right, the British cavalry under the Earl of Uxbridge. This gave Lord Uxbridge an opportunity of charging them with the English Life Guards upon their debouching from the village of Genappe, upon which occasion his Lordship has declared himself to be well satisfied with that regiment.

The position which I took up in front of Waterloo crossed the highways from Charleroi and Nivelles, and had its right wing thrown back to a hollow way, near Merbe Braine, which was occupied, and its left wing extended to a height above the farmstead of La Haye which was likewise occupied.

In front of the right centre, and near the Nivelles highway, we occupied the house and gardens of Hougoumont, which covered this flank, and in front of the left centre we occupied the farm of La Haye Sainte. By our left we communicated with Marshal Blücher at Wavre, through Ohain; and the marshal had promised me that, in case we should be attacked, he would support me with one or more corps, as might be necessary. The enemy collected his army (with the exception of the 3rd corps, which had been sent to observe Marshal Blücher) on a range of heights in our front, in the course of the night of the 17th and yesterday morning, and at about 10 o'clock he commenced a furious attack upon our post at Hougoumont. I had occupied this post with a detachment of General Byng's English Brigade of Guards, which was in position in its rear; and it was for some time under the command of Lieutenant Colonel Macdonell, and afterwards of Colonel Home, and I am happy to add that it was maintained throughout the day with the utmost gallantry by these brave troops, notwithstanding the repeated efforts of large bodies of the enemy to obtain possession of it.

This attack upon the right of our centre was accompanied by a very heavy cannonade upon our whole line, which was destined to support repeated attacks of cavalry and infantry, occasionally mixed, but sometimes separate, which were made upon it. In one of these the enemy carried the farm house of La Haye Sainte, as the light battalion of the German Legion, which occupied it, had expended all its ammunition and the enemy occupied the only communication there was with the battalion. The enemy repeatedly charged our infantry with his cavalry, but these attacks were uniformly unsuccessful and they afforded opportunities to our cavalry to charge, in one of which Lord Edward Somerset's brigade, consisting of the Life Guards, the Royal Horse Guards and the 1st Dragoon Guards, highly distinguished themselves, as did that of Major General Sir William Ponsonby, having taken many prisoners and an eagle. These attacks were repeated till about seven in the evening, when the enemy made a desperate effort with cavalry and infantry, supported by the fire of artillery, to force our left centre near la Haye Sainte, which, after a severe contest, was defeated. Having observed that his troops retired from this attack in great confusion, and that the march of General Bülow's corps by Frischermont, upon Plançenoit and Belle Alliance, had begun to take effect, and as I could perceive the fire of his cannon, and as Marshal Blücher had joined in person with another corps of his army to the left of our line by Ohain, I determined to attack the enemy, and immediately advanced the whole line of infantry, supported by the cavalry and artillery. The attack succeeded in every point. The enemy was forced from his positions on the heights and fled in the utmost confusion, leaving behind, as far as I could judge, 150 pieces of cannon with their ammunition, which fell into our hands. I continued the pursuit till long after dark, and then discontinued it only on account of the fatigue of our troops, who had been engaged during twelve hours, and because I found myself on the same road with Marshal Blücher, who assured me of his intention to follow the enemy throughout the night. He had sent me word this morning, that he had taken 60 pieces of cannon belonging to the Imperial Guard, and several carriages and baggage belonging to Bonaparte, in Genappe. I propose to move this morning upon Nivelles, and to continue my operations without interruption.

Your Majesty will observe that such a desperate action could not be fought, and such advantage could not be gained, without great loss, and I am sorry to add that our loss has been immense. In Lieutenant General Sir Thomas Picton, His Britannic Majesty has sustained the loss of an officer who has frequently distinguished himself in his service. He fell gloriously leading his division to a charge with bayonets, by which one of the most serious attacks made by the enemy on our position was repulsed. The Earl of Uxbridge, after having successfully got through the arduous day, received a wound by almost the last shot fired, which will, I am afraid, deprive His Britannic Majesty for some time of his service. HRH the Prince of Orange distinguished himself by his gallantry and conduct, till he received a wound from a musket ball through the shoulder, which obliged him to quit the battlefield.

It gives me the greatest satisfaction to assure Your Majesty that the army never, upon any occasion, conducted itself better. The British

Guards, under Lieutenant General Cooke, who is severely wounded, and Major Generals Maitland and Byng set an example which was followed by all, and there is no officer nor description of troops that did not behave well. General Kruse, of the Nassau service, conducted himself much to my satisfaction, as did General Tripp, commanding Your Majesty's heavy cavalry, and General d'Aubrêmé who commanded an infantry brigade of the 3rd Division. General Pozzo di Borgo, General Baron Vincent, General Muffling, and General Alava were in the field during the action and rendered me every assistance in their power. Baron Vincent is wounded, but I hope not severely; General Pozzo di Borgo received a contusion. I would not do justice to my own feelings, or to Marshal Blücher and the Prussian army, if I did not attribute the successful result of this arduous day to the cordial and timely assistance I received from them. The operation of General Bülow upon the enemy's flank was a most decisive one, and even if I had not found myself in a situation to make the attack which produced the final result, it would have forced the enemy to retire if his attacks should have failed, and would have prevented him from taking advantage of them if they should unfortunately have succeeded. We have already got here 7,000 prisoners, among them General Comte de Lobau, who commanded the 6th corps, and General Cambronne, who commanded a division of the Guard. Wellington.

No. 2 From La Belle Alliance

Pflugk-Harttung's letter no. 122
Report of the Württemberg General and Commissioner von Hügel on the Battle of Waterloo

Brussels, 19 June 1815, at 12 o'clock noon

Your Royal Highness,
Be herewith most obediently advised that the rallying of the Prussian army has taken place during the night from the 17th to the 18th, as promised by the marshal, and that Prince Blücher has set up his headquarters at Wavre. Yesterday at midday, at half past twelve, Napoleon vigorously attacked the Duke of Wellington at his position at Mont St Jean, half an hour distant before Waterloo. Never before have I observed a similar persistence in an attack or a defence. Despite the strenuous efforts of the French, they were always repulsed at great loss to themselves. At 3 o'clock, the Duke had the British cavalry charge at a French column that was about to storm the village of Mont St Jean. The cavalry cut down a large part and captured 3,000 prisoners and several eagles.

In such manner, attacks were made and repulsed until the evening at 6 o'clock. At that time, the Prussian army debouched impetuously upon the right flank of the French. The prince intended to bar Napoleon's route to Genappe. Napoleon concentrated all kinds of troops to tie down the Prussians. On his part, Wellington advanced in full strength. For a brief time, matters remained undecided; but all of a sudden, such utter confusion gripped the ranks of the French army that it became disbanded in all out flight. At this moment, I am unable to accurately inform Your Royal Highness of the enemy's losses; the entire length of the highway is covered with cannon and munition wagons that he left behind.

The Prussian army pursues the enemy with its full force; only part of Wellington's army follows in the enemy's footsteps, as it had suffered immense losses that, of course, were to be expected. All of us generals, who are accredited to the headquarters, have been riding to Brussels in order to prepare and send off these reports . . . The Crown Prince of the Netherlands has received a shot in his arm, but it is not serious.

The Earl of Uxbridge, who has commanded the English cavalry, is dead, as is also the quartermaster general of the English army [De] Lancey, an enormous loss to the Duke of Wellington; several of the Duke's aides de camp have been severely wounded, among them Lord Somerset. The Austrian General Vincent has a slight wound in one of his hands; Generals Pozzo di Borgo and Muffling* were wounded by ricochets. The Netherlands General Count Rede who, like ourselves, was accredited to the Duke, suffered a very light contusion when his horse was shot dead under him. The Hereditary Prince of Nassau is in good condition.

At this moment, a 6th Bulletin has been issued, according to which all of Napoleon's carriages and 300 cannon have been captured.

von Hügel, General†

* Charles Andre Pozzo di Borgo was the Russian representative at Wellington's headquarters. Friedrich Karl Ferdinand Freiherr von Müffling (1775–1851) was Prussian commissioner at the Duke of Wellington's headquarters in the Waterloo campaign.

† Ernst Eugen Freiherr von Hügel (1774–1849) was a Württemberg general, having fought for many years as part of the French Grand Armée and later became minister of war.

No. 3 From La Belle Alliance

Pflugk-Harttung's letter no. 127.
Major General Count Vincent to Field Marshal Prince Schwarzenberg[*]
on events after the battle of Belle Alliance

Brussels, 26 June 1815

Dear Prince,
Your Highness honoured me with sending Major Baron de Schell to me on the 18th who has arrived here in the evening of the 21st; he has left again the next morning to deliver to the Duke of Wellington the clarifications that I had been charged to inform him of. He is returning this moment and will himself provide Your Highness with an account of the status of the things of which he has been a witness. The advance of the Anglo-Prussian armies since the battle on the 18th of this month will allow Your Highness to assess the condition in which the French army finds itself. At the same time it is to be desired without doubt that, as soon as a pertinent plan has been adopted, France is entered on a broad front so that not a single group could take hold in the provinces which would not be subject to attack.

Could the circumstance of the enemy's attacking Belgium since the 15th and the victory in the battle of the 18th have introduced some changes in the dispositions that have been settled in the conferences of which Your Highness has kindly provided me the protocol although still suffering severe pains,[†] I count on going to the Duke of Wellington's headquarters as well as to the King [Louis XVIII], after I have received the instructions that I had asked Minister Prince de Metternich to send me. I wish that Your Highness will kindly have Major Scarampi return to me as soon as possible. Be assured, dear Prince, of my respectful devotion and of my high regard.

Vincent

---

* Count Vincent was the Austrian representative at Wellington's headquarters. Karl Philipp Fürst zu Schwarzenberg (1771–1820) was an Austrian field marshal and commanded the Austrian force poised to invade southern France.

† Pflugk-Harttung's footnote: This is the only written document from the hand of Count Vincent, the Austrian Military Commissioner. He is unlikely to have sent a report on the battle due to his wound at Waterloo.

No. 4 From La Belle Alliance

Pflugk-Harttung's letter no. 80.
Casualty list of the German Legion and of the Hanoverian troops

List of the officers of the King's German Legion and of the Hanoverian army killed or wounded in the battles of 16 and 18 June to the extent that these were known on 19 June.*

1 Killed

King's German Legion: Colonel von Ompteda, 5th Battalion; Colonel von Linsingen, 5th Battalion; Major Bösewiel, 2nd Light Battalion; Captain C. Holle, 1st Line Battalion; Captain Tilee, 2nd Line Battalion; Captain von Wurmb, 5th Line Battalion; Captains Holtzermann, von Marschalck, Gilsa, and Lieutenant Albert, 1st Light Battalion; Captain Schaumann, 2nd Light Battalion; Captain Peters and Lieutenant Levetzow, 1st Light Dragoon Regiment; Lieutenant Kuhlmann, 2nd Light Dragoon Regiment; Captain Krauchenberg, 2nd Hussar Regiment; Aide de Camp to General von Dörnberg Captain von Kerssenbruch and Captain Jansen, 3rd Hussar Regiment; Lieutenant Schulzen, Artillery Regiment.†

Royal Hanoverian Troops: Lieutenant Colonel von Wurmb, Grubenhagen Field Battalion; Captain Count von Bazoldo,‡ Bremen Field Battalion;

---

* The list is by no means complete (particularly for the Hanoverian Landwehr) and was clearly prepared very soon after the battle as many known to have been killed are here recorded as wounded.

† Colonel Christian von Ompteda, Beamish no. 972.
Lieutenant Colonel William von Linsingen, Beamish no. 559.
Major Adolphus Bösewiel, Beamish no. 975.
Captain Charles von Holle, Beamish no. 989.
Captain Charles Tilee, Beamish no. 984.
Captain Ernst Christian Charles von Wurmb, Beamish no. 981.
Captain Gottlieb Thilo Holtzermann, Beamish no. 987.
Captain Henry von Marschalck, Beamish no. 991.
CaptainFrederick von Gilsa, Beamish no. 298.
Lieutenant Anton Albert, Beamish no. 1,008.
Captain Frederick Melchior William Schaumann, Beamish no. 988.
Captain Frederick Peters, Beamish no. 803.
Lieutenant Frederick Charles Lewis von Levetzow, Beamish no. 810.
Lieutenant Otto Kuhlmann, Beamish no. 812.
Captain Augustus Krauchenberg, Beamish no. 221, died at Celle, Hanover, in 1818.
Captain Agatz von Kerssenbruch, Beamish no. 801
Captain George Janssen, Beamish no. 802.
Lieutenant Charles Detlef von Schulzen, Beamish no. 787.

‡ In fact it was Lieutenant Colonel Langrehr of the battalion who was killed, and

Captain von Bobarth and Ensign von Platho,* Lüneburg Field Battalion.

2 Wounded

King's German Legion: Lieutenant General Charles von Alten, lightly; Major General Halkett, severely; Colonel von du Plat, severely; Lieutenant Colonel von Bülow, 1st Dragoon Regiment, wounded and missing; Lieutenant Colonel von Maydell, same regiment, lightly; Lieutenant Colonel Meyer, 3rd Hussar Regiment, severely; Majors von Robertson, 1st Line Battalion, Müller, 2nd Line Battalion, Lurtermannn, 3rd Line Battalion, Georg Chüden, 4th Line Battalion, severely; von dem Bussche, same Battalion, lost an arm; von Angerstein, 1st Light Dragoon Regiment, Kuhlmann, of the Artillery, lightly; Captain Gerlach von Schlütter, Lieutenant Wilding, Lieutenant Müller and Lieutenant Schnath, 1st Line Battalion; Captain Purgold and Lieutenant Claus von der Decken, 2nd Line Battalion; Lieutenant Heise, Lieutenant Leonhart,†

Captain Bazoldo was only wounded.

* These two officers were killed along with Captain Korfes of the same battalion.

† Major General Charles Count Alten, Beamish no. 292.

Lieutenant Colonel George Charles Augustus du Plat, Beamish no. 1,017, died of his wounds on 21 June.

Lieutenant Colonel John von Bülow, Beamish no. 87, severely wounded but survived.

Major Charles von Maydell, 3rd Hussars, Beamish no. 248.

Lieutenant Colonel Frederick Lewis Meyer, Beamish no. 816, died of his wounds on 6 July 1815.

Major William von Robertson, Beamish no. 376.

Major George Muller, Beamish no. 423.

Major Gottlieb Frederick von Luttermann, Beamish no. 471, died at Gelliehausen in 1831.

Major George William Cyriacus Chüden, Beamish no. 1,019, died of his wounds on 19 June.

Major Hans von dem Bussche, Beamish no. 294.

Von Angerstein is actually Lieutenant Otto von Hammerstein, Beamish no. 105.

First Captain Henry Jacob Kuhlmann, Beamish no. 28, died at Stade in Hanover in 1830.

Captain Gerlach von Schlütter, Beamish no. 383, severely wounded and died at Stade in 1818.

Lieutenant Ernest Wilding, Beamish no. 391.

Lieutenant August Müller, Beamish no. 402.

Lieutenant Frederick Schnath, Beamish no. 417.

Captain Frederick Purgold, Beamish no. 427.

Captain Claus von der Decken, Beamish no. 434.

Lieutenant Christoph Heise, Beamish no. 305.

Lieutenant Harry Leonhart, Beamish no. 312.

Ensign Heise and Ensign Gentzkow, 1st Light Battalion; Captain von Bothmer and Captain Sichart, 1st Light Dragoon Regiment; Lieutenant Brüggemann and Lieutenant True, 3rd Hussar Regiment, the former severely; Captain Braun and Lieutenant Heise, of the Artillery, the former severely; Captain von Einem, Brigade Major.[*]

Royal Hanoverian Troops: Colonel von Berger, of the General Staff, lightly; Lieutenant Colonel von Langrehr,[†] Bremen Field Battalion, lost a leg; Lieutenant Colonel von Klenke, Captain Korfes,[‡] severely; Captain von Lepel, severely; Lieutenant Volger, Lieutenant von Plato and Ensign von Weyhe, Lüneburg Field Battalion; Major von Schkopp, Verden Field Battalion; Lieutenant Hanbury, Lauenburg Field Battalion; Aide de Camp to Count Kielmannsegge; Lieutenant von Mahrenholz, Osnabrück Field Battalion; Lieutenant Westphal, Ensign Stieppel and Ensign Ernst, Grubenhagen Field Battalion; Major von Hammerstein,[§] Gifhorn Landwehr Battalion; Captain von Papet, Osterode Landwehr Battalion; Lieutenant-Colonel von Hake, lightly; Captain von Schenk, most severely; Lieutenant von Offen, lightly, Cornet von Plate, lightly, Hussar Regiment of His Royal Highness, the Duke of Cumberland.

---

* Ensign Adolphus Heise, Beamish no. 324.

Ensign Adolphus Augustus von Gentzkow, Beamish no. 320.

Captain Bernhard von Bothmer, 1st Dragoons.

Lieutenant Philip von Sichart, Beamish no. 89, became a brevet colonel on half pay and died at Osnabrück in 1836.

Lieutenant Henry Bruggemann, Beamish no. 808, was actually killed.

Lieutenant Hermann True, Beamish no. 266.

Second Captain William Braun, Beamish no. 38.

Second Lieutenant Lewis Heise, Beamish no. 64.

Brigade Major Gottfried von Einem, Beamish no. 3.

† He was actually killed.

‡ He was actually killed.

§ He was actually killed.

THE CAVALRY

3rd Brigade of Lieutenant General William Dornberg

No. 5 From La Belle Alliance

Pflugk-Harttung's letter no. 79

Statements by General von Dörnberg regarding 15 and 16 June

... Early on the 15th, I learned that the Prussian advance posts had been attacked, and I sent this information to Brussels.* I then rode towards Binch and saw that the Prussians were retreating. Towards evening, I rode from Mons to Brussels in accordance with my orders to only stay [at Mons] until the start of hostilities, and not to become surrounded. I arrived at Brussels in the morning between 4 and 5 o'clock and immediately went to the Duke (of Wellington), who was still in bed. He jumped up right away, told me that this day we would probably be fighting at Quatre Bras, and ordered me to ride at once to Waterloo with the order for General Picton to have his division march to Quatre Bras without delay. [He said that] my own brigade, cantonned at Mechelen, had already received the order also to march there. I then rode to Waterloo. The division had just set off on its march when the Duke himself arrived. He halted briefly at Mont St Jean and inquired about several roads and where they ran to. On arrival at Quatre Bras, we found the Netherlands troops under the Prince of Orange engaged in skirmishing with the French in the direction of Frasnes; there was also a cannon shot now and then. The Duke here made out an order to Lord Uxbridge to have the cavalry, assembled at Enghien, move at once to Quatre Bras.† A Prussian hussar patrol came here also,

* Dornberg's first report which mentioned an attack on the Prussians was timed 9.30 a.m. at Mons, but unfortunately this was sent to the headquarters of the Prince of Orange at Braine le Comte where it lay unopened as the prince was away at the front. This and further messages were eventually forwarded by Perponcher at approximately 2 p.m. to the prince who had ridden to Brussels, which he then received around 5 p.m.

† It is clear from the memoirs of cavalrymen on the 16th that many regiments were delayed at Enghien for a considerable period awaiting further orders. Dornberg's statement would corroborate the fact that the orders for the cavalry to proceed to

who informed the Duke that Marshal Blücher was near Sombreffe. He [Wellington] told me he would ride there and asked me to accompany him. Apart from several [of the Duke's] aides de camp, General von Müffling was also riding along. We found Marshal Blücher at the mill at Bry. After exchanging a few words, the Duke said to General von Gneisenau, 'Do tell me your opinion as to what you wish me to do!' Gneisenau took the map in his hand and said, 'If you are able to overthrow whatever is opposing you at Quatre Bras and advance quickly, this would have the most desirable result in that you then would take the French army in the rear. But since only narrow roads lead in that direction, it would be safest if you were to tie down whatever is in front of you and march to the left with the remainder of your army; in this way you would come on to our right flank and take the French army in the left flank.' The Duke answered, 'Your reasoning is correct; I will see what is standing against me and how much of my army has arrived, in order to act on that basis,' without saying anything that he would decide in favour of one or the other, and without promising anything. As we rode off, brave Blücher accompanied us for a short while, and when he rode back, the Duke remarked to me, 'What a fine fellow he is!'

From the ridge where we halted, the approach of the enemy columns could be distinctly seen, as also Bonaparte and his suite. On the return ride, we heard the firing at Quatre Bras becoming stronger. As we arrived there, the French kept up a fairly strong cannonade but did not show much of their troops. Since Gneisenau's proposal 'to overthrow whatever was in front of us and to move into the rear of the enemy army' I still had in mind, I said to the Duke that I did not believe that the French were present in any strength and that it appeared to me that they were more into making noise than wanting to attack. The Duke replied, 'It may be so, but I don't believe it' and shortly thereafter he proved to be right, because they now attacked in earnest.

Quatre Bras were severely delayed and that some of Wellington's cavalry could have arrived during the afternoon at Quatre Bras, but for this delay.

2nd Light Dragoon Regiment, King's German Legion

No. 6 Excerpts on the Battle of Waterloo by Lieutenant Ernst Meier

*War Archive of the General Staff, Berlin: Section II, Kap. XII, Nr 3663, from the diary of Major and City Councillor Ernst Meier, LLD, 1809–15.**
Printed manuscript (no date)

On 15 June Küster† and I hosted a dinner to which Fernetti, Braun, Schäeffer, Poten, and Hugo‡ were invited. We were full of cheer and had no idea what the next days would bring.

On the 16th, Wachendorff§ woke me up, shouting: 'We will march off!' I rose at once, packed my things in good order, had breakfast, and then went to Rijmenan where the squadron was assembling. At around 10 o'clock we arrived at Mechelen where we were held up until about 2 o'clock by the procuring of forage and foodstuffs. Here we heard that Napoleon had attacked and pushed back the Prussians at Namur (Ligny), and that today we would be off on a fairly long march. We were all of the belief that today we would once more be properly quartered, or that at the least our baggage would stay with us, and therefore had taken no precautions for the contrary case. Soon after passing through Brussels we heard the sound of a vigorous cannonade, and a little later we encountered wounded men of the Brunswick and other corps. A cavalry sergeant of the Brunswick hussars brought me the first news of the Duke's death, which affected me deeply. We marched through Waterloo and halted in a cornfield close to Genappe. It was about 1 o'clock at night that we here set up our bivouac. We had covered 11 lieues.¶

On Saturday, 17 June 1815, we were awakened at the dawn of

* Lieutenant Ernst Meier, Beamish no. 145, served in the Peninsula, southern France, Holland and the Waterloo campaign.

† Lieutenant Ferdinand Küster, 2nd Light Dragoons, KGL, Beamish no. 148, was later a captain on half pay at Herzberg in Hanover.

‡ Lieutenant Joannes Justinus von Fernetti, 2nd Light Dragoons, KGL, Beamish no. 141, was later a captain in the Hanoverian Garde du Corps.

Captain George Braun, 2nd Light Dragoons, KGL, Beamish no. 137, later became a major on half pay.

Lieutenant Charles Schaeffer, 2nd Light Dragoons, KGL, Beamish no. 143, later a brevet captain on half pay at Campen in Brunswick.

Captain August Poten, 2nd Light Dragoons, KGL, Beamish no. 138, became a captain in the Hanoverian Garde du Corps.

Lieutenant Ludolph von Hugo, 2nd Light Dragoons, KGL, Beamish no. 140, he became a captain on half pay at Harburg.

§ Private Frederick Wachendorff, his batman.

¶ About 35 miles.

morning, towards 3 o'clock, by the order to saddle up. Since everything remained quiet, we unsaddled again after a few hours and remained undisturbed until about 10 o'clock. Almost the entire English cavalry had been concentrated next to us, and large infantry columns had passed us since daybreak. Towards 10 o'clock, almost the entire British army commenced a retrograde movement that went as far as the edge of the forest of Soignes, which extends between Brussels and Waterloo. As the infantry began to retire, all of the cavalry moved forward at the same time and took up position to the right and left of Genappe. From the heights near there, the entire wide plain could be overlooked. After the infantry had retreated without being disturbed, we also moved back for a short distance and dismounted. The heat was oppressive; a spring of clear water on our right flank offered us much refreshment.

After a few hours we remounted again. Everybody believed that the moment had come for a great cavalry charge. Instead, a sudden shower soaked us through and through so that it was impossible for us to get any wetter.

After the rain had ceased we continued our retreat. This retreat of almost the entire British cavalry, as a cover for the position near Waterloo, was most impressive. Three lines had been formed with large squadron intervals. As soon as it was possible, with due regard for the retiring infantry and artillery, the foremost line broke off by squadrons to the right rear and drew back through the intervals of the other two lines, which then moved forward at the same time. The French made some noise but did not attack. At the onset of darkness we moved close to Waterloo, formed close columns of troops, and dismounted. As it had quit raining, we now tried to dry our clothes somewhat. The men had brought some straw, and after I had silenced my stomach with some cold meat I still had with me, I expected to reinvigorate my tired limbs with refreshing sleep next to the camp fire. But another rain shower deprived me of all thought of restful recovery.

Half a cup of coffee without sugar that Thiele[*] gave me, and that I shared with Küster, and a piece of bread was all I had in the way of breakfast. Afterwards, I warmed my cold limbs with a moderate portion of Krambambuli.[†] Thus began the memorable 18 June 1815.

Soon after daybreak we changed our position. The soil was softened to such an extent that on dismounting one sank at once ankle deep into the mud. I searched out a spot where some straw was next to an almost expired camp fire. Seeger[‡] and Küster had also come there. The men brought some

* Captain Lewis Thiele, no. 132 Beamish.

† Krambambuli is a kind of cherry liqueur.

‡ Captain William Seeger 2nd Light Dragoons, KGL, Beamish no. 135.

wood, and we began again drying our clothes. After some time we again changed our position. Here also a fire was lit, and he, who had something left, cooked a meal while the others watched. Generals Dornberg and Bobers* also came to our fire and prepared some mulled wine. Due to uncalled-for modesty I begged off from participating. Afterwards, I rode the horses to a watering place, where I had an opportunity to talk to many Brunswickers, Mahner, Berner, Griesheim, Pott, Cleve and Holn among them.† Upon returning to my regiment, I still had time to dry and clean myself, also to change shirt and stockings, since these had remained fairly dry in my portmanteau. At around 10 o'clock we took up our post in the position forward of Mont St Jean near the rural road from Wavre to Braine where it intersects the Nivelles highway. The 1st [Light Dragoon] Regiment stood in front of us, which together with us and the Cumberland Hussars formed a brigade under General Dornberg [3rd British Cavalry Brigade]. Next to us were many more cavalry regiments, all in columns of squadrons or half squadrons. One might say that we formed the right wing of the centre.

Soon thereafter our artillery, placed in front of us at the rim of the plateau, opened a vigorous cannonade that soon elicited a response. Balls and shells were flying from all sides and in all possible directions, but it took a fairly long time for something to strike our regiment. The only one hit by a shell splinter was Corporal Gerke‡ of No. 8 Company. He fell down right away, and it turned out that his right arm had been smashed. At about this time, probably at 1 o'clock noon, it happened that the Cumberland Hussar Regiment, which was detached to our brigade and was standing in column some several 100 paces to our left, at first fell into some agitated movements and then took off in the wildest of flights. Of that regiment, nothing and nobody was to be seen anymore except Adjutant Dachenhausen who then joined us. This incident was all the more peculiar as that regiment was not at all in an exposed position. After spreading panic among the baggage, its men were said to have ridden all the way back to their quarters at Mechelen. Later on, Colonel Hake was to be the only one at fault!?§ A dragoon of my detachment shouted:

---

* Brigade Major Charles von Bobers, Beamish no. 777, was killed at Waterloo.

† The writer had served with the Brunswick Corps earlier in his career.
Captains Mahner and Berner of the Brunswick Jäger Corps.
Captain von Greisheim of the Avante Garde Light Infantry.
Major Pott of the Brunswick Uhlans.
I have been unable to identify Cleve in the Brunswick Corps.
Captain von Holln Hussar Regiment.

‡ Corporal Henry Gerke.

§ Lieutenant Colonel George von Hake, who commanded the Cumberland Hussars at Waterloo was court-martialled and cashiered.

'What are those Hussar Guards up to? They are going to the devil!'

After the artillery had been relieved several times and the infantry had often been reinforced and the cavalry had cleared the field several times, and as the enemy's attacks became more violent, our regiment received orders around 6 o'clock to move to Braine l'Alleud, a village on our extreme right flank where we had to keep an enemy cavalry detachment under observation. We remained there for about an hour and were outside the range of fire. A good thing in this matter was that we could buy a few bottles of wine at Braine.* At the same time, the cannonade was renewed with redoubled intensity. A new and more desperate enemy attack was apparently to follow.

We then returned to the battlefield where the army was getting ready for a general advance. During this march, with our flank exposed, Küster's horse was struck by a ball. I asked him if he was wounded, which he denied. He jumped off his horse and found that it had one leg less than before. The regiment formed up immediately thereafter. The enemy projectiles struck all over the battlefield and from all directions that one was no longer safe anywhere. Everywhere men and horses were mangled. The horse of Dragoon Wermetch† was thrown down next to me. The cannon ball had passed through the entire length of the horse's body.

It was in this indescribable rain of balls that an aide de camp came galloping up and brought us orders to advance. With a few words, Lieutenant Colonel de Jonquières reminded the men to do their duty, then had us break off by squadrons in divisions and drew the regiment ahead of all the other cavalry regiments.

After we had evaded the enemy's solid shot in our advance, we suddenly came under canister fire from two sides; but we quickly rode ahead, shouting Hurrah all the time. In front of us we saw a broad line of French cavalry. Red lancers were on the left, next to them blue dragoons, then chasseurs à cheval, and then cuirassiers, extending widely beyond our right flank. They were all posted behind a ditch. It was about 50 paces distant from their front and looked like a berm from afar.‡ On passing this obstacle we received a volley from their carbines. When the enemy noticed that we were not impressed, he turned around and fled, and our pursuit was such that we reached him instantaneously. Being superior in numbers, however, the enemy soon reformed, wheeled his two wings towards us, and in this way we were attacked from both sides. A desperate

* This is the first note I have discovered to date of trade being continued in the area of the battlefield; most references to obtaining goods indicate looting of abandoned properties.

† Dragoon Pierre Wermetch.

‡ A berm is a narrow flat ledge at the top or bottom of a slope.

affair was now developing. Two squadrons of cuirassiers now vigorously charged the right flank of our regiment. Captain von Bülow and Cornet Drangmeister were killed, Lieutenant Colonel von Jonquières, Captain Harling, Lieutenant Ritter, and Cornet Lorentz were wounded.* In time, Major Friedrichs† had the 'Rally' signal sounded, and as soon as we had formed at squadron strength, we threw the cuirassiers into flight. Captain Thiele was about to attack also some cannon standing opposite from our extreme right wing; but Major Friedrichs considered this imprudent because our regiment had become disordered and dispersed to such an extent that our strength on the spot was only about one squadron. Moreover on the road to the right appeared large masses of troops of whom one did not know whether they were friend or foe. We therefore let the pursuit be taken over by the cavalry that followed us. A patrol, that was sent to the road where these troops had appeared, did not return. I therefore rode there myself. Here I met Cavalry Sergeant Kölle‡ who told me that it was Prussians who marched on that road in pursuit of the totally defeated French army.

Since full darkness had set in, I was unable to find the regiment, but met Poten and Schaeffer who had the same problem. We remained at the bivouac of the 1st Dragoon Regiment. We kept up a conversation for a while, then I wrapped myself in my coat and closed my tired eyes.

We already departed on 19 June. Bivouacking all the time, we continued our march to Paris in the direction of Ham and Pont Sainte Maxence. On 30 June we arrived in the area of that capital city.

---

* Captain Frederick von Bülow and Cornet Henry Drangmeister, 2nd Light Dragoons, KGL, Beamish nos 805 and 814 respectively.

Lieutenant Colonel Charles Frederick de Jonquières, Beamish no. 127, died at Plate near Lüchow in Hanover in 1831 as a major general on the retired list

Captain Christian Theodore Leopold George von Harling, Beamish no. 136, died at Hanover in 1823

Lieutenant Hermann Heinrich Conrad Ritter, Beamish no. 144, was severely wounded

Cornet Ferdinand August Lorentz, Beamish no. 152, died at Detmold as a brevet captain in 1831.

† Major Augustus Friedrichs, Beamish no. 128, became a lieutenant colonel on 18 June 1815 and became a brevet colonel at Hameln in Hanover.

‡ Sergeant Henry Kölle, 2nd Light Dragoons, KGL.

6th Brigade of Major General Sir Vivian Hussey
1st Hussars, King's German Legion

No. 7 From La Belle Alliance

Pflugk-Harttung's letter No. 55
Report of the 1st Hussar Regiment of the German Legion on its participation in the Battle of Belle Alliance

On the 16th [June] at 12 o'clock noon, the regiment marched off from Tournai through Ath to Enghien. In the night to the 17th, the march was continued to the Brussels highway, where the regiment, on the 17th, formed the rearguard on the way to the position near Waterloo. It was a long, fatiguing march, the men wetted through to their shirts by the rain, and the country roads made barely passable by the continuing heavy rainfalls.

Early in the morning of the 18th, the regiment was detached from its brigade to the extreme left wing of the position, with the order to continuously send patrols behind the plateau into the defile towards St Lambert and search for the vanguard of the expected Prussian columns. Finally after 5 o'clock in the evening, the hussars met the head of the Prussian army not far away from the battlefield. After an attack by the Prussian vanguard on the enemy's right flank had been repulsed, the former returned to the edge of the wood where the path to St Lambert begins, reformed its ranks, and awaited here the advance parties of the other Prussian columns.

At about half past six in the evening, General Bülow commenced the successful attack on the enemy right flank. A part of von Ziethen's Corps relieved the 1st Hussar Regiment, which, recalled to the centre of the position of the English army, went there at the trot and gallop and there joined its brigade. The brigade advanced at a trot. General Vivian ordered the 10th and 18th Hussar Regiments to charge 2 squares of the French Young [Middle] Guard, but he ordered the 1st Hussar Regiment to stay in reserve with the words [in English]: 'I know you 1st Hussars, therefore I keep you in reserve.' Both squares were broken and dispersed. As is well known, Bonaparte says in his description of the lost battle, it was this broken Young Guard who caused the cries '*Sauve qu'it peut!*' [*sic*] in his army.

It seems appropriate to note here that the enemy either did not send any patrols towards St Lambert during the battle to contact Marshal Grouchy, or that these patrols were poorly led. Otherwise one of the patrols of the 1st Hussar Regiment should have clashed with one of the enemy. In this memorable Battle of Waterloo, the 1st Hussar Regiment suffered only insignificant losses: one officer, Captain von Bobers, killed*, several hussars killed, and about 10 horses, from cannon fire.

Note: Late in the evening our picket found a [dead] French cuirassier who had been shot through his chest and both parts of his cuirass by a single musket ball, proof that the enemy cavalry did its utmost to break our squares, and also that the latter opened fire at the right moment.

19 June. The Brigadier General Sir Hussey Vivian expressed his thanks to the regiment for the intrepid and soldierly conduct that it displayed during the Battle of Waterloo.

Hanoverian Cavalry Brigade of Colonel Baron Estorff
Bremen and Verden Hussars

No. 8 From La Belle Alliance

Pflugk-Harttung's letter no. 81
Report of Colonel von Estorff about the 1st Hanoverian Cavalry Brigade during the days from 17 to 19 June

Contribution to the description of the Battle of Waterloo and later events.

The Hanoverian Cavalry Brigade of about 1,100 horse, under my command at the time, consisted of the Prince Regent and Bremen Verden Hussar Regiments. During these days, being part of the corps of His Royal Highness Prince Frederick of Orange, it stood on the right flank and was not present at the battlefield of Waterloo. I am therefore unable to make a report regarding the first seven items of the General Order of 28 October.† However, I am convinced that the positioning of the said corps, ordered by the Duke of Wellington, served an extremely important purpose. It covered the right flank for any contingency, either during the battle, or in case of an unfavourable outcome of the battle, of a retreat, should this have been necessary, whether towards Brussels or Antwerp.‡ In my opinion, this contribution deserves some consideration and I therefore allow myself to comment in particular on Item 8 and also on Item 10 as follows:

In the context of a description of matters regarding the Hanoverian

* Captain von Bobers was attached to the Staff at Waterloo.

† The requirement for official reports of the actions of each corps during the Waterloo campaign.

‡ It is of note that a retreat on Ostend is not mentioned. British historians generally presume that Wellington would order a retreat on Ostend, but such a flank movement, away from his Prussian allies would have been dangerous in the extreme. There is much evidence that a retreat north towards Antwerp and possibly beyond was the more likely route of retreat for Wellington's forces.

Cavalry Brigade, I need to point out first of all that it was assigned since mid-March to the observation of the French troops near Condé and [its] environs. While hostilities had not yet commenced, the three months of service as border guards were disagreeable in regard to their political aspects.

On 16 June it moved to Lens and from there sent out strong detachments to keep Mons and the surrounding area under observation. In the afternoon of the 17th, an order was issued to march through Ath and Enghien to Halle and join the Corps of Prince Frederick of Orange. The brigade arrived there in the morning of the 18th. This corps, of a strength of about 19,000 to 20,000 men, included, apart from the Hanoverian Cavalry Brigade, the division of Lieutenant General Colville[*] the Indian Brigade,[†] the Netherlands division of Lieutenant General Stedmann [1st] and three Netherlands cavalry regiments.[‡] Its assignments were the observation of the roads from Halle to Enghien and to Braine le Comte, and the maintaining of a position at Braine le Chateau as liaison to the main army whose right flank stood two hours away at Braine l'Alleud.

On the 18th, I sent out several patrols and a detachment to reconnoitre in the direction of Nivelles with the instruction to advance as far as possible and to ascertain whether, and how, Nivelles had been occupied by the enemy.

On the 19th, HRH Prince Frederick had his corps march off to Braine le Chateau, pick up the troops posted at that location and then move towards Nivelles, as the circumstances would permit. There was a halt on this march, I believe near Ittre, in order to await information about the advance of the column directed towards Braine le Comte, as also from the patrols sent to Braine l'Alleud. It was here also that Cornet von Laffert of the Prince Regent Hussar Regiment returned with the report about his scouting mission, for which he had been sent out on the day before and which he had handled with great circumspection. An excerpt of the report is attached.[§] It caused the prince to move immediately on to Nivelles.

At Nivelles I received the order from Lord Hill to return with my brigade to his command, to advance as far as Gonesse and to position pickets for the security of the 2nd Corps . . .

---

* Most of 4th Division, the 4th Brigade and most of the artillery were detached at Waterloo.

† A brigade of infantry under Lieutenant General Anthing which had been formed to sail to regarrison the Dutch East Indies possessions.

‡ This is possibly an error of dates. There is no evidence that any of the Dutch/Belgian cavalry was at Halle on 17th/18th; however three cavalry regiments certainly joined Prince Frederick's Corps after Waterloo.

§ Not included here.

THE ARTILLERY

The Staff

No. 9 From La Belle Alliance

Pflugk-Harttung's letter no. 28

Major Heise, Commander of the Artillery of the 5th Hanoverian Brigade, report to the Chief of Staff of General Count von Alten about the conduct of the Artillery at Quatre Bras and Belle Alliance*

To Colonel von Berger, Chief of the General Staff

Montmartre, 13 July 1815

In compliance with the order from His Excellency the Commanding Lieutenant General Sir Charles Alten, I have the honour to most obediently report to Your Honour the following: During the battles of 16 and 18 June, the officers of the Hanoverian Artillery have distinguished themselves and have performed well, as did the officers of the [King's German] Legion, who have been detached to this artillery. They have acted to the highest satisfaction of the commander of the 5th Division, Major General Sir James Kempt, who has expressed his highest satisfaction about the performance both of officers and men of the two batteries. I need to commend in particular Lieutenant d'Huvelé† and Lieutenant Adjutant Muller.‡ The former assumed command of the 1st Battery on 18 June during the battle, after Captain Braun had been wounded while his cannon were being emplaced against the enemy, and Lieutenant von Schulzen§ had been killed shortly after the beginning of the battle. Lieutenant Adjutant Muller took over the command of a division because Lieutenant Hugo¶ had been absent in order to procure ammunition. The two officers have done all that can be expected of

* Major Henry Lewis Heise, Beamish no. 796.

† Lieutenant Friedrich d'Huvelé, 1st Hanoverian Foot Battery.

‡ I have been unable to identify this officer.

§ Lieutenant Charles Detlef von Schulzen, Beamish no. 787, was killed at Waterloo.

¶ First Lieutenant Carl Anthony Hugo, KGL Artillery, Beamish no. 49.

experienced artillery officers.

Lewis Heise, Major and Commander of the Hanoverian Artillery with the army.*

* Note that Major Heise omits any reference to Rettberg's 2nd Hanoverian 9-pounder Battery under his command. On his part, von Rettberg does not mention Major Heise in his battle report.

THE INFANTRY

Second Division of Lieutenant General Sir Henry Clinton

No. 10 From La Belle Alliance

Pflugk-Harttung's letter no. 111

General Clinton praises Colonel Halkett for the conduct of his Brigade and of the Hanoverian Troops in general and will communicate this opinion to the Duke of Wellington

Beauregard,* 7 December 1815

Dear Sir!

I enclose to you the route for the march of your [3rd Hanoverian] Brigade to Brussels on your way to Hanover. The first day's march from your quarters would be too long; I therefore suggest that Count Schulenburg's† Battalion be assembled between Le Chesnay and Rocquencourt and that the remainder of your brigade be entering Versailles on the 9th. I would have greatly regretted taking leave of your brigade without having seen your officers be appropriately awarded for their merits, had I not received the most satisfactory assurances from the Duke of Wellington of his high regard in which he holds your brigade and all Hanoverians who fought in the Battle of Waterloo, as well as of his approbation of their general good conduct. I am authorised to assure you that it has been, and still is, His Grace's desire that the Hanoverian army and those of the other nations receive due awards for their services. Since those foreign orders granted to him were intended exclusively for the British army, it was not in his power to use a part of these to reward the services of officers of the other nations. As to those awards that it is our government's prerogative to give, I know that it is the Duke's recommendation that they be conferred to the officers of the Hanoverian army as if they had served in the English army.

* Near La Celle Saint Cloud, Paris. Le Chesnay and Rocquencourt can both be found just to the south.

† Schulenburg commanded the Hanoverian Bremervörde Landwehr Battalion at Waterloo.

I believe that this recommendation will certainly be considered, and I am convinced that a large part of these marks of esteem will be apportioned to your brigade at the time that they are granted. These details should not be made public, but I request that you pass them on to the commanding officers of your battalions.*

I ask that you express to them my thanks for their eagerness with which they without exception have supported me in the performance of my duties. Allow me to say the same to you, and let your brigade know that your outstanding leadership under any and all circumstances and calm bravery on this trying day of Waterloo have been such as to justly entitle you to the Duke of Wellington's fullest praise and to your country's gratitude. I wish you luck on your return to your homeland after your glorious service; as a soldier I much regret seeing you leave. I remain, dear sir, your obedient servant,

Henry Clinton

1st King's German Legion Brigade of Colonel du Plat
3rd Line Battalion, KGL

No. 11 Lieutenant Henry Dehnel†

Henry Dehnel, Lieutenant Colonel of the Royal Hanoverian Artillery (retired), A Retrospection of my Military Career in the Years from 1805 to 1849, *Hanover 1859*

On 4 April, the Duke of Wellington arrived at Brussels to assume the supreme command of the English–Hanoverian–Netherlands army. By General Order of 11 April, the army was divided into corps, divisions, and brigades; the Duke herewith decreed that the English, Hanoverian, and Netherlands nationalities be intermingled in the different corps so that they became used to joint action and to get to know each other. The army thus gradually took on the following formation for the impending campaign: The 1st Corps, commanded by the Prince of Orange, consisted of the 1st and 3rd Divisions, under the command of Generals Cooke and Sir Charles Alten, with one horse artillery battery and three foot batteries, as well as the 2nd and 3rd Netherlands Divisions of

* A Hanoverian Waterloo Medal was produced for participants in the battle. It is of a similar size but different design to the British Waterloo Medal which was issued to the King's German Legion.

† Lieutenant Henry Dehnel served with the 3rd Line Battalion, KGL, at Waterloo and later served with the Hanoverian Artillery. Dehnel's description of the Battle of Waterloo includes a detailed recapitulation of the major events copied from other battle histories. Those parts of the text have been omitted from this translation.

Generals Perponcher and Chassé, and two foot and one horse artillery battery, for a total of 25,082 men and 48 guns.

The 2nd Army Corps was commanded by General Lord Hill; it consisted of the 2nd and 4th Divisions of Generals Clinton and Colville, with 1 battery of horse artillery and 3 foot batteries, of the 1st Netherlands Division of General Stedmann, with two foot batteries, and the Netherlands–Indian Brigade of General Anthing, in all 24,033 men and 40 guns. The Netherlands troops of the 2nd Army Corps were commanded by Prince Frederick of the Netherlands.

All of the cavalry of the army were under the command of Lord Uxbridge, in all eight English and German brigades, and also the Brunswick Hussars and Uhlans and three Netherlands brigades. Of its seven horse artillery batteries, one consisted of howitzers only, and a second one was equipped for launching rockets. In all, the cavalry numbered 14,482 men and 44 guns.

The Army Reserve consisted of the 5th and 6th Division of Generals Picton and Cole, the Brunswick Division of the Duke of Brunswick, the Hanoverian Corps of General von der Decken, and the Nassau Contingent under General Kruse, with 3 horse artillery batteries and 8 foot batteries, for a total of 32,796 men and 64 guns.

The 2nd Division under General Clinton, to which we belonged, was constituted of the 3rd English Brigade of General Adam, the 2nd Hanoverian Brigade of Colonel Hugh Halkett [actually the 3rd Hanoverian Brigade], and the 2nd Legion Brigade of Colonel du Plat [actually the 1st KGL Brigade], the Legion's Horse Artillery Battery of Major Sympher and the British Foot Battery of Captain Bolton.

The 1st, 2nd, 3rd [and] 4th Line Battalions of the Legion formed the infantry brigade of Colonel du Plat, who was one of the most capable higher ranking officers of the Legion, a leader who by his appearance alone instilled confidence, and who gave the impression of a perfect gentleman.

In order to take care of the lack of experienced officers in the Hanoverian army, the Duke of Wellington, by General Order of 9 May 1815, had the men of four companies of each Legion battalion distributed to the six remaining companies, and had the officers and non-commissioned officers, thus set free, transferred to the Hanoverian infantry.[*] As a result of this order, within the 3rd Line Battalion the command of the rifle company went to Captain Diedel,[†] as Captain Lueder entered a Hanoverian battalion at the rank of major.[‡]

---

* See appendix 4 for a full list of these transfers.

† Captain Frederick Diedel was killed at Waterloo, Beamish no. 990.

‡ He joined the Landwehr Battalion Peine, Beamish no. 476.

We regretted to have this well liked company commander leave us. Lieutenant Brauns* was also transferred to another company, whereby I became the senior lieutenant in the rifle company, with von Sode now joining us as second lieutenant, while Ensign von Rönne remained with us.†

At the same time, an order was issued that the light companies [rifle companies] of an infantry brigade were to form a battalion, commanded by a staff officer or captain, on all occasions that the brigade was deployed, whether in line or in column, on the march or before the enemy. In our case, the rifle companies of 1st, 2nd, 3rd, and 4th Line Battalions were combined into a battalion, to be under the command of Captain Heise of the 4th Line Battalion,‡ most senior of the four company commanders. After our brigade had been stationed in the area of Lens on 8 April, and then been transferred to Ath on 16 April, more exercises took place, not only by brigades, but also by the entire division. In May and in the beginning of June this caused several temporary changes in quarters between Ath, Lens, Beloeil and Huissignies.

On 19 April was my first opportunity to see the Duke of Wellington and Lord Hill, who reviewed our brigade on the road from Ath to Mons. The stern facial expression of the Iron Duke and the kind look of Lord Hill left me with a deep impression; I would have immediately recognised both generals again under any circumstances.

The division as such performed its exercises under the command of Sir Henry Clinton himself . . . Particular attention was given to the line formation four deep and the rapid change into squares, both from line as well as from a column, formed by two battalions and by one, also at the company level; it was even required that nine men, each form up in orderly groups that are capable of resisting cavalry charges.§

Apart from going through the various forms of deployment, some training was also undertaken in building little tents, with the soldiers' woollen blankets, some pegs, and two muskets, which were to house six men. But as far as I can remember, very little use was made of this kind of covering in the ensuing campaign, and only whenever the regular tents were not available, something that occurred on occasion during the first days of marching in France.

---

* Lieutenant Charles Brauns, Beamish no. 486.

† Ensign Charles Augustus von der Sode, 3rd Line Battalion, KGL, Beamish no. 499; he died at Hanover in 1835.

Ensign Frederick von Rönne, Beamish no. 504.

‡ Captain George Heise, 4th Line Battalion, KGL, no. 1029 Beamish. He died from wounds sustained at Waterloo on 27 June 1815.

§ An interesting reference to the formation of 'rallying squares' during exercises.

During the time that the Battalion was cantonned in Lens and Huissignies and environs, from 10 May to 16 June, . . . news was spreading from various sources, and at first among the local population, of unusual troop movements in the neighbouring French border provinces; that Napoleon was expected to be with the French army and that one would have to face the outbreak of hostilities in the near future.

On the morning of 16 June we were engaged near Lens in field exercises, when an orderly came galloping up and interrupted the exercises. After reading the order that had just been received, Colonel du Plat convened the officer corps and told us that the brigade would immediately march off to Enghien. Only the officers' batmen and other indispensable men would be allowed to stay behind and, under the supervision of the regimental quartermaster, collect all effects left behind in the quarters and transport them to the brigade as fast as possible. The brigade went off on its march without delay; there was none of that good hot coffee with extras, although most of us had not eaten anything in the expectation of a certain return to quarters. But as a precaution and according to regulations there was a small store in each haversack of bread, biscuits, and a drink, which served us very well indeed.*

Several hours after our departure, after not only our brigade but also the entire division had been assembled near Meslin L'Evêque,† we arrived at Enghien at 5 o'clock, from where our march took us over some very poor country roads to Braine le Comte. On our way, some distant rumbling could be heard for quite a while, as if from an approaching thunderstorm. But since at the time the skies were still clear and without clouds, I could not concur with the opinion of a thunderstorm coming up. In my opinion those were not weather phenomena that announced themselves; I believed it to be the thunder of battle. The further we moved in the direction assigned to us, the stronger the rumble of the thundering noise, in which one could distinguish single muffled blows of greater intensity.

It was indeed the uproar of battle . . . On 16 June the Allied Armies put up the utmost resistance to the French army, under Napoleon at Ligny and St Amand, and under Ney at Quatre Bras. Blücher commanded the Prussian army at the first mentioned locations, and the Duke of Wellington led at the latter location those troop bodies of the English–Hanoverian–Netherlands army under his command that he was able to concentrate there in the course of that day under the Prince of Orange. The roaring of the heavy guns and the rolling fire of small arms from the different armies fighting at Ligny and St Amand and at Quatre Bras was

---

* Another interesting reference to useful preparations. Many other divisions starved throughout the campaign because of lack of such foresight.

† This village can be found 3 miles north-east of Ath.

now the thundering noise that was heard, sometimes weaker, at other times stronger, by us and probably all those of Wellington's columns, who had left their cantonments during the night from the 15th to the 16th to arrive at the points of concentration as soon as possible, in accordance with the orders of the British supreme commander.

Our brigade approached that point apace. The rural roads that we had to march on from Enghien, by way of Braine le Comte and through the Forêt de Soignes, were in such poor condition from the past rains that particular places could be passed only in single file. Having arrived on the far side of the forest at 1 o'clock at night, we set up our bivouac, totally fatigued, on an open field.

We broke camp at daybreak and marched through Nivelles without delay on the road to Quatre Bras. We had just passed Nivelles when we encountered a large number of wounded, partly on carts, partly on foot. It was here that I learned from a wounded officer to my deepest sorrow of the death of my former commander-in-chief, the Duke of Brunswick, who had been felled by an enemy bullet on the day before . . . After we had continued our march towards Quatre Bras for an hour, we rested by the side of the highway until an order was received, early in the afternoon, to return to Nivelles . . .

The English army retired to Waterloo in two columns. One of the columns led by the Prince of Orange used the highway through Genappe to Waterloo, and our division and part of the 4th Division were assigned the major highway from Nivelles to Waterloo as line of retreat . . .

Crowds of country people, loaded with their possessions and driving their cattle ahead, fled with wives and children in all directions. The heat was oppressive, but thunderstorm and rain clouds already covered part of the horizon. Behind us to the left, artillery fire could be heard from time to time, which clearly marked the fighting that went on between our rearguard and the cavalry of the French Emperor, that advanced through Genappe towards Waterloo and that he followed with his major force. Off and on, the battle noise was joined by the thunder of the skies, and eventually interrupted by the heaviest thunderclaps and torrential rains. It was almost evening when our brigade halted to the left of the highway on a field between Braine l'Alleud and Mont St Jean and piled arms to get some rest. That rest did not last very long. Two French batteries took up position between La Haye Sainte and La Belle Alliance and began to fire at the army; some of its balls dropped in our vicinity. Several English 9 pounder batteries advanced quickly and soon silenced the French ones. After pickets had been placed by both sides, a real period of rest now set in and we could begin to make ourselves comfortable. But there were limits to our comfort on that evening.

Without any kind of breakfast but what our haversacks had held [when] we had marched off in the morning of the 16th, and since that time no foodstuffs had been delivered. But since then we had been moving almost all the time, and had been thoroughly soaked several times. These intermittent showers were only moderate precursors of what kind of discomfort was yet to come; because now we were struck by a truly violent storm. The rain came down in sheets so that the few camp fires could hardly be kept burning. Added to that was my empty stomach's reminder of the empty haversack. In this miserable situation the appearance of my stalwart batman Geige[*] was most agreeable: he arrived with a few full bottles in his right hand, and in his left hand and under the arm some meat and a large piece of bread. I was greatly delighted in beholding this truly revitalizing sight, and his own pleasure shone all over his face from being able to be of such great help to us.

Without a moment's hesitation did we, (Sode, Rönne, and myself), intend to begin our delicious meal when I thought of our captain. This man, a truly disagreeable superior, had done almost anything to make himself unpopular, both with the men who had not forgotten the humane Captain Lueder, and with the officers; von Rönne in particular had had to put up with many a fit of his bad temper; but one readily forgets all discord in the camaraderie of a warrior's life. I then hurried over to where the captain was lying at the camp fire, touched him on his shoulder, and invited him to have a share of our delectables. He angrily turned himself over on his other side and forbade any further disturbance in his customary rough manner, with the ominous words; 'I don't want either wine or anything else; tomorrow everything will be over anyway!' Upon my repeated encouraging words there was no response except sullen grunts, I let him lie there and thoroughly treated myself and my two dear comrades with what Geige had brought. Sode mentioned also that Captain Diedel[†] had been particularly gloomy all day. When Rönne expressed being glad that the first of the day's activities had begun, Diedel had told him, 'that he would soon have to forsake his gladness'. After having finished our meal, every one of us still had a piece of bread and some wine that was carefully stored away. Then we laid down on our wet bedding, with our feet towards the fire, and slept passably well into the new day, in spite of the pouring rain, and of the troublesome thoughts that may occupy one's mind on the eve of a battle, that was generally expected to happen, and with the occasional thunderclaps.

On the following morning, the 18th, we got up from our completely softened muddy place of rest, near which not a trace of the high

* Private Conrade Geige, 3rd Line Battalion, KGL.

† He was killed at Waterloo.

undulating corn existed anymore which we had found on our arrival. The rains finally let up somewhat, and now the men had to busy themselves in earnest with putting their arms back in order. While doing that, a large number of muskets were discharged, although strictly prohibited, in order to quickly get rid of the charge in them. This gave the impression of a regular fusillade, which was misleading people at a distance about the actual beginning of the battle.

Upon completion of this essential and most important business, Lieutenant Colonel von Wissel had the battalion form up, and with terse, simple yet heavy words, told us that we would have to face on this day some hot and heavy fighting, and urged us to perform [our duties] with courageous steadfastness and show patient endurance under the privations imposed on us by the circumstances. The battalion thanked its well respected commander with a spirited Hurrah!

The Duke of Wellington and Lord Hill, as well as the Prince of Orange, rode up quite close to where we were, obviously engaged in determining the deployment of the individual troop bodies at this position chosen by the British commander in chief for the impending battle to cover the city of Brussels . . .

The position of our brigade was to the west of the Nivelles highway and to the south of a road that leads from the area of the right centre of the line to Braine l' Alleud. The four rifle companies were posted on the left flank. These had been combined into a provisional battalion under the command of Captain Heise in accordance with regulations issued earlier, for that day as well as all the later concentrations of the brigade of the campaign. The brigade, by left rearward wheeling of the companies, had formed an open, right-marched-off column, with its front to the southwest. Afterwards, the arms were piled and the men were allowed to rest.

The ridge on which the first line of the army was posted, about 650 to 700 paces from our location, to our regret, kept us from being able to see from our position the deployment of the French army in line, often described as unusual for a Napoleonic battle. It was later said to have been a most impressive and grand spectacle for our troops in the first line. But then we, and with us the entire second line, formed in accordance with the Duke of Wellington's instructions, were hidden from observation by the enemy. Our view to the west was more open; however, only the extreme left wing of the French army was stationed in that direction, of which a small part could be seen to the side of the advance post of Hougoumont that was occupied by our troops. Towards the east, we could view the space between the first and second line for a considerable distance.

Shortly after the brigade had piled arms, a continuing loud shouting could be heard coming from the direction where the enemy must have been standing. The distance from where the shouts originated was too great for us to distinctly understand anything, but we could only assume that those were the *Vive l'Empereur!* shouts of the French army, whereby it used to salute its great and much adored leader. A period of quiet then set in, during which the commander of our division, Sir Henry Clinton, on horseback with his aides de camp halted some 50 paces before the centre of our brigade. His person stood out not only because of his tall figure and stiff military posture, but also by the unusual manner in which he wore his cocked hat. He always put it on sideways and different from other English officers who wore their hat, ornamented with a drooping white and red feather, so that its extended tips served as peaks in front and back.

The time might have been half past eleven when the quiet was interrupted by individual musket shots to our front at the outpost of Hougoumont which soon were followed by several cannon shots, that must have originated on the right centre of our side, judging by their sound, and then by a continuous rolling musketry and cannon fire. Very soon we had occasion to notice that the artillery fire did not only emanate from the British side, because solid shot now howled not only above and about us, and shells hissed through the intervals between the companies standing in open column order. Soon, balls and the shell splinters flying about us from exploding shells between and above us felled both officers and men. The wounded were taken to the hollow way near the rear of our position, where several surgeons put on temporary dressings . . .

During the course of the continuing attacks and defensive manoeuvres, Wellington decided to reinforce his front line, which had been greatly weakened by the considerable losses it had suffered, by advancing the 2nd Division under Sir Henry Clinton, together with Sympher's and Bolton's batteries, and by replacing them with General Chassé's Netherlands Division, which until then had been posted near Braine l'Alleud. The time might have been about 5 o'clock when du Plat's [1st KGL] Brigade left its position, where we had rested for five long hours under a cross fire of artillery, as it were, but with remarkably low losses. It then advanced beyond the Nivelles highway towards Hougoumont after having changed fronts in a left-marched-off column of companies, with the rifle battalion at its head. After we had marched for 300 to 400 paces and had passed a small elevation, it became necessary to close the column to ¼ distance to be able to rapidly form square in the customary four deep ranks because of the French cavalry being engaged with ours on this side of the main position. The stretch of way that we passed over was covered with the fallen; it had been the 1st Light Dragoons of the Legion under the command of the brave Dörnberg and Major von Reizenstein* who had here made a splendid charge against enemy cuirassiers by whom the regiment had been surprised on its flank. I was particularly struck by the sight of the dead body of the youthful Lieutenant Kuhlmann, an officer of great promise with the 1st Light Dragoon, who was well known to me. Our rifle battalion was ordered to move in the direction of three trees which stood some 300 paces away from the nearest hedge of the Hougoumont outpost. We had hardly arrived there and formed square when enemy cuirassiers charged us. Upon their approaching to within a few feet, our commander, Captain Heise, gave the order to fire which made them turn back with considerable loss. All the other battalions of our brigade had a similar experience; but soon afterwards we lost, apart from a good number of other officers, our brave and noble brigadier, Colonel du Plat, who had been severely wounded by an enemy bullet. Command of the brigade was taken over by Lieutenant Colonel von Wissel, who in his turn had been replaced by Major von Luttermann in the command of the 3rd Battalion.

The various attacks of the enemy cavalry upon the squares of our brigade ended as they did earlier. Soon after these heroic horsemen had turned back towards some lower ground , pursued for a short stretch by the advancing battalions with shouts of Hurrah!, and the well-directed cannon fire of Sympher's and Bolton's brave batteries, our rifle battalion faced a most critical situation.

Both the fire from an enemy battery that had moved up to our left, and the skirmish fire directed at us from the Hougoumont gardens [orchards] all of a sudden became extremely deadly. Captain Heise, our battalion commander, was mortally wounded, and killed on the very same spot were captains von Holle and Diedel, of whom the latter had been a great example for us with his brave and calm demeanour, and had now succumbed to the fate whose foreboding had caused his low spirits on the previous evening. The fourth captain of the battalion, Beuermann,† received a glancing shot to his head, through which he lost consciousness for a considerable time and had to be laid down near Hougoumont a short time later. At the same time, grape shot blew down a corner of the now small square so that from that moment on the battalion changed to more of a round formation than a square one, as the men were drawing together. Since the enemy musketry from the hedges of Hougoumont before us kept causing us losses, and remaining further in this position

* Major Augustus von Reizenstein, 1st Light Dragoons, KGL, Beamish no. 88, was severely wounded at Waterloo, but later became an aide de camp to the king of Hanover and died at Celle in 1830.

† Captain Charles Beuermann, 2nd Line Battalion, KGL, Beamish no. 428.

would completely annihilate our small group, I then, together with the fellow officers of my company von Sode and von Rönne, and with us all the other officers of the battalion, stepped before its front and led it against the nearest of our annoying enemies. The brave riflemen followed us at the double-quick, with firm determination, with an Hurrah! and levelled sword bayonets. The enemy did not wait for the clash of arms, however; they yielded and withdrew behind the next line of hedges.

Shortly thereafter, swarms of enemy tirailleurs pushed ahead past the hedges and toward the main position, but were energetically thrown back by General Adam's advanced brigade, upon the Duke of Wellington's personal instruction. This brigade also had to repulse several cavalry attacks before it withdrew behind the crest of the position, to where the remaining battalions of our brigade had also retired, with the exception of the 2nd Line Battalion, which was sent to reinforce us between the hedges of Hougoumont that we were holding . . .

The arrival of our rifle battalion, much weakened as it was, and of the 2nd Line Battalion, provided both necessary as well as welcome and energetic assistance to the Guards fighting at Hougoumont. The attacks and advances of the French tirailleurs, until then of increasing vehemence, diminished at that moment, and there was a pause in the fighting, as sometimes happened in a battle. During that period, Corporal Brinkmann, of the rifle company now under my command after Diedel's death, made a French tirailleur officer his prisoner, who had not immediately followed his retiring men, by a quick jump over the hedge that we had occupied.*

Our riflemen put up a great fight throughout; although wounded several did not go to the rear and kept on fighting. After Captain Beuermann joined us in observing the enemy tirailleurs – he had recovered from unconsciousness for some time and had taken over his command again – an English soldier approached us, whose left arm had been smashed by a cannon ball so that his lower arm seemed to hang on by just a strip of flesh or a tendon. His right arm he held in to his lower body. His bronzed face that may have seen many an enemy in all parts of the world was slightly contorted from his pain. He calmly asked us to cut off his injured arm, or have somebody do it, since it was inconveniencing him very much. To my question why he did not hold the arm with his right hand until he had had medical help, the badly wounded warrior held his hand off from his lower body for a brief moment, looking reproachfully at me, and now I saw that the hand had covered two holes from enemy bullets from which blood was flowing. Without any moaning nor repeating his wish, the unfortunate man took a few steps, then tumbled and, crying 'Oh dear Jane!' suddenly fell down and was dead . . .

---

* See appendix 2 for his citation.

The impression made on me and those around me of the death of this British warrior was soon effaced when an officer galloped up with the information that the French right wing had already been attacked for some time by the Prussians . . .

In the meantime, in our particular part of the battlefield, between the orchard hedges and the wood of Hougoumont, the Allied troops had become mixed up and interspersed due to the incessant attacks of the enemy tirailleurs and the open order of fighting, the moving up of reinforcements and the frequent alternating between advances and withdrawals.

When about 8 o'clock in the evening the attack of the Imperial Guard was beaten back, only the smaller part of our much weakened rifle battalion happened to be near Captain Beuermann, who was in command. He ordered me to search for any of our men in the walled garden, the chateau building, the farm buildings and the adjoining spaces and to gather them and bring them back.

My prompt and eager efforts had no significant success. I found only a few men who had brought up from the basement of the chateau a drink of beer, where some was still available.* I do not dare describe the scenery that I faced on the inside of the estate: it would be a picture full of blood, with burned and mangled corpses, with dying, wounded and fatigued warriors, surrounded by burning and smoking ruins. This scene of a contest fought most bitterly for long hours I left as fast as I could and rejoined Captain Beuermann.

Of the advancing British troops on the extreme right wing, who passed by Hougoumont, a number also moved into the environs of the estate. With their help, the enemy tirailleurs who still resisted energetically, ignorant as they were of what had happened elsewhere, were now completely driven out of the wood. Beuermann, with all the men of the battalion he had been able to gather, now rushed on with the tumult of the advancing troops; the other part of the riflemen had joined the 2nd Line Battalion. In the vicinity of the tavern of La Belle Alliance . . . the British troops were told to halt. The daylight already began to yield to the darkness of night. Most of our totally exhausted men sank down on the wet ground not far from the well known observatory, and let themselves be embraced by the god of sleep, to the extent this was possible, so did I myself. But as is easily understood, this rest would not remain undisturbed. Apart from the incessant monotonous noise peculiar to such scenes of war, there was here and there a thunderous blowing up of a powder wagon or a limber. In their anger and utter despair, badly wounded enemies would fire their muskets at groups of our men who had gathered around camp

* This is the only mention I have found that Hougoumont had a cellar; while it would not be unusual, I cannot find any corroborating evidence.

fires; or there was small arms fire for other unknown reasons. Added to that was the moaning and groaning of innumerable wounded who were imploring in different languages for a drink to still their terrible thirst, or for any help, even often for their deaths. A large number of horses without their riders were running loose and caused unrest, not to think of the disturbances that were visited upon those, who had lain down, by scavengers and other vagrants crawling about, and not least of all by one's own excitable state of mind . . .

The 3rd Line Battalion's losses were 3 officers killed and 3 wounded, 37 rank and file killed and 93 wounded; 31 men were missing; of all the battalions of the brigade it had suffered the highest losses.

The troops took up arms early in the morning of 19 June. This served the purpose of facilitating the reassembling the men, who had been scattered, partly due to helping back the wounded – a duty that an undeniably larger number than necessary had engaged in – partly from the fighting as such, as well as from the search for a more comfortable place to rest in the dark or for something to eat or for other kinds of things . . .

Entire ranks of fallen warriors all over the vast field indicated those well recognizable places where the most violent fighting had occurred: a horrifying, heart-rending scene met the terrified eye, of mutilated and often already nude corpses, of fallen and mortally wounded horses, which wrenched the stomach almost more than the gnawing hunger could do. In our brigade, that hunger was eased somewhat by the distribution of frugal portions. As we were eating the food we had just received, a part of the Prussian army was passing by our camp ground in its pursuit of the French. Not much later, our own army also marched off to take part in its turn in the pursuit of the remains of the enemy army.

4th Line Battalion, KGL

No. 12 Ensign Ferdinand von Uslar-Gleichen*

From H. Dehnel, Royal Hanoverian Artillery Colonel (retired) Reminiscences of German Officers in British Service from the Wars 1805 to 1816, collected from notes and oral accounts and supplemented with individual historical comments, *Hanover, 1864*

As was related by the Royal Hanoverian Lieutenant Colonel Baron Ferdinand von Uslar-Gleichen, in the year 1815 in the Netherlands, the rifle companies of the 1st, 2nd, 3rd, and 4th Line Battalions of the German

* Uslar, Beamish no. 547, served in the Holland and Waterloo campaigns and eventually became a lieutenant in the Hanoverian Grenadier Guards.

Legion were combined under the command of Captain Heise of the 4th Line Battalion. Those line battalions formed the brigade of Colonel G. C. du Plat, in the division of Lieutenant General Sir Henry Clinton in the 2nd Army Corps of Lord Hill.

On the day of battle at Waterloo, I, a very youthful ensign, happened to be with the rifle company of the 4th Line Battalion. During the course of the battle we left the position assigned to us on the right wing in the second line of the battle order and moved towards Chateau Hougoumont in support of the troops that had been engaged in and around it for some time.

Near the chateau at a place where the battlefield was marked by three trees we had to fight off several vigorous cavalry charges and then suffered considerable losses from a battery moved against us at a distance of about 400 paces, and also by skirmish fire from the hedge of Hougoumont.

After Captain Holle of the 1st, and Captain Diedel of the 3rd Line Battalion had been killed, the commander of the rifle battalion, Captain Heise, was mortally wounded, and many men had fallen, the fourth captain, Beurmann of the 2nd Line Battalion, was struck by a ricochet on his head that rendered him unconscious for a short time.

It was urgently necessary for us to extract ourselves from this critical situation; Lieutenant Dehnel, of the 3rd Line Battalion, took the initiative, with his sabre raised, he stepped in front of the square and shouted: 'Forward!'

With him in front were the remaining officers, Ensign Heise of the 1st,[*] Lieutenants Dawson and Lowson[†] of the 2nd, Lieutenant von Sode and Ensign von Rönne of the 3rd, and von Lasperg[‡] and my humble self of the 4th Line Battalion of the German Legion. We immediately advanced to the attack, followed by our brave riflemen, against the French tirailleurs behind the first of the hedges surrounding the orchard of Chateau Hougoumont, and with the bayonet drove them out and also out of a second one behind the first hedge.

Because the French received reinforcements we had to fall back to the first hedge, and then the fighting continued back and forth until we eventually retook the second hedge and held on to it. During this action I was on the extreme left flank of our skirmish line.

At the point where the second hedge adjoins in a right angle that hedge which encloses the Hougoumont orchard on its east side there

* Ensign Arnold Wilhelm Heise 1st Line Battalion, KGL, Beamish no. 409.

† Lieutenants William Dawson, 2nd Line Battalion, KGL, Beamish no. 444, and George Lowson, Beamish no. 451.

‡ Lieutenant Charles Frederick William von Lasperg, Beamish no. 539, later became a brevet major and retired at Bernburg in Anhalt Bernburg.

was a narrow opening which led to the field between the opposing armies. I walked through this opening for a view of the lay of the land. But on stepping outside I at that very moment, faced a French officer on horseback who was riding along, and close to, the hedge.

Having hardly outgrown my boyhood at the time, I – to tell the truth – was caught unawares. Without further thought I grabbed the reins of the horse with all my might. If the strong enemy horseman had resisted, things would have turned bad for me. But I received help from the wing corporal of the company who had come through the opening directly behind me and ensured that the officer remained our captive.

After our prisoner had dismounted from his horse he gave me his well filled purse, his watch and other precious things, which I passed on to the corporal with the instruction to return half of the money to the officer. I was then thinking what to do with the captured enemy and the horse when Captain Beurmann of our rifle battalion, who just had somewhat recovered from his contusion, walked up to me and said: 'My dear little huntsman' [Schütz] – [which became] my nickname that was often jestingly used at that time by my officer comrades – 'that horse is indeed too large for you, just let me have the animal'.

My liking of the older brave officers and a heavy dose of bashfulness prompted me to say 'yes' immediately. Apart from a certain, albeit somewhat questionable and dampened victor's elation, nothing much remained to the 'little huntsman' of the extraordinary feat of capturing an enemy officer, on horseback besides, but the humble role of beholding how Captain Beurmann sent horse and prisoner back under escort and the corporal pocketed both purse and watch.

3rd Hanoverian Brigade of Colonel Halkett

Salzgitter Landwehr

No. 13 From La Belle Alliance

Pflugk-Harttung's letter No. 47
Colonel Hugh Halkett to Major von Hammerstein
Regarding the Conduct of the Hanoverian Landwehr Battalion Salzgitter at La Belle Alliance

The fact that the Salzgitter Battalion under Your Excellency's command was not mentioned in the report on the battle of 18 June can only have been caused by the loss of my original battle report to His Excellency, General von Alten. I was able to name only the Osnabrück Battalion in my preliminary report because of the haste in which it had to be prepared, and because I was with the Osnabrück Battalion until the last moment, while yours had to operate on its own. In the meantime, I have already expressed to you in person, and repeat it herewith, that your battalion distinguished itself in the battle in particular with the seizing and occupation of the well known wood [at Hougoumont]. This I have not only brought to the attention of His Excellency, General von Alten, but will do everything to assure that he extends to you his appropriate recognition.

H. Halkett, Colonel and Brigadier

Third Division of Lieutenant General Baron Alten
2nd King's German Legion Brigade of Colonel Ompteda
2nd Light Battalion, KGL

No. 14 Lieutenant Emanuel Biedermann*

Extracts from Von Malta Bis Waterloo, Erinnerungen aus den Kriegen Gegen Napoleon I, *Emanuel Biedermann, Berne 1941*

From the Camp in the Bois de Boulogne near Paris, 19 July 1815

What a series of events since I last wrote you from Ecaussines! In the evening of the 15th of last month, at 6 o'clock, we were sitting quite calmly at our communal dinner and did not have the slightest idea of an approaching army when the news that the Prussians had been attacked by the French put an end to our peaceful existence.

At first, the word was that the French had made only a minor incursion. A quarter of an hour later, the Brigade Adjutant came galloping with the order to rally immediately and form up near the village on the Nivelles road. The order was quickly followed; we remained under arms until 10 o'clock in the evening and were then released again to our quarters.

At 2 o'clock in the morning of the 16th, the alarm was again sounded, and our bugles signalled our immediate departure. We marched to Nivelles by way of Braine le Comte, where the 3rd Division was concentrating. During the action at Quatre Bras our brigade and several Netherlands regiments were detached to keep the road to Charleroi under surveillance, from where an attack was suspected to come.† We could distinctly recognise the advance of our troops by the slowly weakening sound of the artillery fire.‡ Late in the evening we had to return to Nivelles and,

* Lieutenant Emanuel Biedermann had served in northern Germany and the Waterloo campaign and died at Steinhütte near Winterthür in Switzerland in 1836.

† This force was detached at Nivelles to watch the road from Charleroi to Nivelles. This provided security on the flanks of the units marching on Quatre Bras which Wellington clearly anticipated.

‡ As the army advanced, the distance apart grew.

after a short rest, we had to move to the vicinity of Quatre Bras, where we were allowed to rest for a few hours. At daybreak of the 17th, the rattling of the small arms fire started again and lasted until 2 o'clock in the afternoon, without leading to any decisive outcome. All we learned about yesterday's fighting was that the French had been pushed back to their positions of the day before yesterday, but also that apart from the loss of many of our brothers-in-arms we had to deplore the death of the heroic and by all beloved Duke of Brunswick Oels.

At 2 o'clock, our riflemen were sent off to relieve the skirmishers, and the army began to retire in several columns. The order for this sudden retreat came as a result of the news of some unfortunate engagement of the Prussian army and its [subsequent] falling back. The French remained all quiet, and there was no firing.

After our army had commenced its retrograde movement in the best order, we received instructions to follow our column as its rearguard in a fighting retreat, as soon as the enemy pressed on after us. But since the enemy remained quiet all the time, we slowly followed our army, and in a low-lying bushy meadow we lay down for some rest and waited for the French to come. All of us were very hungry and fatigued, and in the oppressive heat of the day most of us fell asleep. But soon a severe thunderstorm and the rain from a cloudburst shook us out of our repose. Also, some Brunswick hussars came galloping up and urged us to retreat speedily because the French were already all around us. We had to move at the trot through sunken roads that had already changed into brooks, and over bottomless cornfields, through Genappe onto the Brussels highway. In the town itself the water went up to our knees; we encountered our cavalry which had just then hurried here from the country's interior. Once we were in the open again, the word was: free the highway for the cavalry and artillery, and the foot soldiers to its left and right on the cornfields! But the corn was standing dense and high, and the clayey soil was quite soft. Hungry and tired and heavily loaded as our men were now, we found it heavy work to keep up with those moving in the same direction on the roadway. To our left we observed strong cavalry formations that we soon recognised as the enemy's. To the right, enemy masses were also pushing forward and began saluting us with artillery fire. The same was done by those moving up the highway. Luckily, the enemy horsemen to our left were unable to advance on the softened soil of the cornfields and had to draw onto the highway, as had the artillery which bothered us from the right, thus putting us in the lead again. Our own artillery unlimbered at purposeful intervals to cover our retreat, and scared off the enemy by its well-directed fire, whenever he followed too brazenly. The enemy nevertheless attempted several times to charge into our rearguard and, in fact, overran an English hussar regiment.* We quickly formed squares. At that moment, the Scottish horsemen of the Royal Life Guard† came rushing like a thunderstorm and chased the enemy away, otherwise we might have experienced some serious rearguard action. As soon as the enemy had been driven back we continued our march.

We officers made some comments about this unexpected retreat and of the various rumours about incidents regarding the Prussian army and its present situation that now made the rounds. Everything seemed to be in a strange contrast to the carefree peace that we still had enjoyed just two days ago in our cantonments. There was no question but that Napoleon had surprised us. Proof of this was the fact that officers of some brigades appeared on the battlefield on the 16th in their ball dress that they had had no time to change. Another proof was the cavalry hurrying from the interior as late as the evening of the 17th.

Napoleon knew that this battle was to decide his own fate; that he would now strike with even more than his usual impetuosity upon his implacable enemies was foreseen by the stern and heroic Duke of Brunswick Oels. He hurried to form a protective dam against the immense onslaught of an enemy who had become more defiant after his past gains, and then the Duke died the sublime death for freedom and fatherland. Without his heroic intercession, the British army would probably have been completely separated from the Prussians, and our situation would have become all the more unpleasant. But Napoleon's tempestuous rage failed completely before Blücher's indefatigable ardour and the courageous determination of his army that was unfazed by any reverses; before also the steadfastness of the British army and the outstanding generalship of our Wellington.

We had to behold the sad spectacle of crowds of country people leaving their homes, in order to bring themselves and their movable possessions to a safe place to escape the enemy who pressed on behind us. There were men driving their cattle ahead, others loaded with bundles, women carrying their children and dragging them along, all of them wailing and crying in their flight in every direction towards the interior.

We arrived shortly before sunset on the ridge of Mont St Jean, where our retreat had then ended and the army took up its order of battle. From our position we could overlook a large part of our line. Austerely and in great calm did the various brigades move to the posts assigned to them.

* This refers to the 7th Hussars who were handled severely by the French lancers at Genappe.

† It was the Life Guards who drove the French lancers back at Genappe, but Biedermann is in error stating that these were Scottish soldiers.

The enemy were hot on our heels and may have had a mind to push us through the forest of Soignes. But now our numerous artillery thundered and bid them such an energetic halt that they had no choice but to comply.

It was already dark, but we still heard to the left, right and behind us commands in different languages to wheel into the battle line. After night had set in, our riflemen were ordered to occupy the farm of La Haye Sainte, which was located before us on the Brussels highway. There were about 400 of us, of whom half were posted in the buildings, and the others in the orchard to their front; I belonged to the latter group. Heavy rains were pouring down on us hungry and tired warriors with few interruptions. We were not allowed to light fires because of the closeness of the enemy, and even if it had been permitted we could not have kept them going because of the rain. The tumults of the day were followed by rest and utter quiet. After sleeping for a while the rains would soon wake us up again.

Despite the unpleasantness of the rain, it later worked greatly to our advantage. It softened the soil to such an extent that the enemy's mostly heavy cannon could be moved from one location to another with only the greatest difficulties. Since our army was posted on a gradual incline, most of the French cannon balls became stuck in the soft ground without rebounding.

There was no doubting that a decisive battle would be fought on the next day, and most men were probably given to grave reflections in the night, that very well could be, and indeed was, the last one for many of us. I was confronted with the question: will you see your homeland and your loved ones again, or will your restless life be cut short by an enemy's sword? Upon the news of your death they will lovingly remember you and say: He has finally found his rest after all! Being on the threshold of death, the past and the future impress one in a more sober light than heretofore. Then again, man is always at the threshold of eternity; it is only that the world around him does not always remind him of it in all its earnestness. This night before the decisive and fateful day thus went by in solemn quiet.

Shortly after daybreak on the morning of 18 June, the rain had ceased somewhat, and permission was given to light some fires, which were readily used to dry the thoroughly wet clothes. Our men then searched the house for any edibles, and they were lucky, finding a bag of peas, some salt, and a pig, which was slaughtered right away, even if not exactly according to the rules of the art. It seems, however, that hunger promotes selfishness because there was little in the way of brotherly sharing. I was glad to have got at least a few peas and some salt. While we prepared our meagre meals, the enemy already made some vehement attacks, first on our right wing, where he suffered a severe rebuff at Chateau Hougoumont that was defended by the British Guards. Afterwards, it was the turn of our left wing, while at the centre we remained unmolested for some time. This was probably to induce our side to send reinforcements from the centre to both wings. Once weakened by these movements, the enemy would be able to break through all the better in a severe onslaught, divide the army and cut off part of it. But our leader would not let himself be misled.

After our peas had been half cooked, we thoroughly enjoyed them. The thundering of the cannonade became more general and came closer. Soon the balls from the artillery on both sides were flying over and beyond us. During the incessant buzz of the cannon balls, which only caused broken tree branches to shower on our heads, the major[*] gave us instructions for the impending action. That cannonade caused considerable losses, however, among the troops posted behind us on the plateau. In the event that we would be driven back, our orders were to withdraw to the point on the ridge that we had occupied yesterday evening in the beginning. All of a sudden the skirmishers of our cavalry now came galloping back. The French rapidly advanced in close columns and began a heavy fire with case shot. Our second major was struck by several bullets and sank off his horse, the first of us to be killed.[†] We vigorously returned the fire for some time, but our men fell by the dozens, and the French pushed on with an ever increasing superiority. The major then had the hornist sound the retreat. As we were about to withdraw towards the plateau, the tirailleurs of Napoleon's Guard already came from there against us, and fired at us. On my side, Lieutenant Robertson, a young man 18 years old, was killed by a shot through his head.[‡] All of a sudden there was shouting 'Cuirassiers! Cuirassiers!' Now we had to take to our heels. Many of us were shot or sabred. Whoever was unable to reach the squares behind us in time was to suffer that fate.[§] When I arrived at a square, its men were

---

* Major Baron George Baring commanded the force defending La Haye Sainte. His own memoir of the defence was published by the editor in *Letters from the Battle of Waterloo*, Greenhill Books 2004.

† Major Adolphus Boseweil, 2nd Light Battalion, KGL, Beamish no. 975.

‡ Ensign Frederick von Robertson, 2nd Light Battalion, Beamish no. 1013, was killed at Waterloo.

§ This is a very interesting statement. The order given to the men in the orchard of La Haye Sainte to return to the ridge rather than to enter the farmhouse is of great interest. Militarily this makes sense; because these troops would have been slaughtered by the French as they crowded in to attempt entry to the farm complex; it would also require the defences piled up at the various entrances to be removed temporarily and would run the risk of allowing the pursuing French troops to enter with them. The losses incurred from the fire of skirmishers and from a sudden attack

already pointing their arms. There was nothing left for me [to do] but quickly drop to the ground and to crawl for a few more paces to get there. My captain was killed there, and so were three of our company sergeants. The first major – B[aring] – lost two horses one after another, and his hat was punctured by several bullets. He himself remained uninjured. After his Adjutant had been wounded and been made a prisoner, Lieutenant R[iefkugel],* who was to replace him immediately, was shot through his thigh. Those of us, who had been saved, now joined the ranks of the square, and soon were glad to see how the cuirassiers, clanking up in their sabre flourishing charge, were forced by a well-directed fire to flee in their turn with heavy losses. With great intrepidity they repeated their attacks several times, but always with the same lack of success.

A period of quiet prevailed for a brief time on the battlefield which we used to rally the few of our men who had survived so far. But soon the turmoil became the severest ever. Returning bodies of our cavalry dispersed whatever small groups of our men we had collected, and as soon as we came together again, we hurried to the nearest squares of our division. While these squares had to fight off many violent attacks and had their ranks weakened by enemy fire, our comrades who defended the farm of La Haye Sainte were in a desperate situation. It was completely cut off, and the French had attacked it several times, and had even succeeded in setting it afire, but the defenders were able to extinguish the flames although only after a great effort. In the end, after having expended all of their ammunition, they attempted to fight their way out, and part of them succeeded.

Our brigade had terrible losses, because the rifle battalion that defended a ditch to our right had been severely mauled, and the 5th Battalion was almost completely annihilated by the cuirassiers. In that action our brigadier, Colonel Ompteda, had also been killed.†

---

by cuirassiers were serious but not overwhelming.

This comment may also help to explain oft misquoted statement by Baring that only forty men from the defence of the farm were still with him at the end of the battle; if one presumes that he did not include in his figure the many that had escaped unharmed from the orchard previously, as many more than forty of his battalion certainly survived the battle. This would also reduce the number of defenders actually in the farm complex and the numbers who became casualties within.

* Lieutenant Bernhard Riefkugel, Beamish no. 348, had replaced Lieutenant and Adjutant William Timmann, Beamish no. 370. Both were severely wounded at Waterloo but survived.

† Colonel Christian Frederick William von Ompteda had been ordered by the Prince of Orange to advance with the 5th Line Battalion, KGL in line, to succour the defenders of La Haye Sainte despite the proximity of cuirassiers. They were attacked in the flank and rear and decimated.

The tumult and confusion on the battlefield were frightful. Abandoned cannon and powder wagons stood here and there. Some of these were ignited by shells and exploded, making a terrible noise. The enemy cavalry often rode through the intervals between our different squares to whose murderous fire they were then exposed. Their frequent attempts to charge into those squares that had already been formed were all unsuccessful and moreover each time they were pursued on their way back by our own cavalry. And so it went on during this never-ending afternoon with its seldom interrupted cannonade and small arms fire. Our ranks shrank all the while; some squares were not even able to close up anymore, and our store of ammunition became depleted to the point that we had to gather what was left in the cartridge pouches of the dead and wounded.

The commander of our army corps, the Hereditary Prince of Orange, and the commander of our division, Alten, stayed at one of these squares until they had to leave the battlefield, the former after receiving a shot through his arm, and the latter upon being shot through his thigh.

The centre of our line began to waver. Reinforcements moved in from our second line, and at the most desperate moment, Blücher, like a saving angel, appeared with his heroic Prussians in the rear and to the right of the French who were pressing us with their much greater strength. Our enemies then began their flight.

At the onset of night, our brigades now moved again to the positions they had held in the beginning. The battlefield offered a most gruesome sight, being covered all over with dead and wounded. Of our battalion only a small troop was left, the others were killed or wounded, or went missing. Overcome with fatigue from the immense exertions, we lay down to sleep among the mangled corpses of friends and enemies. A ghastly place to bed down in. Without being asked, one of our sergeants, Wittopp by name,* brought a bundle of straw, put it under my head, and covered me with a coat.

A great many camp fires could be seen in the distance. They were those of the Prussians who restlessly pursued our common enemy. A full moon shone over the gruesome battlefield, with its deep stillness only interrupted by the groaning of the poor wounded men.

On the morning of the 19th, after all the remaining wounded had been gathered, we collected the dead bodies of the officers of our brigade that had been disfigured by blood and mud, and placed them in a large [mass] grave.

---

* Strangely his name is missing from the Waterloo Medal Roll, but this would appear to be a mistake in the Roll as a Sergeant Friedrich Wittopp, 2nd Light Battalion, KGL received a Military General Service Medal with 7 bars for Talavera; Busaco; Fuentes d'Onoro; Salamanca; Vitoria; San Sebastian; and Nivelle. He therefore most certainly received a Waterloo Medal in addition.

Towards noon, the wagons with foodstuffs finally arrived, and right away began the portioning out and cooking. Defaced as we were by powder smoke, mud and blood, we sat down in groups among the corpses, had the multitude of saddles, knapsacks, drums, and similar equipment lying around us to serve as chairs, and the coat of many a cuirassier as a tablecloth, who yesterday was all out to make us do without food forever. It took the kind of ravenous hunger that we had to make us enjoy our food as much as we did in these surroundings.

As soon as our hunger was sated we received the order to break camp, and then marched across the ghastly battlefield to the area of Nivelles where we set up our bivouac. It was now time to wash ourselves in the stream that was flowing by the side our camp. As I walked along that stream, looking for a suitable place to do so in my turn, I noticed a crowd of many people at a nearby isolated house. I walked there to satisfy my curiosity about what was going on. They were stragglers from various English regiments who were about to extort foodstuffs and other goods from the inhabitants of the house. There was absolutely no need for this, since we were amply supplied with provisions and since, moreover, it was strictly prohibited. Only with great effort did I succeed in driving off this pack, which included a group of drunken women who excelled in brazen insolence. Two English non-commissioned officers were faithfully helping me in this incident. In gratitude for my interference, the inhabitants of this house, a motherly old woman and her daughter, prepared a hot bath for me, which was most invigorating. When afterwards I was about to return to the camp, the two still terror-stricken women asked me to stay with them as their protector. They always called me Monsieur François and would not let me explain to them that I was not their friend François, who may earlier have been in this area with the French army. They were asking me all the time why I would not admit that I was he. 'You may say what you want, you are none other than François, and you have come here for our protection'. But I could not stay away from the camp much longer without the permission of my superiors, and it was painful for me to almost have to use force to turn myself loose from these people. I promised I would do my very best to have our commander provide a protective guard for them. Upon my return to the camp, I reported the incident and these people's wish; I hoped that they would not be molested in the future.

Early on 20 June we broke camp. As we passed by Nivelles, we encountered on the highway many of our friendly hosts from Ecaussines whose interest in our fate had brought them here. How anxiously did they not inquire into what had happened to their former house guest! How cast down were not those who missed theirs! For us who had remained unscathed they offered the heartiest handshake, and they assured us that they had eagerly said many a prayer on our behalf. The good people followed our army column for a good stretch of the road and related the events in their area and their own fates during the terrible three days of the 16th, 17th, and 18th. After wishing us all the best, our friendly former hosts were leaving us. May they fare well, those stout-hearted people.

On our march we encountered already a great number of country people who had returned from the battlefield and carried all kinds of equipment. Some had woollen blankets, cavalry coats, harnesses; others had weapons and other implements in their collection. Many now drove there with wagons, to gather any leftovers. We did not begrudge them this kind of harvest as small compensation for the devastation by both armies of the cornfields far and wide.

We were much gladdened by the return of many of our brothers in arms who had succeeded in escaping from their captivity during the confusion prevailing in the enemy army. They were sent back to the battlefield, there to re-equip themselves with weapons, uniforms, and knapsacks, of which there were only too ample stores left by their fallen brothers.* At night we camped at the small town of Binche.

On the 21st, we marched across the French border.

Upon Napoleon's reappearance, the French newspapers untiringly described the enormous defence preparations, by which every village seemed to have been turned into a fortress. But these announcements were only idle boasting by the French because we did not see a single trace of all this. On the other hand, the white flag† fluttered above all roofs, which had probably been raised more in fear of the victors than from love for the Bourbons. Except for the riff-raff, most inhabitants viewed our arrival with mute resentment. But he would not be a good citizen who would rejoice over the entering of an enemy army into his fatherland, and who would just fake being glad. The French certainly could not expect much good to come from our occupation because only too vividly would their conscience remind them of their own arrogant behaviour in all those countries through which they had marched as victors. In the evening we camped near Bavay, and the French now had a good opportunity to see how unfounded their concerns had been. We bivouacked on a very wet meadow. After the tents had been erected we went with a few men to a nearby village and picked up some straw so that we would not have to lie on the wet ground. We had hardly taken care

* An interesting comment on soldiers being sent on to the battlefield to collect equipment to put right any shortages they had. An obvious solution, but one I have not come across before.

† The Bourbon flag was white.

of this matter when an adjutant of the general-in-chief [Oberfeldherr] came to see our commander with the strict order to desist from any and all extortion in this friendly country. We were then informed by way of a most splendid proclamation directed both at the French people and at our army that the war had been conducted exclusively against Napoleon. Louis XVIII now was our ally, and consequently all the French were our good friends. In compliance with this, the straw earlier taken to our camp therefore had to be returned immediately to our new friends. All this we did not fully understand. The French, having as victors become used to act by entirely different principles, could not explain this extreme generosity; instead they viewed it as a sign of fear of the grand nation, and now became all the more insolent towards us.

On the 22nd, the march continued as far as a camp between Maubeuge and [Le] Quesnoy.

On the 23rd, we bivouacked near Cateau Cambresis and spent the 24th as a day of rest. We then learned from a very edifying report that on 18 June the false rumour of our loss of the battle had spread a terror within the baggage train that had halted several hours behind our position, and had caused the train crews to hurry to the rear at full speed. In the resulting disorder, a large part of the baggage had been lost in various ways. I thus lost my nice portmanteau; what little I had left was what our Surgeon Müller* had kindly packed in his box. During the campaign of 1813, I had twice lost my baggage, and now I had lost it for the third time. Thank God I did not lose any of my limbs, and these are infinitely more valuable than any baggage that can easily be replaced.

On the 25th we camped for the night near Reumont on the road to St Quentin.

On the 26th, our camp was near Caulaincourt, and on the 27th near Crécy that has become known for the victory that Prince Edward of Wales, the Black Prince, there had won over the French in 1346, through which he gained possession of Calais.†

On the 28th we camped near Roye.

On the 29th, we passed the Oise River near Pont Sainte Maxence and set up camp two hours away from Senlis.

On the 30th, we arrived at a camp on this side of Senlis.

On the 30th, we moved into a bivouac near Aulnay [sous Bois], a few hours away from Paris that the Prussians just had vacated. We did

---

* Assistant Surgeon Henry Frederick August Muller, Beamish no. 373. He died at Luneburg in 1819.

† This is a consistent case of misidentification in memoirs of this period. The Crécy of battle fame is Crécy-en-Ponthieu near Abbeville on the coast, not here. The division was at Cressy-Omencourt.

not find a single person in the town itself. All inhabitants had fled to Paris. The Prussians must have marched off unexpectedly and in a great hurry because they had left behind pigs, sheep and calves that had just been butchered, as well as broiled and half-broiled pieces of meat in any amount that we were most grateful for and that we thoroughly enjoyed eating. There were ample stores of tables, chairs and any other kind of household goods.

On 5 July, we finally left the boredom of this camp behind us as it was said, to enter the capital. As we came up to the barrier, the command was: 'Right turn!' and on to Montmartre. From this Montmartre, which, however, is only a hill of moderate height, we all of a sudden had the view of Lutetia* once so proud but now humiliated. All of us were greatly impressed by this spectacle of the place of origin of many revolutions that had such wide effects in political and moral respects, and by all of its cathedrals and palaces.

We had hardly occupied the hill when we were already joined by many hucksters of all kinds of wares. Almost all of our officers provided themselves with maps and descriptions of this famous city that we hoped to enter in a few days. We in fact, left Montmartre on 7 July, but at the barrier, the word was again: 'Right turn!' We now had to move into the Bois de Boulogne, where the greatest part of Wellington's army set up camp; the remainder went to the area of Neuilly and St Denis.

The Prussians went about this matter in an entirely different way than we did. In the very beginning, every officer received a significant compensation in the form of money; then they were billeted in the houses of the lordly Parisians where they were properly regaled, as was their due. Furthermore, their army corps, one after another, were newly uniformed by their newly won friends†.

Tomorrow or on the day after tomorrow, the monarchs, those that are present, will hold a big parade of our troops, and then, according to hearsay, we are to move to Normandy.

* Lutetia Parisiorum was a pre-Roman town in Gaul, the predecessor of Paris.

† It is perhaps over generous to the Prussians to say that the Parisians who had Prussian officers billeted upon them and who made heavy demands on their funds, were received as friends.

5th Line Battalion, King's German Legion

No. 15 Lieutenant von Brandis,* Aide de Camp to Colonel Baron Ompteda

From H. Dehnel, Royal Hanoverian Artillery Colonel (retired) Reminiscences of German Officers in British Service from the Wars 1805 to 1816, collected from notes and oral accounts and supplemented with individual historical comments
Hanover, 1864

At the beginning of March [1815], a large number of our men were discharged, something that had already happened a few weeks earlier. This order greatly dampened the cheerfulness of our officers because, without doubt, it soon would be our turn to be discharged.

The command of the 5th Line Battalion was taken over by Lieutenant Colonel von Linsingen.

On 9 March, the news arrived of Napoleon's escape from Elba and his landing in France, which raised like magic the depressed spirits. In our delight we made three hurrahs to dear little Boney, as the emperor was jestfully called by the English, although there were doubts about the truth of the news. During the following days, several sources fully confirmed this portentous information which was particularly significant for us legionnaires. Napoleon had already advanced to Lyon, and even to Paris.

The joyful excitement of many of the inhabitants [of Tournai] was obvious, although their elation was for a very different reason than ours. They wanted to fight for Napoleon, we, however, hoped to fight against him and to prolong in this profession our agreeable existence in the British army.

We already received orders on the 17th to be ready to march off, along with instructions to send the heavy baggage to Ostend. All the time, things became more lively in our garrison. Rumours, one worse than the next, changed by the hour and increased everybody's excitement including ours. At one time it was said that Napoleon had been surrounded by troops loyal to the king, then again that he approached France's capital in giant steps. Re-enlistment was offered to a number of [our] soldiers who had served their time, which was accepted by many.

The official notice of Napoleon's arrival in Paris was soon followed by the certainty that Louis XVIII had yielded to him and had gone to Lille.

As early as 13 March, a ban against Napoleon was declared in Vienna, and it was agreed that the Peace of Paris was to be maintained in all of its

* Lieutenant Eberhard von Brandis, Beamish no. 570; he later became a captain in the 12th Line Battalion.

points, and that the Allies were to field large armies in Italy and on the upper and lower Rhine.

The order given to the garrison to post pickets along the French border confirmed the warlike turn of events that was now the order of the day. Every morning at 4 o'clock, the garrison had to stand to arms; work detachments were formed that had to repair the citadel and the fortress walls, some cannon were also moved onto the market square; two Hanoverian Landwehr battalions under Colonel Hugh Halkett also arrived, in short, for us everything again took on an agreeable warlike appearance. On 4 April the Duke of Wellington arrived to take over the command of the Allied troops who had a strength of about 50,000 men, who were however, constantly being reinforced. A few days later our officers received an inquiry if anybody, and if so who, would be inclined to join the Hanoverian Landwehr. Colonel von Ompteda was gladdened that nobody was willing to leave his unit at this time.* On the 8th we were moved to Lens, on the 9th to Chaussee-Notre-Dame[-Louvignies], by way of Ath. A General Order from the Duke of Wellington of 15 April notified us of the organizing of the army in two army corps with newly formed divisions and brigades, the divisions for the most part in a mixed combination of English, Hanoverians, and Netherlanders.† The 1st and 2nd Light, and the 5th and 8th Line Battalions [KGL] were made up into a brigade under Colonel von Ompteda, which, together with the Hanoverian Brigade of Major General Count von Kielmansegge and the 5th English Brigade of Major General Sir Colin Halkett, formed the division of General Sir Charles Alten, in its turn part of the 1st Army Corps.

The 1st, 2nd, 3rd, and 4th Line Battalions of the Legion were likewise made up into a brigade under Colonel du Plat which, with the Hanoverian Brigade of Colonel H. Halkett and the English Brigade of General Adam, formed the 2nd British Division under Lieutenant General Sir Henry Clinton that had been assigned to the 2nd Army Corps.

The 1st Army Corps, commanded by the Prince of Orange, consisted of 2 infantry divisions – English and Hanoverian – with 4 batteries, and of 2 divisions and 1 brigade of Belgian and Nassau infantry with 2 batteries and 7 regiments of cavalry.

The 2nd Army Corps, under the command of Lord Hill, consisted of 2 divisions – English and Hanoverian – with 4 batteries, and 1 division and 1 brigade of Belgian infantry and 2 batteries of artillery. The Reserve included 3 batteries of artillery and 2 divisions - English and Hanoverian, also 4 batteries of the artillery reserve. Then there was the Ducal Brunswick

* Actually three officers from the 5th Line Battalion, KGL, transferred to the Hanoverian Landwehr. For details see Appendix 4.

† Actually the Dutch/Belgian troops remained within their own corps structure.

Corps, commanded by its heroic prince, the Duke Frederick-William of Brunswick-Oels, consisting of 2 artillery batteries, 1 hussar regiment, 1 uhlan squadron, 2 infantry brigades, and 4 companies of light infantry and the Hanoverian Reserve Corps under Lieutenant General von der Decken, consisting of 4 infantry brigades and 1 cavalry regiment. The cavalry under General Lord Uxbridge numbered 7 English and 1 Hanoverian brigades.

On 19 April, we and a number of other troops were inspected on the highway between Mons and Ath by the Duke of Wellington who appeared with a numerous suite. As he passed along the brigade, we saluted him with a loud Hurrah! On the next day, Colonel von Ompteda favoured me with offering me the position of Aide de Camp that I gratefully accepted. It had been my wish for a long time to serve on the Staff, although I relinquished my command over my trusted and much tried riflemen with much regret.

At about this time the battalions of the legion were reduced from 10 to 6 companies, each, because of they were under strength. The officers thus freed were transferred to Hanoverian service because of the lack of experienced officers among the Hanoverian troops. On 1 May I commenced my duties as aide de camp to Colonel von Ompteda and moved into his quarters at the castle of Brugelettes.*

During the following period, there were exercises without interruption in good and bad weather by battalions, brigades, and divisions, and also inspections and parades, etc., for which reason the troops were cantonned closer together. These concentrations of the military now led to splendid *déjeuners* of the generals, in which the ladies also participated, who enhanced the social life and, of course, the general contentment.

On the 10th, the brigade marched to Ecaussines and environs. Colonel von Ompteda, a stern disciplinarian, let the baggage feel his wrath because it did not move in the proper order, as earlier in Spain.

In Ecaussines† we moved into the castle of Count van der Burcht, colonel and aide de camp to the king of the Netherlands.‡ His wife, the countess, was lady-in-waiting to the queen, lived at the castle and was so kind as to assign our living quarters to me in person. She was about to arrange a large formal dinner for the two princes of the Netherlands, to which she also invited the colonel and myself. I rode ahead to the brigade and brought the colonel the invitation, which obviously did not please him; upset as he was with the affair of the baggage. On our arrival at the castle he immediately excused himself, whereupon the countess had the

* The castle of Brugelettes is now known as Château Attre.

† The castle of Ecaussines-Lalaing purchased by the Burcht family in 1642.

‡ Author's footnote: In February 1815, the Prince of Orange, 'Father of our Serene War Companion in the Peninsula', had been proclaimed king of the Netherlands.

invitation again extended to him in an urgent manner, but in vain. He even declined the subsequent invitation by the crown prince with the excuse that the baggage had not arrived yet and that he was unable to dress for the occasion.* But now the crown prince changed the invitation into an order that the colonel could not very well disobey. He appeared, and was most warmly received by both princes with the assurance that he would be welcome in any kind of garment.

During the meal I had the misfortune that a large piece of pastry slid not just off my plate but off and under the table where it fell on the feet of the guests on the opposite side. The matter struck me as so funny that I laughed out loud, in which laughter the other guests merrily joined in. The countess in particular showed in this her exceptional kindness, as she also by her friendliness made my stay in Ecaussines one of the most agreeable ever offered me in my life. She asked me to regard her family as my own, and to spend time in her family circle whenever circumstances would permit. The countess was a most vivacious and kind lady of between 30 and 34 years of age, had three sons and as many daughters. She had a relative living with her, la Comtessa de Peralta, about 30 years old, not pretty but no less vivacious and kind than the countess herself.

The count's brother, Mr Aimée, had earlier been in French service and seemed to me to be an inveterate Bonapartist who obviously wished us to go to the devil. Besides him, the castle's chaplain, an amiable priest named Mr Ledoux, and a quite inane music teacher had access to the family circle.

On the morning after the formal dinner, Colonel von Ompteda rode with me through charming scenery to the Prince of Orange's headquarters, which was one hour away at Braine le Comte, to pay the prince our respects. He received us most kindly and congratulated us on our good quarters in Ecaussines.

On 8 June, at 4 o'clock in the morning, I was awakened by a sergeant with the information that the brigade was to immediately march to Soignies. I rose in a great hurry and, ready for travelling in a few minutes, went to Colonel von Ompteda.

Upon arrival of the brigade at Soignies we learned that General von Alten only intended to test the mobility of the division, and that we would return to our quarters. A few days later, an order from higher authority was received to be ready any minute for marching off. News had arrived at headquarters of the movement of French troops at the border.

---

* To be fair to Ompteda, the editor of his memoirs reveals that it was at this time that Ompteda learnt of the death by natural causes of his beloved brother Ferdinand; it may be presumed that the lack of baggage was therefore a convenient excuse in an attempt to be left alone.

When on the 14th I returned from a muster of the division, the countess mentioned to me the receipt of a letter from Roeulx of the Princess de Sort, according to which that lady would arrive in Brussels that same day; she urged the countess to be prepared also for an immediate departure because of the approach of the French army under Napoleon. We nevertheless spent the day cheerfully and in peace in the family circle.

On the 15th, I accompanied Colonel von Ompteda on a visit to General von Alten at Soignies. He had just then received information that early in the morning the Prussian advance posts had been attacked by the French. The general now requested of the colonel to rally the Brigade at Ecaussines without delay, to be ready to march off immediately if necessary. The colonel sent me at once to the 5th and 8th Battalions in order to expedite the concentration of the brigade. I then hurried to Ecaussines to take care of everything else, pack the baggage, etc.*

By 3 o'clock in the afternoon, the brigade was assembled in the bivouac at Ecaussines. In the evening I was sent once more to Soignies to General von Alten. Upon my return I threw myself exhausted fully clothed on my bed.

At 1 o'clock in the night to the 16th, the order to march was received. On taking leave from the family, the thought saddened me that this kind, hospitable castle might perhaps soon become part of the theatre of war and be exposed to its horrors. The countess was in tears; she intended to depart with her family to Brussels in a few hours.

The brigade marched to Braine le Comte, where it was ordered to move on to Arquennes and there take up position. After a march of two hours, during which we passed a Belgian corps, we arrived at the prescribed location.† No enemy was in sight, and we stacked arms; two brigades of Netherlands dragoons halted to our rear.‡

Towards noon we heard heavy cannon and small arms fire in the direction of Quatre Bras, and saw heavy clouds of smoke rising there. The

---

* There is clear evidence that the Prince of Orange had sent orders for his corps to assemble while he went to Brussels to apprise Wellington of these early reports of a French attack.

† In *Memoirs of Baron Ompteda*, London, 1894, the editor of this work wrongly states that these troops arrived at Quatre Bras before any other British or Hanoverian troops but were ordered away to Arquennes. A simple glance at any map will show you the error of this statement. The road from Braine le Comte to Arquennes does not lead through Quatre Bras, that place being a number of miles beyond Arquennes. The editor of the work has been confused by the mention of Dutch/Belgian cavalry. These were not the cavalry at Quatre Bras, but those sent along with the Hanoverian troops to watch the road from Charleroi to Nivelles on Wellington's flank.

‡ The brigades of Ghigny and Trip were ordered here by the Prince of Orange, only van Merlen's Brigade of cavalry marching on to Quatre Bras.

firing continued heavily and kept us in great suspense. Towards 5 o'clock in the afternoon we eventually received orders to advance to Quatre Bras as fast as possible. A Netherlands brigade relieved us and sent us off with three cheers. At the onset of darkness we arrived at Nivelles, where we had to halt for a time in order to let two splendid English dragoon regiments ride past us at the trot, a magnificent, stirring spectacle. We then followed them and encountered many wounded near Quatre Bras.

The wounded English Captain Havelock* told us that the other brigades of the division had been engaged and had had significant losses, and that the Guards and the Scottish had suffered in particular.

We arrived on the battlefield at our position at 11 o'clock in the evening. There had been some severe combat, but the traditional bravery of the British and their sharp bayonets had left their mark; Marshal Ney had attempted in vain to follow his Emperor's orders and seize the Quatre Bras position.

We also learned here that the Duke of Brunswick had fallen, and that his corps had fought bravely as always, preserving its well deserved renown of long standing. On that evening, a splendid view was offered by the camp fires of the two armies. In general, a solemn quiet prevailed, which was only interrupted now and then by 'Who comes there?' or '*Qui vive?*' and by the distant murmur and muffled noise of newly arriving troops. I had the reins of my horse attached to my hand and, wrapped in my coat I lay down on the ground and slept calmly towards the events to come. On the 17th, at 2 o'clock in the morning all troops stood to arms. At daybreak the tirailleurs on both sides began to fire although there were no movements. The firing soon ended. From the opposite side we often heard shouts of *Vive l'Empereur!* presumably from newly arriving troops.

As soon as there was broad daylight, our brigade changed to a different position on the highway. We noticed here many signs of yesterday's fighting. The shells had thrown up numerous holes in the ground, and there were many dead scattered about. The enemy remained calmly in front of us and gave no sign of renewing the fighting; we assumed that he was waiting for reinforcements.

Towards 11 o'clock noon, I rode with Colonel von Ompteda to General von Alten who stayed in a house nearby. Here we learned that Napoleon had beaten the Prussians near Ligny yesterday and that therefore our army was about to fall back. Ompteda was given instructions to form the rearguard with our brigade. The general gladdened us also with the information that yesterday our compatriots had held up the reputation of the Hanoverians by their good performance.

---

* Lieutenant William Havelock, 43rd Foot, aide de camp to Count Alten.

After the army had gradually left the position, we commenced our retreat at 1 o'clock The enemy followed only slowly and without hindrance let us cover the 1½ to 2 hour's distance to the area of the town of Genappe. The division marched up sideways on a ridge a quarter hour distant from that locality, stacked their arms, and attempted to light a few camp fires. These were, however, extinguished by a severe thunderstorm and heavy rain. Our rest period soon ended as artillery fire was coming closer, and upon the order to continue our march.

The roadways had badly deteriorated due to the heavy rain, and it was only with great efforts and exertions that we reached the highway in Genappe. The road was packed with troops of all arms and baggage that moved ahead side by side at a good rate of speed. Lord Wellington and his suite passed by us, horses and riders splashed with mud all over.

From Genappe onward, the enemy was hot on our heels and pushed us mightily, while our cavalry and horse artillery had much work to do on the softened ground. At 6 o'clock in the evening we eventually arrived at the village of Mont St Jean near Waterloo, where our brigade took up position not far from the farm of La Haye Sainte and directly to the right of the highway. The enemy formed up opposite us and, while there still was daylight, saluted us with cannon shots which received a heavy reply from our artillery. At the onset of darkness the brigade deployed a picket line. The 2nd Light Battalion occupied the farm of La Haye Sainte on our left wing, the other battalions took up position in the surrounding cornfields. The other two brigades of our division lined themselves up from our brigade towards Hougoumont. The Brunswickers and the Guards attached themselves further down the line, to the extent to which I was able to observe in the twilight. The 5th Division rested on our left flank. The situation of the troops was extremely uncomfortable on the soft soil, under the incessant rains, and at poorly burning camp fires. I carried my observations to the colonel, who had occupied a room at La Haye Sainte, together with Baring, the two Bussches, and Brigade Major von Einem, where a cosy fire was burning and I was very much refreshed by a cup of hot bouillon.

At daybreak of the 18th, all of us expected the enemy's attack who was standing opposite from us at a distance of about 2,000 paces on a ridge, but our expectations did not come to pass. The morning hours of that Sunday were used by the troops for the cleaning and repair of their arms, and to cook their meals to the extent that provisions were available. On the Genappe highway, a makeshift abatis of tree trunks was installed, and the 2nd Light Battalion, which had occupied the farm of La Haye Sainte, barricaded the doorways and pierced loopholes through the walls. Various troop bodies now moved into their more definitely determined positions. The two armies thus calmly faced each other until about 11 o'clock when we noticed brisk activities in the enemy's ranks. Several strong columns of all arms moved from the right to the left wing. A short time later a strong infantry column advanced there, preceded by swarms of tirailleurs, and attacked Chateau Hougoumont in front of our right wing, that was occupied by British Guards, Nassauers, and a small detachment of Hanoverian Jäger.

On the enemy's advance in that direction he was saluted by the 9-pounder battery of Captain Cleeves of the legion artillery with the first cannon shots fired on that day of battle.

When the enemy column moved on unflinchingly and entered the range of the small arms fire, this also commenced and kept rolling without let up, accompanied by the lower roar of the field artillery.

The assault of the French upon the garden of Chateau Hougoumont failed before the determined resistance of the defenders. But they renewed their attempts with greater numbers; the small wood in front of the chateau was lost, was retaken and lost once more; even part of the chateau went up in flames; this important post was nevertheless held by the stout-hearted defenders.

During this engagement on our right wing the French made an attempt on the left wing of our battle line which however, was easily repulsed by Colonel Best's Hanoverian Brigade. Towards 2 o'clock, it was our turn who, until then, had only been exposed to some artillery fire from both sides that had spread over much of the entire battle line.

But Napoleon was now about to execute his principal plan, that of breaking through the British centre. To that purpose, he had some 80 cannon emplaced opposite from us, and these now raged in all violence against the divisions of the centre, those of Alten and Picton.

At that time, Colonel von Hake, whose regiment – the Cumberland Hussars – was standing to our rear, galloped up to Colonel von Ompteda and in the greatest agitation asked him for 'an order to withdraw his regiment from the artillery fire which had become unbearable'. Ompteda referred him to Lord Uxbridge, commander over the entire cavalry. By the way, besides the Cumberland Regiment, several English and Netherlands cavalry regiments were stationed behind us who, like ourselves, suffered under the cannonade but still stood calmly in the places assigned to them.

During the onslaught of the enemy cannon, large infantry and cavalry formations were lined up against us. While our guns replied vigorously to the French artillery, four strong infantry columns eventually advanced towards us in echelon – d'Erlon's Corps – supported by Roussel's massed cavalry.

The battalions of our brigade formed square immediately and received the cavalry, which charged ahead of the infantry, with a murderous fire at close distance that forced it to retreat speedily.

In anticipation of the enemy infantry attacks to follow, deployment in line was to be quickly executed when ordered. The powder smoke was so dense however, that nothing could be seen. After a few minutes, Colonel von Ompteda sent me ahead of us to determine whether it was enemy infantry or cavalry that was approaching. I soon found myself in front of a line of enemy cuirassiers, which advanced at a walking pace. I therefore quickly turned my horse around in order to notify the brigade. But at the same moment a brigade of heavy English dragoons came towards me at the trot in line, about to attack the cuirassiers. It was impossible for me to pass through that line. Much against my will I had to turn around again, and to avoid being overrun I had to charge against the cuirassiers. Having to make the best of this awkward game did not appeal to me at all. Still, I flourished my sabre and was forced to ride in front of the dragoons, I tried to enhance their fighting spirit by shouting some strong encouraging words at them. I nevertheless steered my ride in a way that, while still some 20 paces away from the enemy, I happened to end up in a squadron interval of the English dragoons. I now let them pass and hurriedly went back to Ompteda in fulfilment of my last assignment; he had already once more received the order to deploy.

A short time later, the English dragoons that I had left in their attack returned to the rear of our squares. But as often happens in cavalry melees, in following the dragoons, the French cuirassiers suddenly charged again and cut at once into our battalions that were about to deploy.

The 8th Battalion in particular suffered terribly, the 5th Battalion less so, which with about half in line formation, was saved by the timely controlled fire of a neighbouring square, in which the brave General Count Kielmansegge happened to be.

The effective fire from this and other squares soon forced the enemy cuirassiers to retire, who then received a rough treatment from the pursuing English cavalry. The enemy artillery fire, on the other hand, caused severe losses in our squares that were formed four deep, and often a single cannon ball would blow away several files.

The enemy repeated his cavalry attacks upon the various squares of our division with the utmost vehemence, but these stood like rock. The French cuirassiers rushed through the intervals between the squares and circled them. A murderous cross-fire drove them back, and many a horse ran off without its rider.

The light company of the 5th Line Battalion was sent in support to Lieutenant Colonel Baring, who with his battalion fought off the incessant attacks of the enemy infantry upon the farm of La Haye Sainte, and was in an extremely hot situation. That company had already lost its commander, Captain C. von Wurmb, over the short distance, and Ensign Walther* was wounded. When a short time later I was at the square of the 5th Line Battalion, a shell landed underneath my horse and spattered me with dirt. I watched the fuse burning below me, but had compunctions about moving away because such movement might be considered a sign of cowardice. The shell exploded, but it damaged only the heel of my boot and the spur, my horse also remained unscathed.

The death defying bravery of the French cavalry on this day filled us with admiration, I have never seen more valorous troops.

At the approach of the enemy charges our artillerymen left their guns that were emplaced before the squares, after having fired as long as possible, and sought protection in the nearest squares with their loading tools. The pieces then fell into the enemy's hands but he could neither use them nor drag them away. As soon as an attack had been repulsed and the enemy horsemen were on their way back, the brave artillerymen hurried back to their guns and sent iron parting greetings after the intruders.

The horse of Colonel von Ompteda was struck in the chest by a cannon ball and collapsed. The colonel entered the square of the 5th Line Battalion near which we had been standing for a while. He then asked me to give him my horse and to pick up one of his led horses. Upon arriving, after great difficulties, at the house where we had earlier left our led horses I met with the greatest confusion, and our horses were gone. A surgeon from the 2nd Light Battalion gave me a captured French cuirassier horse. I had just mounted it, and was on my way back to the brigade, when a cannon ball smashed one of the horse's forelegs. As the horse tumbled down, I found myself next to a dead English cavalry officer and a fallen comrade of the 1st Light Battalion, Captain Holtzermann, whose body had been trampled into the mud and was almost unrecognizable.

After I had freed myself from the saddle I tried again to locate our led horses, and, in fact, found them. I hurried back to the brigade on a splendid black horse owned by the colonel, but had great difficulties getting through on the highway: demolished artillery pieces and other vehicles, cavalrymen and foot soldiers, wounded and healthy ones, all of them had taken over the highway, filled with the desire to remove themselves out of the range of the deadly cannon balls.

On my arrival at our position I received the sad news from Captain von Einem that Colonel von Ompteda had just then led the 5th Line Battalion in a bayonet attack against enemy infantry and had been killed;

* Ensign and Adjutant William Walther, 5th Line Battalion, KGL, Beamish no. 597.

the 5th Battalion had successfully beaten back the infantry but was then surprised and dispersed by enemy cavalry; one of the colours had also been lost. The few of the battalion's men who had remained together then had joined what was left of the 1st and 2nd Light Battalions who, some time earlier, had to yield the farm of La Haye Sainte to the enemy because of lack of ammunition, and had temporarily retired somewhat in order to re-assemble.

Of our brigade only the 8th Light Battalion was still formed in square, but its numbers were greatly diminished.

The enemy used the capture of La Haye Sainte to direct a violent fire upon our position. Von Einem was struck by a bullet in his lower body. Sinking down on the neck of his horse, he said with a broken voice: 'I am done for.' He then asked me to take his money and his watch and to handle these according to instructions still to be given to me.

I declined; however, I attempted to impart courage to him, which, incidentally, I did not have myself; took the bridle of his horse and led him to a Hanoverian square nearby, where I had four men carry him in a blanket to the rear.

The time might have been about 7 o'clock, but the battle still raged on with unchanged violence. I encountered Colonel Baring who happened to be all alone on the battlefield without a single man from his battalion. We then looked for the remains of the brigade that had been re-assembled by Lieutenant Colonel von dem Bussche. They were already on their way back to our position where they formed up again.

The roar of a cannonade could be heard, coming ever stronger from the direction of the extreme left wing of the army: we hoped this was the Prussians.

Some time elapsed, and the enemy's assaults became visibly weaker and his movements uncertain. Then finally, we received the order to advance. It revived our blood and our muscles. I, and certainly the entire line of weakened battalions, stepped forward against the enemy, with an indescribable feeling, who without waiting to face us, yielded in disorder and left us his entire artillery.

Darkness set in. Our day's work had been done; whatever remained of the division and had kept together, returned to their former position on the battlefield. I now searched for the body of my revered commander with the help of a few soldiers. We found him, almost without clothes - his neck pierced by a bullet – near a hedge of the farm of La Haye Sainte. I was greatly saddened not to have been by his side at his death. Still, his life's end was glorious and enviable.

With the last cannonshot fired at Waterloo, Napoleon's rule had irreversibly been terminated. But our warriors' life, our battles with the

French, and the army service we had grown fond of, were to come to an end. The British army followed the Prussians who closely pursued the remains of the French army to Paris with an energy that thwarted any re-assembling or resistance of the adversary. From time to time we still heard the rumbling of artillery fire from the two antagonists still fighting before us, as parts of our army were still engaged in front of the French border fortresses. But as early as 3 July a military convention was concluded between the allied commanders, Blücher and Wellington, and the provisional commander of the French – Prince Eckmühl,* that required the French army to withdraw behind the Loire and to surrender Paris to the Allies.

On 7 July, Paris was in fact occupied by the allied troops, and on 8 July Louis XVIII re-entered his capital from which he had to flee a few months earlier. On the same day, Napoleon went aboard a French frigate at Rochefort with the intention to escape to America, but was forced to surrender to the English† who brought him as their prisoner to St Helena.

The greater part of our army set up camp in the Bois de Boulogne on 7 July.

After the death of my revered Brigadier von Ompteda, the Hanoverian General Count von Kielmansegge offered me a position on his Staff that I gratefully accepted; I was also given the promotion to captain in the 5th Line Battalion of the Legion as of 27 July 1815.

My days in Paris in my position of aide de camp passed away most agreeably because through my noble and dignified superior I not only had the honour of being presented to various monarchs and princes, but also to make the acquaintance of many excellent and interesting personalities in the different armies, and of many distinguished French families, something the service on a regimental level would hardly have offered me.

But regardless of how amusing and stimulating the entertainments and diversions affected me that were offered in Paris in such abundance and variety, the thought would not leave me of the approaching dissolution of the legion upon the conclusion of a general peace. It burdened me like a nightmare, as it did my dear comrades in the legion, and spoiled all the enjoyment that this capital offered us in greater wealth than any other place in the world.

On 30 November, the Duke of Wellington issued the order of the discharge of the army that had fought under him at Waterloo and had entered Paris as victors.

---

* Marshal Davout, Prince Eckmühl.

† Napoleon had intended to board a French frigate and sail to America, but seeing no chance of evading the Royal Navy, surrendered to Captain Maitland on HMS *Bellerophon.*

1st Hanoverian Brigade of Major General von Kielmansegge
Bremen Field Battalion

No. 16 Lieutenant Frederick von Bülow

From J. Kannicht, All of This Because of Napoleon: From the war diary of George von Coulon, Major in the Royal German Legion, and the letters of his wife Henriette 1806–1815, *Bernard & Graefe Verlag, Koblenz, 1986*

Dear Coulon!
Since you, a former member of our battalion,* will be interested in its fate, I will let you know a little bit about its experiences during the bloody days from 16 to 18 June.

At 5 o'clock in the evening of 15 June, the battalion suddenly received marching orders. We thus marched from Neufvilles, a village between Soignies and Mons not far from the border, to Soignies where the divisional commander, General von Alten, had his headquarters. Since this is a small town at which the entire division had been assembled, many battalions had to set up their bivouac, and our battalion and several others had their quarters for the night in the local church. At 2 o'clock in the morning, camp was broken and we marched to Nivelles by way of Braine le Comte. On the way, we met some Prussian stragglers whose regiments had been attacked yesterday by the French and had been driven back. We bivouacked half an hour beyond that town.

Hardly had we spent a few hours here in very hot weather when we heard cannon fire from about 2 hours in our front. We were ordered to break camp, and while we marched in the direction of the sound we already met some wounded Dutch. We passed through a village named Quatre Bras, and as we just had reached the far side of the highway we were already exposed to the enemy cannon fire. Several battalions of our brigade were sent ahead, and we remained in reserve and were ordered by our general to lie down in the ditch alongside the highway because the fire was so violent.

Towards 7 o'clock in the evening, the enemy tirailleurs moved up so rapidly that we suffered severely from small arms fire. At that moment, Captain Bazoldo† was struck by a ball in his head that dented his skull. The 1st and 8th divisions [half companies] of our battalion were therefore sent against the skirmishers, and soon our brave fellows, already angry

---

* Both Bülow and Coulon had transferred from 1st Line Battalion, KGL, to the Bremen Field Battalion in 1814, but Coulon had then joined the Veteran Battalion, KGL, in which corps he was in the Netherlands in 1815. Coulon's own letter is no. 49 in this volume.

† Captain Bazoldo was wounded.

because of our previous inactivity, boldly drove them back. The enemy abandoned the battlefield, and since night had brought matters to an end, that was where we encamped. No. 3 Company, where I was, had been ordered to do picket duty and was so close to the French that we could hear them talking and shouting.

At daybreak at 2 o'clock on 17 June, the French engaged the Osnabrück Battalion to our left, and soon we also came under fire. The battalion was posted behind a hedge, and the enemy tirailleurs drove up so heavily that the battalion had to close ranks and keep up a rolling fire several times. Eventually, our wounded included Lepel, Bruel and Meyer* formerly a sergeant and now an ensign. Our men fired off 3 times 60 cartridges, and my company was withdrawn some distance to clean the muskets which would not fire any more.†

At 1 o'clock midday, we received orders to retire to a village named Genappe. The entire army retreated and we made up the rearguard while exposed to a thunderstorm and a terrible downpour, closely pursued as we were by the French army with Napoleon at its head. After we had marched for about 2 hours, the army took position on a ridge (Mont St Jean) in front of the village of Waterloo. The French sent many skirmishers and light troops forward, but things soon became as quiet as night set in. The battalion's losses for yesterday and today amounted to 100 men [16–17 June].

18 June. We had not eaten anything since the day before yesterday; the rain continued all night and we were soaking wet. All agreed that this was the most terrible night that the battalion had gone through since its beginnings. The Duke of Wellington, who had only arrived this night (until then, the Prince of Orange, commander of our corps, had been in command), passed all alone through our camps in completely unrecognisable attire.‡

Towards midday, we observed some general manoeuvring on the enemy side. We broke camp and formed up. During the advance of the French, our artillery kept up a terrible cannonade to which their side did not at first respond. But they eventually deployed their masses, and there commenced a cannonade, the likes of which not even the oldest of veterans had ever experienced before. We had already spent 1 hour lying down inactive in line, when suddenly the call came to form square as enemy cavalry was approaching. We formed square together with the Verden Battalion in 4 ranks. It was commanded by Langrehr;§ he reminded

* Captain Lepel and Ensigns Bruel and Meyer.

† Intensive firing clogged the musket and caused numerous misfires.

‡ Clearly this was an unfounded rumour.

§ Lieutenant Colonel William von Langrehr, commander of the Hanoverian Bremen

the men to stay calm and not to open fire until ordered. A formation of cuirassiers, at least 2,000 strong, moved up. It approached as close as 30 paces towards our left face and then received a very effective fire, wheeled round our rear and right faces which also sent some powerful volleys their way, and then took off, with shouts of 'Hurrah' from our square and pursued by our cavalry. The Prince of Orange had witnessed all of this and rode up and shook Langrehr's hand, asking him to thank his men in his name for their bravery. This was a magnificent moment.

There soon followed another cavalry charge. Langrehr's beautiful English horse now fell, being struck by a cannon ball. To avail himself of another horse he stepped outside of the square, but hardly had he mounted it when a cannon ball tore off his left foot. He stammered 'keep up your bravery' and 'farewell' and was then taken to the rear. Major Schkopp[*] assumed command; we deployed in line again to suffer less from the enemy fire, but soon had to form square again upon the approach of cavalry; we repulsed 4 more charges. Majors Schkopp and Muller[†] also fell, and a captain of the Verden Battalion[‡] assumed command, and I also commanded one face, which consisted of only half a battalion.

About this time, we were the only infantry still standing at this point on our side. The French advanced ever more heavily; their guns fired at us from a distance of 100 paces, and their grapeshot blew away all of the front face at once. A very strong square of enemy infantry moved against us. There was a call for skirmishers, and at this moment when nobody believed anyone could come out alive, there were many volunteers. The square of our two battalions was shot up to a point where no space was left for an officer on horseback.[§] We now received orders from an aide de camp to withdraw, and while we retired to the village, the French also took off in wholesale flight. We returned to the battlefield and bivouacked among thousands of dead. Our battalion's strength was 80 men. On 20 June we passed the border and arrived before Paris on 1 July, without a day of rest and without beholding an enemy.

Judgement was passed on several of Napoleon's adherents, several colonels have seen their last, and Ney[¶] will be shot dead one of these days. All the best,

Frederick Bülow

Field Battalion, was killed at Waterloo.

* Major von Schkopp, commanded the Verden Field Battalion.

† Major Muller Bremen Field Battalion.

‡ Captain von Bothmer took command.

§ The would indicate the high number of casualties in the battalion who would be dragged into the centre of the hollow square. There were so many that there was no room for a horse.

¶ Marshal Ney was shot by firing squad on 7 December 1815.

Fifth Division of Lieutenant General Sir Thomas Picton
5th Hanoverian Brigade of Colonel Vincke

No. 17 From La Belle Alliance

Pflugk-Harttung's letter no. 94
Parting letter of Major General Sir James Kempt to the Hanoverian Colonel von Vincke, in which he praises the conduct of the 5th Hanoverian Brigade at La Belle Alliance

Meulan [en-Yvelines], 5 December 1815

My dear Colonel,
I enclose to you a Route for the march of the Hanoverian Brigade under your command to Brussels on its way to the Hanoverian Dominions. You will perceive, that your are to leave the 5th Division on the 9th instant, but I cannot permit you to depart without expressing my entire approbation of the conduct of the officers and men since I have had the honour to command them. Though very young soldiers, they evinced the greatest steadiness and very best spirit in one of the greatest battles fought in modern times. Qualities which I feel persuaded will never leave them and their general discipline and regularity in camp and quarters has also been highly commendable.

You will have the goodness to convey these, my sentiments, to the officers and men of the brigade with my best wishes for their honour and welfare and be pleased to accept yourself of the assurance of my particular regard.

James Kempt, Major General commanding 5th Division

Gifhorn Landwehr Battalion

No. 18 Lieutenant Friedrich Hemmelmann

From Gunter Weinhold Reminiscences of Waterloo: The ways and the fate of the Gifhorn Landwehr Battalion *1985*

Lieutenant Friedrich Hemmelmann of the battalion's No. 1 Company, wrote to his mother after the battle. The address shown on the last page of the folded letter sheet is as follows:

Open Letter
To Madame Hemmelmann at Celle, by Military Post.
Lieutenant Hemmelmann.

Battlefield near Genappe, 5 hours distant from Brussels, 20 June 1815

Yesterday [actually 18 June] we were engaged with Napoleon in a terrible battle. The fighting began at 10 o'clock in the morning and continued until darkness set in. The French fought like lions. Our brigade was exposed for 7 hours to the most dreadful canister fire. Of our battalion, Major Hammerstein, Major Leue,* Captain Wiedenfeldt, Lieutenant Schmidt are the officers that have been wounded, we have considerable losses. I have lost 10 men of my sharpshooters. The French have been completely beaten. We have captured 50 artillery pieces with powder wagons and have taken several thousand prisoners. Greater details are not yet available; you will read about them in the newspapers. More than 100,000 Frenchmen fought against us. The number of our columns was immense. The Landwehr stood like lions; it was most admirable. Bonaparte himself was in command and was said to have been wounded in the leg. The Prussians, Dutch and Brunswickers put up a tremendously brave fight. The Duke of Brunswick is dead, he had already fallen in the battle on the day before yesterday. The French cavalry has been thrashed soundly, particularly the cuirassiers.

I am in good shape, only we have not had any brandy; we have not had any for 3 days, but always hope to get some. Do not be anxious about me. As you well know, ill weeds do not perish; I hope we will be in France tomorrow. Cheers to Hanover. Greetings to acquaintances and friends and trust in God and the rightful cause.

Your ever loving Fritz Hemmelmann, Lieutenant

No. 19 Private Ernst Christian Schacht

From Gunter Weinhold Reminiscences of Waterloo: The ways and the fate of the Gifhorn Landwehr Battalion *1985*

Landwehr Private Ernst Christian Schacht from Ettenbüttel had joined the battalion in Gifhorn on 18 March 1814 at 19 years of age and was assigned to No. 1 Company. He had participated in the march to the Netherlands and in the Battle of Waterloo. Afterwards, he and his comrades had marched to Paris, and he then had the time to write to his relatives in Ettenbüttel. He describes in moving words his participation in the murderous contest and a soldier's hardships and privations.

Camp near Paris, 25 August 1815

My dearly beloved ones back there!
I must not fail to write you once again, and you will read this letter very

* Major George Lewis Leue had transferred from the 4th Line Battalion, KGL, Beamish no. 1025; he died of his owunds on 23 June 1815.

carefully, because to describe everything just now is quite impossible, so here in brief are the main occurrences. So it was on Friday morning the 16th of June that the drums sounded the alarm for marching. In front of Halle, a small town, the battalion formed up and so it went. At 11 o'clock we heard artillery fire; the word was that the Brabanters did their exercises there. The General Order said that we should move to Waterloo; we eventually arrived there at 2 o'clock, and saw 3 regiments march on the highway in the greatest hurry. The cannonade now became heavier, and we were told, to make ready for the attack in the battle! Oh the very thought! Thoughts, and more thoughts; sighs upon sighs were sent up to God. Everybody became disheartened; still, nothing could be done about it but to pluck up courage. We remained at Waterloo until half past five. Some 40 thousand Dutch came back with many wounded, saying that nothing was accomplished, the French were just too strong. At half past five we marched off to the battle field with the song: 'A free life we live etc.' The terrible sound of the cannonade became ever closer on the road before us. In the evening at half past ten we had already encountered the corpse of the Duke of Brunswick. We spent the night lying in a green meadow near Nivelles. On the next morning, the 17th, at 2 o'clock, we were awakened by the cannon; at 5 o'clock we marched through this little town and for another half an hour to Quatre Bras, a single farm estate, where the enemy attack had occurred. One believed that now one's life would soon end, and so very soon.

At 11 o'clock [a.m.] we turned around and retired for about 3 hours in a hurry until before Waterloo (a village) because 180 cannon had first to be in place. In the evening at 7 o'clock, the guns were firing throughout the area, in a 3 mile circle, and then suddenly it was all over. Heavy rains began to pour down and lasted through the night; that night I will not forget in all of my life.

On the next morning, Sunday the 18th, nothing was happening, the skies were clearing, and everybody tried to get something to eat. And so it was that the stomach was soon filled, but it was not to be, all the pots were taken off the fire and put aside. It was just 11 o'clock when the cannonade erupted so very terribly, one side against the other, as if everything was to be smashed. 500 great cannon thundered and fought against each other, and the firing of the small arms also went on ever so dreadfully. The screaming and the groans of the wounded was so pitiable on this day that I can not even put it on paper. The French left wing attacked our right wing where the English were posted. We stood along a small ridge, so everything could be observed, in a square eight ranks deep for 3 hours until 2 o'clock. During that time, more than 80 large balls flew quite low over our heads, until some flying lower struck and wounded some and turned others into corpses. So we beheld these cruelties going on and on as in a huge slaughterhouse. I am still shaking, my pen is too weak to describe this pitiable misery, and so it went on from 2 till 7 in the afternoon; full of suffering, until finally at 9 o'clock in the evening there was jubilation, 'Hurra! Hurra! Victory, victory, victory is ours, God be praised!' But the battlefield was now only consecrated to be a field of death; dead men everywhere! Thousands upon thousands had lost their lives, only for what is right and for the fatherland. The mind stands still in beholding all this, and stays in agonies. I said my prayer: 'Lead me, oh Lord, and guide me' and so on. During these three terrible days I have often thought of you, and had you before my mind's eyes in the hope of seeing you again in the future. May God grant that this will come true because then I will relate to you everything better and to the smallest detail. In telling all this, the mouth shall flutter, the tongue take on wings, the hands weave about, the veins pulse strongly, the heart overflow with feeling, and there shall be questions and answers and the mind will properly recall and describe and remember well, so that it will be a great delight for all of us. I only wish I could gabble my story for you very, very soon, only now it cannot be done, I am too far away.

We are staying here in a camp near the capital city of Paris and are now more than 62 hours distant from Brussels. We have marched for 14 days from sunrise to sunset, and had hardly anything to eat or drink, while sleeping at night under bare skies. Yesterday we were assigned quarters for 8 days in a city named Saint Denis, one hour outside Paris. I will no longer think of the miserable past, instead write about my good quarters. One drinks French wine here; and so I will drink my health and yours, Vivat and cheers, let us live. In this friendly outlook do I commend myself and you to God's merciful blessing and I conclude with this verse: 'Keep the faith and do right, and so on, and stay righteous under Our Father who has given me my life, and who will preserve it in days to come, as also all of yours.'

Now the news about the war. Every day the Prussians come marching up, and also the English. Now the army of the cruel war is gathering here. As it was entering France, it has brought along King Louis the 18th; God knows where Napoleon happens to be now. Nobody knows how long we are going to stay here. On 24 July, we had a big parade where the Emperor of Austria, the Emperor of Russia, the King of Prussia, the King of France, our Duke of Wellington, in short, more than 200 princes and generals appeared on this day. The march past took place in front of the royal palace in Paris; you see, all of this earth's majesties were present on this day. 180 thousand took part in this march past; I am amazed no end about this huge army; everybody was under arms from 5 o'clock in the morning until 5 o'clock in the evening. But one fell down here, two there, and three more, who lay there, having become sick. From that day on, I also have been very sick for three weeks, but thank God, I am in good health again. By the way, we have exercises every day near our camp. We are provided with bread, meat, firewood, every day a little wine, but no side dishes, they do not know any better, and so we will have to make do. Dear mother! In my younger years I would never have believed what happened to those who are away from their father and mother, as it now is my case. But it is not my fault because it is on behalf of what is right and for the fatherland, and as it is wisely ordained. Finally, I ask you to please save this letter so I can retrieve it when I come home. In the expectation of its coming true in the future. I send greetings, thousands of them, to all of you, even to strangers who share this with you. And so I remain your son, brother, brother in law, most devoted and now farthest from you, as always, Amen.

Ernst Christian Schacht, Hornist

Do write to me again, you know my address

6th Division of Major General Lambert
4th Hanoverian Brigade of Colonel Best
Verden Landwehr Battalion

No. 20 Lieutenant von der Horst*

From 'Reminiscences of a Hanoverian Officer in the Verden Landwehr Battalion of the days of the Battle of Waterloo', Hannoversches Magazin,*Hanover, nos 95 and 96 for 25 and 29 November 1816, cols 1505–20 and 1521–34*

Of the memorable days of the Battle of Waterloo, the following reminiscences have remained in my mind. I do not believe that my memory has deceived me, not even in the very minutest details. The first events here described were witnessed by the company with which I served. The greater part of the following ones can be verified by the officers who were forced to share my fate.

'Halt!' And the battalion stood in lifeless calm on the ridge [at Quatre Bras].† A wide expanse opened up before the eyes. Rigid lines, surging

* The name in the original article is partly hidden, but a quick look at the list of officers in the Bremen Field Battalion reveals this officer as the only possible candidate. See Appendix 5.

† Lieutenant Von der Horst and Ensigns Plate and Kotzebue were captured at the Battle of Quatre Bras. See Colonel Best's report, *Waterloo Archive* vol. II, letter no. 38, for further details. Best, however, thought these men were captured because of a

squares on the opposite hillside. To the side extend the ranks of the companions in arms far off into the blue yonder. Heavy clouds of steam hang over the regiments. Now and then the wind tore up the haze and threw shades over the scenery. Sudden death spewed forth from the batteries, balls howled through the air, shells turned up the ground. The general on his charger stood there in an icy calm. Bullets hissed into the battalion. French tirailleurs lay hidden in the corn before us and went about their trade of hunting big game with good success. 'Forward! No.1 Company!' the major shouted loudly. And happy to escape the deadly calm they stormed jubilantly against the crafty enemy. Thus rushes roaringly the mountain torrent into the valley when the dam breaks that stemmed its flow.

Young soldiers are little afraid of battle when they can use musket butt and bayonet to their heart's delight; but it is a severe trial when bullets from afar strike the idle limbs. Some faces glowed as red as sunset; from others the blood had vanished to boil all the hotter in the heart! The young soldier is searching for his fate in the demeanour of the officers, and many picked up courage from the cold and calm gaze of the major. About me I hear whispering; those were prayers. 'My God, my mother!' was what one of them was sighing; 'Father who thou art in Heaven!' from another one; 'God bless this meal' from a totally bewildered one.

Finally, we were turned loose to relieve No. 1 Company. No. 2 Company with which I served hurried ahead as if released from a dungeon. We noticed that some good work had already been done. The tirailleurs had been driven out of the field before us and had been chased through a hedge, and now had taken position behind a second hedge that was separated from the first one by a meadow. For a time we fired at each other. No. 3 Company had joined us, and an English light company fought together with us. About 400 paces to our right a body of troops moved through the hedge from the enemy's side. They could not be clearly made out because of the tall corn. The English fell back, and they had done the right thing, as borne out by events. From what I saw glittering, I estimated the number of bayonets at 50. I thought I could overpower them and make prisoners some part of them. But it was a risky undertaking because we would have to pass through a shower of bullets. I saw that the soldiers were burning for a fight. My decision had been made, I addressed them for a few seconds and concluded with the appeal: 'Whoever is a brave soldier will follow me!' At the head of a platoon I considered myself strong enough to take on 50 Frenchmen. But the heavily loaded soldiers had been too exhausted by the long march from Brussels and from fighting in the burning heat of the sun to be able

---

case of misidentification rather than Horst's more adventurous version.

to advance on the run. The tall corn was also of such height that men of low stature became invisible. To sustain my volunteers' courage, I carried my shako up high on the tip of my sabre.

These moments I cherish as the happiest of my life. A like opportunity to gain distinction does not offer itself to a subaltern officer in a line unit, not even in more than three battles. I was certain of a favourable outcome, in my imagination I already visualised myself with a small group of prisoners that I handed over to my superior. I did not hear the bullets that whistled past myself. The sight of some of my men falling even raised my spirits; I felt as if I was floating between death and life, and to me both were like a game to me. Glory was all that my burning self was thirsting for, and trusting in a flattering foretaste I partook of it in full measure in advance.

But man proposes – and God disposes!

Now I had the enemy before my bayonets. My companions stormed in on him, as I expected, like the Numidian lion on his prey. I was certain of our victory when suddenly we were surrounded in an ambush by a French tirailleur regiment, which had risen out of the corn.

Who has never experienced the tumult of battle cannot fathom the state of mind in a fighter who is engaged in a struggle for life and death with another man. All thinking, all feeling is consumed by the mad craving to strike down the enemy. All the muscles of the face are distorted. He hardly hears another's voice, he does not feel the pain of a light wound. Such was the state of my companions when they found themselves overpowered. No path open to escape! Spasms of desperation show on everybody's face. Stifled curses are hemmed in by teeth. Nobody heard me praying! One officer, Lieutenant W,* had been killed by a bullet. I gathered 24 men around me to attempt to break through somewhere: but the enemy stood in tightly packed ranks! One by one my men were falling with arms still in their hands. Four were still standing, the others lying crumpled on the blood drenched soil. All our cartridges had been fired. The soldiers struck the enemy with the butts of their muskets, which they preferred in their rustic ways, in spite of my urging to use the bayonet. A French officer jumped at me, and we duelled with our swords. One of his men stuck his musket at my chest, but the officer held him off, and at the same moment I was struck to the ground by a blow in my back with a musket butt. My falling was observed. Our army afterwards included me in the first list of those killed.

Oh how terribly was I thrown from the height of my expectations down into an abyss. The fire within my chest was extinguished with one stroke and in the first seconds it was replaced by an unfeeling numbness.

* Lieutenant C. E. Wegener, Verden Landwehr, was killed at Quatre Bras.

A sergeant and two men led me away from this site of misfortune. Painful thoughts arose in me about what the major, what the colonel might think of me, that I let myself be captured. The entire campaign and perhaps years on end, will be lost for you! Battles will be fought, and here you sit in idle inaction, a miserable prisoner! That same quarter hour that promised the fulfilment of my plans and of my boldest desires, it had now smashed with blood, my golden future!

But my pain soon dissolved into agreeable sensations. I had arrived at the hedge, into which we had fired earlier, where the sight of killed and wounded Frenchmen scattered all around inwardly delighted me. Man thus can squash all humane feelings in the bloody work of a battle!

I had to pass the French lines. Ever more formations moved up on the highway, cavalry in particular. Wildly jubilant shouts of '*Vive l'Empereur!*' emanated from the ranks. It seemed to me that nobody among them had any doubt of a complete victory, as far as I was able to judge the mood of the French army. At the onset of darkness I arrived at a farmstead, one and a half hours from the battlefield, where I was handed over to a sentry.

Thus left to my own thoughts, surrounded by some twenty captured and wounded Hanoverians and Englishmen, I felt the full weight of my depressing situation. I designed plans on how to remove myself away from the sovereign power of my wardens, but nowhere was there a glimpse of a possible salvation. I was stirred out of my projects by the arrival of one of my battalion's officers, Ensign K,* who had been my companion in battle and was now forced to share my fate. A sad reunion but a consolation for both of us. Sleep, the angel of suffering souls, took us in its arms, until the rays of the morning sun and the bustle in the guard room woke us up. On first beholding the highway I saw another of my battalion's officers, Ensign P,† among a group of prisoners passing by. I shouted at him. He was permitted to join me. He had suffered the same fate as the officer who was already with me. At my request, one of the guards took me to the courtyard to look for water. A pretty girl viewed us from the door of an adjacent building, I asked her for water and a bit of bread. Water she promised me, but the bread her father had given to the French, and if any was left she would give it to her friends. I realised at this moment that my face was still buried under a crust of dust and burned powder. I therefore did not say another word to her; I took the water and washed myself. Taking up our conversation, I told her that I was a Hanoverian and that I had had the misfortune of being taken prisoner during the battle, and that now I was to be transported to the

* This has to be Ensign Kotzebue.

† This must refer to Ensign Plate.

interior of France. Still, I was not too concerned about my fate because I had found the French to be friendly people; and as was rumoured in my fatherland, the ladies in particular were said to excel in the tenderness of their sentiments and in the kindness of their hearts. The longer I looked in her eyes, the more did I become convinced that these rumours were true. I had hardly finished when she offered me bread, butter and brandy. My guard laughed and joined in the repast. While thus talking, I received so much more from her that the two other officers and all the prisoners received a wholesome breakfast.

We then continued our well escorted march to Charleroi. Although I cannot complain about being a prisoner of the French, we had to suffer much from the curses and ridicule of passers by. A drunken sergeant of grenadiers, who had joined us, excelled in that regard. With his wounded left arm in a sling, he brandished his sword over our heads with his right arm. He paid particular attention to me because of my tall figure and because of the expression of contempt with which I looked at him. He demanded that I shout '*Vive Napoleon*'. I could easily have done that; but the sound of cannon behind me reminded me all the time of the feats of my fellow countrymen and their Allies, and I therefore would not debase myself by an act unworthy of them. My refusal enraged the sergeant so much that he bellowed '*Foudre!*' several times, hit his head with a clenched fist, and '*Foudre!*' At that, he jumped at me and was about finish me with a stab of his sabre, but I parried his thrust and flung him sideways several paces into the ditch at the side of the highway. I shouted at the sergeant, who commanded the escort: that if he did not protect me against assaults I would make a complaint about him with the next general or commander [I saw]. I knew of Napoleon's order to treat prisoners well because he had made it known: the Belgians, Hanoverians, and Brunswickers had been so happy under his government that they fought with the greatest reluctance against him, and they looked upon the French as their liberators. The sergeant in charge put me under his personal protection and would not tolerate anybody coming near me who did not belong to the escort. We eventually arrived in Charleroi where we were taken to an enclosed courtyard that already held 500 prisoners, Belgians and Prussians. I searched out the commandant from whom I obtained an agreement that the wounded among the Hanoverian prisoners, who were with me, be brought to a hospital. They thus avoided a cumbersome march that the wounded Prussians were forced to make, and were freed the next day by the allies. On my part, myself and the two officers were quartered in a private house, with a soldier as our guard.

The rain came down in sheets.* The sound of the cannonade was

* This must refer to the 17 June, when the torrential rains hampered the French

muffled by the damp air. I sat in a corner of my small room, lost in numb brooding. Now I deplored my undertaking in the battle, then again I delighted in the thought of some of those moments. Long trains of wounded passed before the front of my window. The French swore that they had won the battle, I did not believe it, but yearned to stand outside and listen as to whether the sound of the battle came nearer or went farther away. If Napoleon were to win the battle, the greater part of the continent would be lost, I could not imagine that the Almighty would again impose such misery upon my fatherland. A painful anxiety drove me from one corner to the other, I have not experienced a more agonizing night in my life. There was some slight consolation in the morning. More transports of wounded I saw arriving and new reinforcements marching towards the battlefield.* I heard that the battle had started over again. The French no longer claimed over confidently that victory was theirs. I breathed more freely. Towards noontime it was announced that the prisoners were to march to Beaumont, a small French town. At 2 o'clock in the afternoon, the column was formed, the wounded in front and the uninjured in the rear. Nine or ten Prussian officers had joined us. We distinctly heard the cannonade from the heights before the city. Several old artillery officers, who had participated in all of the preceding war, affirmed that they had never heard anything like it before. The cannon shots followed each other at such rapidity as if it were small arms fire. All of us felt renewed courage and gathered fresh hope.

We arrived at Beaumont at night. The commandant was there to inspect us, he wanted to confine the officers together with the rank and file in one courtyard. I represented to him that this was not according to the conventions of war; he apologised but said that the town was completely filled up and no space was left. 'But yes, I can accommodate your request.' We were separated from the soldiers and brought into a well lit church. On entering we wished we were back with our men because it was crowded with wounded Frenchmen. I halted at a pillar to consider what to do next. The moaning of the wounded, interrupted by the yelling of the female and male nurses, aroused mixed feelings in me of compassion and disgust. The deplorable condition, the groaning of these thousand sufferers, would certainly have evoked pity in the hardest heart! This was the first time that I felt how lucky I was to still be in good health. I thanked God and vowed to bear steadfastly whatever I was to face in the future. In my state of utmost resignation I accepted my situation and thought of ways to improve it. Bread and sleep were my greatest needs; to obtain here the former without money could be the subject of a prize

---

pursuit as Wellington's army marched back to the ridge at Mont St Jean.

* This refers to infantry moving up to join the French army near Waterloo.

puzzle. All the valuables that I had with me in the battle I had given to the sergeant who had escorted me to Charleroi. He had earnestly advised me to leave them in his safekeeping otherwise they would be taken from me by his greedy comrades. There they have remained to this day unless a courteous Prussian has relieved him of his safekeeping concerns. Resting against my pillar I watched the attendants, male and female, pass by me one by one. They had been forcibly recruited from the lower classes of the town. I noticed a cheerful young girl among them, I addressed her and talkative as French women are, she stopped at once to rest up from her hardships by keeping her tender tongue in motion. I expressed to her my admiration of the patriotism and the self sacrificing ardour of the French ladies to lessen the pain of a suffering mankind; and that as my eyes made me see, even she with her tenderest build would not refrain from willingly performing the worthy, although arduous duty of caring for the sick and wounded. 'Well, dear Sir,' she replied, 'you would not be surprised if you knew how full of tender emotions the hearts are of the French!' Indeed at this time, full of emotion towards the commandant's execution! But I did not give vent to this naughty thought. 'But, dear Sir, who are you? And where do you come from? Where do you want to go?' Hardly had I started to answer when an untold number of more questions interrupted my answer. Only at the last one, 'Had I had supper yet?', did I cut her short. I intimated to her that it was just this trifling matter that next to our conversation would give me the greatest pleasure. The girl understood my hint when I subtly pointed at my comrades and a short time later she refreshed us with soup and bread. I expressed my heartfelt thanks with a warm handshake; she seemed to be delighted thus to have done a good deed. After my brief experience, I resolved to address only members of the fair sex in moments of distress and if my captivity should extend for any length of time; their tender traits would assure kind sentiments. I yearned for rest and sleep, the girl offered to accommodate me and some of my comrades in her house, but the guards would not permit it. I searched for an empty small space in the church and noticed that there was no light below the tower; that is where I went. I found some straw and did not hesitate to lie down. My foot struck something that seemed to be a leg.

I investigated my neighbourhood persuaded myself that corpses were scattered all about me that had been thrown out of the church. A living person, even one not afraid of death, will not crave their companionship, I therefore rose and went off, telling my comrades of my discovery, and we kept away from the tower. A step at the altar served this night as my surrogate for a bed.

The sun had hardly risen above the horizon in its purple morning gown when we were called up to march off. This was the 19th of June. I noticed a hurried running to and fro of the French military; it did not attract my attention because I had observed similar things at Charleroi, but what made me curious was their secretive whispering instead of their former boasting; questions were not allowed that I wished to ask. In front of the gate I saw several dirty and damaged cannon and wagons standing in great disorder, with their vehicle shafts turned towards France. Single officers and riders passed by our column in great haste. Those were lucky omens for us! Joyful feelings spread among the prisoners; a special effort was needed to keep the men from expressing their exultation too openly. The number of fugitives was increasing, we saw a group of some 20 officers from different regiments galloping from behind us. They had hardly caught up with us when some men of our escort shouted '*Napoleon! Mon Dieu Napoleon!*' My heart jumped for joy. I observed him at their head, cowering on a black English horse and untiringly driving his horse ahead with a little whip and with his spurs. It was a remarkable sight to me! This man, whom I had seen in the most brilliant glow of human magnificence, who with a single word bent a million necks, the terror of many countries and kingdoms, this same man now careered past my person, a homeless fugitive! I held him in my eyes for a long time! Noble Scipio now shed tears on the ruins of the great Carthage, proud Rome's hated enemy to the death. I was gripped by an awestruck feeling on beholding the sudden downfall of this monstrous man; then I thanked God for the salvation of my fatherland.

The captain who was in command of the transport awakened me somewhat heavily from my musings. All of his men had thrown away their knapsacks. He ordered everybody to run. The prisoners in front shouted 'Why run away now from our own people?' But those in the rear pushed ahead as they received slight pricks with the bayonet and in a few minutes our entire column was trotting like a cavalry regiment. The captain announced that anybody would be shot immediately who attempted to flee. After an hour we arrived at a deep torrent of a creek in a wood. There was a bridge that we passed; we then climbed up a hillside that was covered with wood and sprayed by the water at its bottom. I had slowly moved back to the end of the column; there were guards marching on both sides; I walked behind the next to last one. The hillside was very slippery, which much encumbered our climbing, I saw the rearmost guard slip and fall and in the same moment I flung myself like lightning into the undergrowth. As I later heard from the other two officers of our battalion who took off from the French at Tours on the Loire, 50 hours behind Paris; my absence was not noticed until several hours later. After I had moved about 60 paces into the undergrowth I lay down on the ground to listen to see if I was followed. I heard nothing but the shouting of the column that slowly faded away. I breathed more freely; I could have leapt like the bird in the branches above. Freedom, that precious gift! Whoever is denied it seems to crave nothing more on earth! And yet so little esteemed by him who has always counted on it as his own.

I heard a rustling noise in the undergrowth, some men were coming. Were they French? And if they find you, was this the last time that you were allowed a glance of the beautiful world around you? A fight was not in the offing because I did not dispose of a weapon. I would have given everything for a sabre; in the heat of a combat I would have cared less for my death! But now, to die like one to be executed; with no defence, no protection in my hideout! A rustling leaf might betray me, it was a situation where even to somebody more courageous than myself the heart would pound with strong beats! Oh heavenly sounds! I heard the German language spoken! At this moment I felt like a wanderer in the Alps who had been buried under an avalanche of snow and then sees the golden light of the sun for the first time!

They were a number of Prussian prisoners who had dared to take the greatest risk rather than remain under the hated enemy's domination. They asked me to be their leader, wherever one would go, there they would go also. A musketeer still had a knife; I had him fashion heavy knotted sticks with which we all armed ourselves. I asked the rifleman to climb to the top of a tree to observe the lay of the land. 'There are some galloping up the highway! Also some running after them on foot!' I had him come down from the tree, and made us move deeper into the wood. While at the top of a tree around noon, I saw crowds of men dragging themselves along, all of them in the greatest disorder. Soldiers of all arms were intermingled, nowhere a trace of a compact regiment or battalion; cuirassiers had thrown away their cuirass, helmet, portmanteau and all arms; only their spurs seemed indispensable to them. Men of the Train chased off on draught horses; cannon or powder wagons were nowhere to be seen. Wagons full of wounded had become stuck in the mud, those in sound health had fled on the horses. Loud shouting and screaming could be heard coming from the highway. Everybody pushed ahead. Never before had I seen this kind of retreat, and never had I heard of a similar one in the more recent wars. Like hunted game, everybody sought to save himself by the speed of his feet. Thus it was that I became convinced of the total defeat of the French.

I looked down on this fleeing crowd with proud, victory-elated eyes! My imagination transported me to my jubilant pursuing comrades, the saviours of my fatherland! 'Now thank thee God!' Called a voice from my innermost self, and I fervently obeyed this sweet command.

The Prussians called to me: 'There is a farmer sitting on a tree trunk.' I approached him and asked who he was and where he was going? He said he was an arms maker and wanted to look for work in Maubeuge but had been unable to get through. He just wanted to watch the retreat for a while and then return home. He lived four hours from here near Philippeville. He said that we were in a large forest which extended as far as Lille, also that he knew every way and path and all the inhabitants in the area around here. This was extremely good news, but I was not pleased to learn that the tradesman was going to leave us. He made it clear to me that he would be massacred along with us if the French were to find us. The question now was: shall I keep him by force, or let him go in peace? If, in the former case, I intended to use his knowledge of the roads in the area, he might deliver us to the French in revenge. If, in the second case, he was a Bonapartist, he might betray us and lead the French towards us. I decided to let the man keep his freedom and not to antagonise him. He left me a few notes and departed in a great hurry. I climbed a tree once more; the crowds on the highway were pushing on ever more heavily, I saw them spreading across country in all directions, and also hurrying towards the forest. I became concerned for our safety; if all those fugitives were to push straight through the wood, it would be a miracle if they did not find us. But the churning waters of the forest creek protected us because everybody had to use the bridge to reach the other side, and thus nobody came to the side into the undergrowth.

Suddenly the arms maker appeared a second time. He said he was unable to get through and wanted to stay with us until evening and then return to his village at night. I took his farmer's frock and hat to disguise myself. He suggested that the two of us go to the side to reconnoitre the area. That would be all right as long as the man could be trusted. Still, I decided to take the risk for the common good. I left my Prussians at a corner of the wood and walked across a large enclosed field. I had hardly arrived at the bushes on the other side when I saw my Prussians rush in a great hurry down into the valley. I shouted at them but they did not answer; they waved downward with their hands for me to see. They probably had seen some Frenchmen nearby. Thus I was separated from all the others, alone with my arms maker. He invited me to stay with him in his village until the first storm had blown over. I accepted and towards evening we started our walk. It was night already when we approached the first village, there were camp fires all around it where French soldiers were bivouacking. I wanted to pass outside the village, my guide, however, explained that this was impossible because it was surrounded by a large moor. He told me to simply walk with him straight through the French; one would assume that I was one of the farmers of the area, and nobody would ask me any questions. I followed his advice and, with good luck, slipped through the village. I eventually arrived where I was to stay at 2 o'clock. My guide was only a journeyman and lived at his master's; he therefore brought me to the humble cottage where his brother, a shepherd, and his family were living. Here I was welcomed with rustic hospitality; I only had a problem understanding the people because they did not speak regular French but the language of the Walloons. No fugitive had yet arrived at this village. It was agreed that in the morning I should go along with the sheep into the wood. As to the farmers, I would be passed off as a cousin who had arrived from the Netherlands. I wanted to sleep for one hour only, the family's daughter was to wake me up and then take me along; the father would already go ahead with the sheep. When I woke up, the sun was already shining bright through the single window. I jumped up angrily because I was afraid that the first Frenchmen might arrive, but my anger soon dissolved into a gentle smile. In front of me stood a slender girl, handsomely rustic, with large brown eyes and a pleasant face. This then was my shepherdess! But this time I was concerned for my safety first of all; I asked if any Frenchmen had been seen yet? 'No, my cousin, but they will arrive soon: I was about to wake you up several hours ago; I extended my hand to you some twenty times to rouse you, but I drew back each time, you seemed to slumber so sweetly that it was impossible for me to disturb you.' I expressed my thanks to her in some fashion for the naïve display of her kind feelings. I had already changed part of my clothing, she gave me a knapsack, a dog on a chain, a shepherd's staff, and so we wandered towards the wood. We found the father with his sheep after one hour; the girl took her leave and promised to pick me up again towards evening. Resting in the shade of a tree, I let the events of the last days pass by my mind's eye. From the roaring tumults of war I saw myself transposed to a calm pastime in the deepest peace; the same hand that only a few days ago swung a sabre in battle was now holding an innocent shepherd's staff. I could not help but be amused about my fate that changed me so suddenly from somebody thirsting for glory to a merry shepherd. I now tended the sheep as carefully as I formerly did the soldiers of the company.

The first French fugitives arrived at our place towards noon; they were so confused and fearful that they hardly dared to look back. They asked for directions which I gave them to the best of my knowledge, and they hurried on without delay. A few more were coming, but those had lost their way, because the village was in a remote location in the mountains.

Towards evening I saw my shepherdess return to me. 'Now, my cousin, have you merrily done your day's work?' 'Yes, dear cousin, the prospect of seeing you tonight again made me gladly do today's work.' So with pleasantries and laughter we hurried back home. The next day I spent in disguise, as on the day before. I was assured towards evening that all the French had left the area and that the Prussians had taken over their places. On the next morning, I took leave from this poor but so very kind family; I had grown very fond of them because of their unaffected kindness. These good people had done me a tremendous favour, which I did not fail to express in my thanks to them. Duty bade me to turn my back on the innocent shepherd's life and to follow in a hurry the call to arms, to trade the beautiful rustic roses for the blood-demanding perils. I took off on the return trip to Beaumont where I sought out General Thielemann, who was in command here, to learn in which direction the English army had been marching. The general suggested that I go to Mons, but 6 hours before that place in front of the gates of Bavay, a small French town, I found some men from my battalion; they told me that it was cantonned in town. With what was left of my energy from my cumbersome march I continued at the double. I wanted to pass the market square in a hurry, when the remainder of my company stormed out of the house, in which they were quartered and surrounded me who was presumed dead. There was ample reward in the joy of their radiant faces for all the perils and encumbrances that I had survived. The majors and the other officers present I met at a cheerful meal. Fate thus led me back to my men and a happy welcome after six eventful days!

Von der Horst Lieutenant in the Verden Landwehr Battalion

Münden Landwehr Battalion

No. 21 From La Belle Alliance

From Major von Berckefeldt, 'Geschichte des Koniglich Hannoverschen Landwehr-Bataillons Munden',* Archiv des Historischen Vereins für Niedersachsen, *2nd double issue, 1848 (Hanover 1850)*

The Battle of Quatre Bras and Waterloo

Among the troops stationed at Brussels, there were no indications on the 14th and on the morning of the 15th that would allow us to assume the opening of hostilities in the very near future. Proof of this may be seen in the fact that on the morning of the 15th the 4th Brigade still followed its prescribed extended march routine and returned to its quarters at 2 o'clock in the afternoon without any disturbance. Towards 6 o'clock in the evening, the news spread in Brussels, however, that Napoleon had joined his army and that hostilities had begun with an attack on the

* Lieutenant at the time, von Berckefeldt was adjutant of the battalion.

Prussian advance posts on the Sambre. At about 9 o'clock the order was issued: 'The troops will stand ready for marching off. The English buglers will sound the signals to break camp and these signals are for all the troops stationed in Brussels'.

Towards 1 o'clock at night, the first signals were sounded on the Place Royale, which then were quickly taken up elsewhere. Even the Scottish bagpipers passed on these signals which made a peculiar impression in the middle of the night. There was now more than a little activity in the streets; 16 battalions hurried to their alarm stations, which were on the Place Royale for the 4th Brigade, and near the park for most of the English troops. Various dispositions that had to be taken in the middle of the night which it was difficult to accomplish in as large a city as Brussels due to the short notice, interfered with the prompt formation of the battalions. These concerned in particular the procurement and distribution of ship's biscuit that had to be given out to the men as a reserve to last for several days. This delayed the marching off in a way such that it was daybreak before the 9th English Brigade (the Scottish) could take off on the road to Charleroi; it was followed by the 8th English Brigade, by von Rettberg's Hanoverian battery,* and, at sunrise, by the 5th Hanoverian Brigade. The 10th English Brigade, which with the 4th Hanoverian Brigade formed the 6th Division, had also formed up on the Place Royale but did not march off with the other battalions.†

Our march went on without delay until the far end of the forest of Soignes, about four hours from Brussels, but we then halted for one hour by the side of the highway in the wood near Waterloo. At that place, the Duke of Wellington and the Duke of Brunswick rode past the columns, the former, dressed in a plain blue coat, white trousers, white neckerchief, and a small cocked hat, looked sternly ahead and riding at a fast trot, hardly seemed to pay any attention to the troops. But the Duke of Brunswick (he wore the well known black uniform) answered with a few friendly remarks to the Hanoverians who saluted him, both here and at Genappe.

---

* Rettberg's battery was actually assigned to the 4th Division, but had not joined them at Oudenarde. Rettberg was ordered to march with the 5th Division and as such was engaged at Quatre Bras. See *Waterloo Archive*, vol. II, letter no. 14, for Rettberg's own report which confirms this.

† Author's footnote: According to Beamish's History of the King's German Legion, the 4th [Hanoverian] Brigade, instead of the 5th Brigade, had joined the 5th Division by mistake. The 5th Hanoverian Brigade, which was part of the 5th Division, was not at Brussels but stood at Hal and its environs, and only linked up with the 5th Division on 17 June. The 4th Brigade received a specific order at the alarm station with the instruction that the brigade was forthwith under the command of General Picton. An officer of the staff of General Picton had brought this order.

During this period of rest, part of the Duke of Brunswick's Corps of troops marched by us, and, after a brief stop at Waterloo, preceded us to Genappe, where it halted and we then took the lead.

After its pause, the column commanded by General Picton advanced by way of Mont St Jean to Genappe where it arrived at about 2 o'clock. Here we heard the first sound of a cannonade coming from the Quatre Bras area that was about one hour distant from us. Our rate of marching was increased and Genappe was passed as quickly as possible. On the far side of this locality, arms were loaded, and all dispositions made it clear that we would soon take part in the action that had developed before us.

About 2 o'clock in the afternoon, the Quatre Bras position had been attacked by French troops and the Netherlands troops had been pressed back towards Quatre Bras. At about 3 o'clock, [van] Merlen's Netherlands cavalry brigade had arrived on the road from Nivelles at almost the same time that Lieutenant General Sir Thomas Picton moved up on the Brussels highway on the ridge of Quatre Bras with his three brigades and Rettberg's Hanoverian battery. The cavalry immediately advanced on the Charleroi highway. The infantry halted at some houses with the name of la Baraque.[*] Rettberg's battery went from here to its emplacement by the side of Quatre Bras; it opened fire right away. The 9th English Brigade and two battalions of the 8th English Brigade (the 28th and 42nd Regiments)[†] advanced and deployed between Quatre Bras and the village of Pireaumont in front of the Namur highway in an extended line in a field of tall corn. Here they were at once engaged in a very violent action that caused significant losses to the Scots of the 42nd and 92nd Regiments. The other two regiments of the 8th English Brigade (79th and 95th) and the 4th Hanoverian Brigade were to deploy at la Baraque as a second line. Before this deployment occurred, the two English battalions and the Verden Landwehr Battalion were instructed to move into the first line. Lieutenant General Picton himself placed the Verden Battalion in its new position, where it soon had occasion to take an active part in the action. The other three battalions were formed in line to the left of la Baraque, where the Münden Battalion was caught in the fire of a French battery and lost a few men without having yet seen an enemy. After the completion of the deployment, the line advanced to the Namur highway. The Luneburg Battalion rested with its right flank on Quatre Bras and then extended from there in the ditch alongside the highway. The Osterode and Münden Battalions formed the extension of this line, although not next to the highway but behind a narrow meadow

[*] Quatre Bras then consisted of the large farm which still stands at the crossroads, a few houses and a tavern called La Baraque.

[†] The 32nd was meant. The 42nd was actually part of the 9th British Brigade.

that was enclosed with tall hedges and formed an obtuse angle with the highway. The battalions were thus covered against the enemy fire; on the other hand, it obstructed the view of the terrain in front, and also [hampered] any prompt movement forward. Of the violent attack that the Scots in the first line had to endure, the two Osterode and Münden Battalions did not see anything, nor were they able to come to their support when it was most needed. The two battalions were under orders to maintain their position until the end of the action and to thwart any advance by the enemy, should he move forward beyond Pireaumont and threaten the left flank.

Several major French attacks occurred on the Charleroi highway against Quatre Bras. In one of these, the French light cavalry threw back the Brunswick cavalry, but in its rash pursuit near and into Quatre Bras it came under fire from the infantry posted there, and suffered significant losses. This body of cavalry scattered in all directions; on that occasion, a detachment of some thirty riders passed through Quatre Bras as far as la Baraque and galloped off close behind the Osterode and Münden Battalions. The fire from part of the Münden Battalion also caused them losses of a few men and horses; most of them escaped, however, favoured as they were by the terrain. Those they had left behind belonged to the 6th Chasseur Regiment.* In a second cavalry attack upon Quatre Bras, the Luneburg Landwehr Battalion was in a position not only to repulse this cavalry attack by its fire at close quarters but also to inflict fairly large losses in men and horses to this cavalry formation which for the most part consisted of cuirassiers. During the forming up at la Baraque, the skirmishers were ordered to advance beyond the Namur highway. As the most senior officer, Lieutenant Brenning took over the command of the skirmishers, including those of the Osterode Battalion, and joined the skirmishers of several English battalions, with whom he advanced towards Pireaumont and was constantly engaged with the enemy tirailleurs for the duration of the action. Lieutenant Jenisch of the Osterode Battalion was killed in this engagement; Private Klute of No. 3 Company of the Münden Battalion killed the commanding officer of a French voltigeur company when he was about to bravely lead his company in an attack against the skirmishers. Upon the arrival of Lieutenant General von Alten's Division, the skirmishers who had used all of their ammunition were relieved by the Hanoverian Jäger company of Captain von Reden, they returned to the battalion in the evening. Towards 9 o'clock in the evening, the firing ceased at all points and bivouacs were set up at

* The 6th Chasseurs à Cheval formed part of Piré's 2nd Cavalry Division, the two lancer regiments of this division causing great devastation within the British infantry squares at Quatre Bras.

the positions that had been occupied. The Münden Battalion posted a number of pickets to protect the left flank of the army. During the action at Quatre Bras, the firing could be distinctly heard of the engagement of the Prussian and French armies at Ligny, a distance of about two hours. That firing also stopped with the onset of night. The outcome of that battle became known to us with full certainty on the morning of 17 June. Some idea of it was already formed from the sound of the firing and by unidentifiable masses of troops that appeared at a great distance to the rear of our left flank as darkness set in.* At Quatre Bras, the Münden Battalion lost 2 soldiers killed and 8 wounded. Among the former was Private Herbold of No. 1 Company whom I mention here because he was the first Hanoverian soldier to die for his Fatherland in this new campaign. He fell at la Baraque when struck by a cannon ball in his chest, next to the battalion adjutant [Von Berckefeldt] who was then designating the point of support for the deployment of the battalion.

During the night, additional troops had arrived, the English cavalry in particular, which formed up between Gemioncourt and Pireaumont.

At daybreak of the 17th, an exchange of skirmish fire near Pireaumont, engaged in by accident between the French and our advance posts, caused a general call to arms for all the troops. The firing ceased a short time later and then things were quiet at the French camp, most of which could be observed and the troops piled their arms again for several hours. During this time, the Duke of Wellington, the Prince of Orange, as well as most of the higher ranking commanding officers met on the right flank of [Colonel] Best's Brigade, in order to make observations from there.

The outcome of the battle at Ligny caused the Duke of Wellington to lead his army then gathered at Quatre Bras to a position on the ridge at Mont St Jean. Towards 8 o'clock on the morning of the 17th, the troops were ordered to break camp, and around 10 o'clock the march back commenced in several columns. The troops commanded by Lieutenant General Picton were with the column which retired through Genappe on the Brussels highway. It was the first column to set off on the march. This column's march was slow and often interrupted by artillery and train columns, which also used the highway and for which the roadway had to be freed, particularly at the defile of Genappe. On arrival on the ridge of La Belle Alliance the 4th Brigade was ordered to move off the highway and march in the direction of Plançenoit and form up in column line. The 5th Hanoverian Brigade, which had just arrived, took up in the same formation next to the 4th Brigade. The men were allowed to rest and some

* Von Berckefeldt's footnote: These masses of troops made even our higher-ranking officers believe that Napoleon had already advanced far beyond the rear of our left flank.

details were sent to Plançenoit to obtain water. They were soon forced to return because at not too great a distance from Plançenoit French cavalry were standing and had sent reconnoitring detachments into Plançenoit. Several men of the brigade were taken prisoner in Plançenoit, including 2 men from the Münden Battalion. The oppressive heat on this day caused the formation of thunderstorms, which erupted at 3 o'clock in the afternoon with enormous violence and heavy rainfall. The ground in the fields thereby became softened to such an extent that moving forward was almost impossible. The troops had to suffer much, unprotected as they were from this rainfall.

In their position opposite Plançenoit the two Hanoverian brigades remained ready for battle and in formation, while observing the enemy detachments on the far side of the village, until the rearguard under Lieutenant Colonel von Alten had arrived at the Maison du Roi. During this period of about 1½ hours, the remainder of the columns were marching behind us to their assigned positions at Mont St Jean. The two Hanoverian brigades then proceeded to march off, with the 5th going first, followed by the 4th. Back on the highway, the rate of marching was very slow on the way to the farming estate of La Haye Sainte. The highway runs immediately past the east side of the farm and cuts through an elevation on the other side, at the bottom of which the farm is located. Upon arrival at this defile, the 4th Brigade had to halt once more and close up because of a stoppage of the preceding columns on the plateau some several hundred paces in front, where the rural road to Ohain branches off and a hedge and berm were located. Before the removal of the obstructions, the rearguard was approaching and its columns marched past the west side of La Haye Sainte. Larger formations of cavalry and artillery also retreated on the highway and pushed past the 4th Brigade and again held up its march for some time. Lieutenant Brenning, of the Münden Battalion, who with his skirmishers had formed the brigade's rearguard, then reported that the last detachments of the army's rearguard had marched by and that no troops were left behind, also that the enemy vanguard, supported by artillery, was closing up on the highway at not too great a distance. In this situation, the 4th Brigade and in particular the Münden Battalion at the rear would have been gravely imperilled in the event of a rapid advance by the enemy. At that moment, the Duke of Wellington appeared on the ridge, a battery moved up next to La Haye Sainte on the side of the highway, sappers hacked openings through the hedge, and within a few minutes all obstructions to our march were removed. The 4th Brigade continued its march, and just as the Münden Battalion was starting to move and march off to the rear of the battery, the enemy vanguard arrived on the opposite ridge at La Belle Alliance.

Several guns moved up at that location and opened fire on the 4th Brigade, which, however, turned out to be totally ineffective as not a single ball hit its target. At the same time, a mass of tirailleurs in open order came down the slope of the ridge. The brigade had to turn about immediately and face the enemy. The Münden Battalion stood next to the battery, and one company of the Osterode Battalion was sent off to occupy the farm of La Haye Sainte,* while the three other companies remained in support. The battery on our side now opened fire, both at the enemy guns and at the masses of tirailleurs. A few shots of remarkable effectiveness sufficed to make the artillery and the tirailleurs retire at speed to the area behind La Belle Alliance. This exchange of cannon fire at the onset of darkness remained the last shots fired this day. The brigade then continued its march to the assigned position, where it arrived in total darkness. The troops under the command of General Picton formed the left wing of the army, from the ridge at La Haye Sainte. For the night, the 4th Brigade was placed some 800 paces from the highway on the slope of the plateau of Mont St Jean, behind the Ohain road. Captain von Rettberg's battery had moved up to the crest in front of the brigade. To the right of the 4th Brigade and nearer to the plateau stood the 9th English Brigade, and at a similar distance to the left the 5th Hanoverian Brigade. These three brigades stood in line of columns.

The troops suffered much discomfort after the night set in; the men were wet through and through; the heavy soil of the camp ground had turned into a swamp; the total darkness and the unfamiliarity with the area prevented the setting up of a regular bivouac. Straw was not available to lay upon or to serve as a cover; nor was there the smallest piece of wood for lighting a fire to be had in the vicinity of the camp. There was no opportunity to dry or to warm oneself; neither was there a means to prepare a hot meal. Of the provisions provided for the 16th and 17th in Brussels, only a few frugal men had retained any small leftovers. In addition, the rain again came down in sheets; it was a cold rain that benumbed the limbs. The men were sitting on their knapsacks, wrapped in their blankets. Around midnight, the troops of the left wing had to stand to arms for an hour because an assault from the French side was suspected. That assumption was caused by a detachment of the Netherlands cavalry that had lost its way in the dark. The scenery changed with the onset of day; the rains had ceased and the weather was improving. Now the first camp fires were lit; parties were sent off to procure foodstuffs and brandy. Owing to an enterprising young officer, Ensign Meder, several of these things were obtained at various

* This company must have only remained in the farm for a short period, until the 2nd Light Battalion, KGL, was sent there. However, the soldiers of the 2nd Light do not mention seeing them.

places, wood in particular, whereby the direst of the present needs were somewhat alleviated. The wet clothes were dried as best as possible, the equipment was cleaned and the muskets were loaded with fresh charges, and after a few hours the discomforts of the past night were forgotten, the men were reinvigorated and ready for battle.

On the evening of the 17th and during the night into the 18th, the French army had taken position on the ridge of La Belle Alliance, which, at a distance of more than a thousand paces, ran parallel to that of the Anglo-Netherlands army. Its camp could be overlooked from our side.

Early in the morning the same kind of activities went on there as on our own; but between 9 and 10 o'clock an increase in movement could be observed over there. The troops took to arms, and it was concluded from their manoeuvring that preparations for the battle were being taken. The French army deployed in several lines and towards 11 o'clock the Emperor could be clearly recognised as he was riding through the ranks of his army, accompanied by a numerous suite. Their continuing shouts of '*Vive l'Empereur*' could be distinctly heard, by which he was saluted by the troops. On our side, arms were also taken up and the lines were formed in proper order. The troops of the left wing, commanded by Lieutenant General Picton, were positioned as follows: next to the highway between Brussels and Genappe the 8th English Brigade, then the 3rd [actually the 1st] Netherlands Brigade (Count Bijlandt), next to this the 9th English Brigade, followed by the 4th Hanoverian Brigade and the 5th Hanoverian Brigade to its left, and on the extreme left flank the 4th [actually the 2nd] Netherlands Brigade (Duke of Weimar), part of which had occupied the farms of Smohain, Papelotte and la Haye that were situated in front of the left flank. The infantry was formed in two lines standing closely together, and most of the battalions were deployed in line. The Münden Battalion was now posted at the crest of the plateau in the first line. In front of the foremost line of infantry four batteries were moved up into suitable emplacements. Several cavalry brigades stood at an appropriate distance behind the infantry lines, and it was the 4th English Cavalry Brigade (Vandeleur) that stood behind the crest on which the 4th Hanoverian Brigade had formed up.

The Battle of Waterloo commenced at about half past one.* French attack columns advanced against Chateau Hougoumont that was located on our right wing and some vigorous fighting developed there. Enemy batteries now opened fire, and before long all batteries on both sides became engaged with each other. Those battalions of the left wing that had been exposed to the enemy cannonade were retired from the first line behind the crest of the ridge, where they remained for some time without

* It actually started at around 11.30 a.m.

anything particular happening. Around, or soon after, 1 o'clock, the 4th Brigade was ordered to join up, at a certain point, with the 5th Brigade to its left. This combining occurred at some distance from Rettberg's Battery, on the slope on this side of the plateau of our position, and having Smohain, Papelotte and la Haye some 800 paces to the left front. Colonel von Vincke, commander of the 5th Brigade, now took over the command of both brigades that he now formed into a compact mass of one large square, of which the front face now stood on the crest of the plateau. The 8 battalions that were to form the square could not simultaneously move up to the point of assembly. As each battalion arrived there, it closed up to the battalion that was already in place, so that the battalions of the two brigades became mixed up. The total number of men of the two brigades now in the completed square was about 5,000.[*] Both brigades remained inactive in this position for a good hour. The French artillery failed to direct its fire at this compact mass, to which a few cannonballs could have inflicted severe losses. Only one cannonball did strike, which killed an officer and a soldier of the Osterode Battalion. Shells bursting in the air and the fire from enemy tirailleurs wounded several men. The skirmishers of the Münden and Verden Battalions had remained with Rettberg's Battery. At this location, they soon became engaged with enemy tirailleurs and kept them at a proper distance, also [aided by fire] from the square of the two brigades.

All of the action on the left wing until about 2 o'clock had mostly consisted in a heavy cannonade and in skirmishing. The enemy attacks had been mainly directed at the right wing and on the centre, but now several strong infantry columns advanced against the left wing. One of these columns made its major thrust against Bijlandt's Netherlands Brigade. The enemy column received heavy artillery fire but pressed forward nevertheless and threw back this brigade's battalions which stood in the first line. At that section, about 700 to 800 paces to the right of us, erupted one of the most violent engagements. The advancing French column was attacked in both flanks by several battalions of the 8th and 9th English Brigades, and in front by the remaining battalions of the Netherlands Brigade.[†] The 2nd English Cavalry Brigade (Ponsonby) galloped up and charged into this column, which now turned back with heavy losses[‡].

* A strange formation, which was particularly vulnerable to artillery fire.

† It is interesting to note that not all of Bijlandt's Brigade fled, but some joined the renewed attack.

‡ von Berckefeldt's footnote: This action deprived the army of two excellent generals, General Ponsonby fell during the pursuit, and Lieutenant General Picton was killed during the fighting. All of us were much saddened by the news of Lieutenant General Picton's death. During the brief period of time that we were under his command we had ample opportunity to learn to hold him in great respect.

There were two more columns apart from this one which moved up to attack the left wing, one of them against the farms of Papelotte, Smohain and la Haye, the other straight in the direction of the two Hanoverian brigades. The attack on the left wing by the three columns was not simultaneous; the middle one in particular, which marched towards our position, stayed far behind the other two columns. This middle column was preceded in the tall corn of Smohain by a skirmish line, and it was followed by the French 3rd and 7th Chasseur Regiments;* they rode up to the large square and seemed determined to launch their first attack against it. The outward faces of the square made ready to receive the approaching cavalry, when the 4th English Cavalry Brigade appeared and charged the French cavalry with great vehemence a short distance in front of us, scattered it and took a large number of prisoners including several staff officers. On their return, the horsemen were saluted by us with a cheerful 'Hurrah'. The repulse of the first attack column by Generals Picton and Ponsonby, the cavalry charge by the 4th English Cavalry Brigade, and the lack of success of the attack against the three farms mentioned earlier, caused the strong infantry column that was moving against us not only to not advance any further, but even to retreat a great distance. While the cannonade from the French side was somewhat reduced during the attacks, it now resumed more vigorously than before and the centre was struck by a powerful onslaught. An officer from the Staff of the Duke brought an order that the 5th Hanoverian Brigade was to march off to Mont St Jean to reinforce the centre, while the 4th Brigade was to hold the position that both brigades had occupied until then. The resulting breaking up of the square proceeded slowly due to several unfavourable circumstances. As already mentioned, the battalions of the two brigades had been intermixed. The disentangling of battalions took as long as an hour, during which the concentrated mass had to remain in one location, and moreover on unfavourable terrain. The heavy soil was soaked by the rain and had turned into a morass on which the men could not stand but sank in, to an extent that many of those at the centre of the square had their shoes and gaiters removed, remaining stuck in the ground. They now attempted to salvage them as the square was broken up, but not very many succeeded in this.† The battalions were drawn out of the square one by one, and marched off immediately.

The 4th Brigade now took up the following position: the Verden Battalion in the first line on the left flank of the brigade, behind the hedge

* The same Chasseurs à Cheval that they had faced at Quatre Bras two days previously.

† Von Berckefeldt's footnote: Of the Münden Battalion alone, some 40 men received compensation for the shoes that had remained stuck in the square.

of the Ohain road; it maintained contact with the Prince of Weimar's Netherlands Brigade. This battalion fought here mostly in open order until the end of the battle. The Luneburg and Osterode Battalions stood in the first line on both sides of Rettberg's battery, deployed in line or square depending upon the circumstances. Towards 5 o'clock in the evening, two companies of the Osterode Battalion were sent forward in open order to reinforce the skirmish line which was under considerable pressure. Both companies fought very well and used up all of their ammunition.

The Münden Battalion was deployed in line behind Rettberg's battery, and its specific assignment was to keep the battery covered. After taking up this position, there were no serious attacks on the left wing for some time, and only the skirmishers of the brigade were continuously engaged. During the later enemy attacks, the brigade's battalions were employed either in support of the centre or of the extreme left wing; when no longer needed they returned to their original position.

The Münden Battalion now found itself in a situation in which there was no opportunity to perform brilliant feats of arms, but it had honourably passed the test of battle due to its courage and endurance. Immediately after its placement behind the battery, the battalion was in the range of fire of an enemy battery on the opposite side, and even had to endure the musketry from enemy tirailleurs. No. 4 Company was particularly exposed to the cannon fire and lost many men within a short time. The battalion now had to calmly view the tumult of battle, its arms at the ready and had to watch how its own ranks became thinner without having the satisfaction of returning the fire, not even with a single shot. When the attacks upon the centre were renewed after 4 o'clock, the battalion was ordered there as a reinforcement, but shortly after its arrival it had to march back to the battery. Then, between 5 and 6 o'clock, it was sent forward to support the Netherlands Brigade which was being pushed out of Papelotte, Smohain and la Haye. But hardly had it arrived at the hedge of the Ohain road and had formed up next to the Verden Batalion, and started firing at the enemy, when it had to speedily march back to its battery. After its arrival there, a cavalry detachment, perhaps of squadron size, showed up in the rear of the battalion, whose appearance indicated that it did not belong to our army; but was very soon identified as Prussian cavalry.[*] An officer came galloping up and asked to see the Duke of Wellington; he left us the agreeable news that Blücher was approaching with his army and would provide us relief with his attack. Soon thereafter, dark uniformed columns moved out of the

* Von Berckefeldt's footnote: It belonged to a Silesian Hussar regiment [presumably from the 6th Hussars who led the Prussian advance of Bülow's Corps].

woods behind Fischermont against the right wing of the French army and were shortly opposed by masses of troops at an angle from us, who until then had been facing our side. The pressure on our troops on the left wing was becoming less for the moment. Before one hour had passed, fighting now commenced which would decide the outcome of the battle. Between 6 and 7 o'clock, the action became most violent at the centre, between the highways from Genappe and Nivelles, and between the area of the farms to the left of the Genappe highway and to the left rear of the farm of la Haye Sainte. The Münden Battalion was also sent to the latter point in support of the Scots and in particular of the 92nd Regiment which was low on ammunition. Posted at the point where the Ohain road branches off the highway, that regiment repulsed the attacking French columns with the greatest bravery, the combatants were only separated here at this moment by the hedge and berm of the Ohain road. The lack of ammunition was alleviated by an officer of the Münden Battalion who chanced on an English ammunition wagon that was arriving from Mont St Jean, and made some of his men carry its contents to the Scottish troops. In no time were the ten barrels with cartridges torn open; the Scots hurried over from their ranks and helped themselves to the cartridges, of which the most effective use was then immediately made.

During this fierce engagement, the Münden Battalion stood less than one hundred paces behind the 92nd Regiment without being allowed to advance and use its arms. The battalion lost a good number of men, and here it was where from the soldiers' ranks the loud request was heard: 'Why don't we go at them and revenge our fallen comrades?' But it was impossible to grant this request. Standing still and with their arms at the ready, the battalion had to remain where it was and at a distance of a few feet had to let the Scots alone fight on in this murderous contest. Our battalion commander was constrained in this regard by the strictest and most definite orders and the splendid opportunity to come to blows with the enemy thus came and went. It hurt deeply that the battalion had been denied here the chance to give proof of Hanoverian bravery in going to the attack and in hand to hand combat.

As soon as a break through at this point by the enemy was no longer to be feared around 7 o'clock in the evening, the Münden Battalion had to return to its battery. Its guns had to cease firing once before because of lack of ammunition, and now kept it up at a slow rate. The French cannon then reduced their fire at this battery and increased it in the direction of the Prussian ones that were moving up near Smohain, etc., which led to repeated requests by Prussian officers for Rettberg's battery to increase its rate of fire. But it had only 3 charges left for each gun.

Towards 7 [8] o'clock in the evening, the army's situation became particularly critical. About this time the French right wing was attacked and thrown over by the Prussian army, and the Duke of Wellington attacked the French Guards that were charging against the centre and also overpowered them.

During the following general advance of the army, Rettberg's battery and with it the Münden Battalion that had served as its cover, remained in the position they had held for some time. The latter then marched off and joined the other three battalions of the brigade which had moved up to a place slightly to the left rear of La Belle Alliance. Two cannon left behind by the enemy were secured by the Münden Battalion and passed on the next morning.

The battalion's skirmishers did not stay with the battalion during the battle. As agreed by the brigadier, they were sent in front of the line to fight off enemy tirailleurs and to act as needed on the judgment of their commanding officer. Together with the skirmishers of the Osterode Battalion, Lieutenant Brenning attacked a much stronger and favourably placed enemy tirailleur detachment near Papelotte and drove it out of its position; he afterwards became engaged with a French voltigeur company and was severely wounded in the attack. Ensign Murray, a courageous young officer, then assumed the command of the skirmishers. This officer was also wounded and replaced by Ensign von der Hellen.* That officer led the skirmishers with great circumspection and bravery until the evening when he was also badly wounded. An officer with the 4th [2nd] Netherlands Brigade now had the skirmishers join his men and led them in an attack, but was mortally wounded. Around 7 o'clock, the remaining skirmishers were called back to the battalion, but even here Sergeant Leonhardt, who now commanded them, was gravely wounded. The skirmishers had been fighting bravely all day, and some with particular distinction. Private Friedeborn of No. 1 Company was wounded three times but nevertheless did not leave the battlefield; he was an excellent shot and, as was witnessed, had inflicted many losses in the enemy ranks. Privates Oppermann and Losekrug of No. 2 Company and Biesterfeldt of No. 1 Company together had jointly aimed at a particular target and had shot dead three French officers, as was also witnessed. Private Stahlhuth of No. 2 Company was promoted to corporal for his exemplary conduct on the battlefield, which, although wounded, he left only when the skirmishers returned to the battalion. Sergeant Leonhardt was later also to enjoy honourable recognition for his brave and circumspect leadership.

The example given by the officers and many non-commissioned

* Ensign Charles August von der Hellen, Beamish no. 484, had transferred from the 1st Line Battalion, KGL, in 1814.

officers and soldiers had a beneficial influence on the younger soldiers of the battalion and contributed much to its serving with distinction on these days in which it was exposed to difficult situations. The number of the men of all ranks would certainly have been great who would have excelled in their personal bravery if the battalion had seen more of the action. There was little opportunity and I thus must confine myself to the names of those non-commissioned officers and soldiers who by their active and brave conduct had served with particular merit and who received appropriate awards. These include the four senior Sergeants Breiding, Harriehausen, Ammer, and Hornbostel, Sergeant Fischer of No. 4 Company, Corporal Utermohlen of No. 3 Company, Privates Schafer of No. 2 Company and Better of No. 1 Company.

But the Münden Battalion was not without individuals who had failed to do their duty. These included: a sergeant of No. 4 Company who had disregarded his duties and had brought back some wounded men and failed to return promptly; the supply sergeants of No. 1 and No. 4 companies and a corporal of No. 3 company who had been dispatched early in the morning to procure foodstuffs and did not return to the battalion until the 19th; moreover two train attendants, 11 musicians, and 13 privates, of whom it was proven that they had dishonourably left the battlefield. All these men were punished appropriately.*

The losses suffered by the battalion were significant in regard to its strength when marching off from Brussels on the 16th, and considering its mostly passive role in the battle, and after deducting those assigned to the baggage. The following would have been with the battalion on 18 June: 2 Staff officers, 1 Adjutant, 2 Physicians, 1 Staff commissary, 1 bandmaster, 1 armourer, 3 captains, 16 lieutenants and ensigns, 19 sergeants, 13 corporals, 7 drummers, 556 soldiers, and 4 train attendants.

Of these were:†

a Killed – 1 sergeant, 1 corporal, and 23 men.
b Wounded and hors de combat – 8 officers, 2 sergeants, 2 corporals, 1 drummer, and 102 men.
c Taken prisoner – 2 men.
d Missing – 1 drummer and 20 soldiers. (The latter includes the 13 men already referred to. Of one man it turned out that he was wounded;

* Refreshing honesty that is extremely rare for any unit at Waterloo! Even Wellington admitted as much when he claimed that a true history of the battle would destroy many reputations!

† These figures given here are much higher than those quoted by Siborne in his *History of the Waterloo Campaign*, but are more likely to be correct, being written by the adjutant.

2 men were deserters; the remaining men were retained as hospital orderlies).

As to materials, the losses of the battalion were:

60 muskets, 43 bayonets, 58 bayonet scabbards, 36 cartridge pouches, 55 woollen blankets, 37 canteens, 20 field kettles, 13 pioneer's hatchets, and one pack horse with medical supplies. Officers and soldiers were reimbursed for losses of private property as late as May 1819.

The place on which the 4th Brigade bivouacked in the night from 18th to 19th June was one of the areas of the battlefield where the fighting had been very severe in the evening. The large number of dead and badly wounded of all nations located here gave ample proof therefore. Not much help could be given to the latter because the surgeons were still busy at distant points and not a drop of water could be obtained nearby.

The battalions had to form up at daybreak; all of their files had been much reduced. Most of the men who had taken the wounded to the rear had not yet returned, although many of them came back in the early hours of the morning. Those who had brought the wounded to Brussels or were retained at the dressing stations returned only after several days. The infantry had to detach large details which collected and buried the corpses and brought the severely wounded to the nearest dressing stations. These detachments had to return by 11 o'clock. Towards 9 o'clock, wagons of the commissariat arrived on the battlefield and the troops received biscuits, rice and salt. These were the first supplies of foodstuffs since our departure from Brussels. After 11 o'clock the order to march off was issued; the 4th Brigade began its movement near 12 o'clock. We now had to leave the stalwart Scots of the 5th Division and join again the 10th English Brigade of the 6th Division.

No. 22 Ensign Theodor Oppermann

From J. Kannicht, All of This Because of Napoleon: From the war diary of George von Coulon, Major in the Royal German Legion, and the letters of his wife Henriette 1806–1815, *Bernard & Graefe Verlag, Koblenz, 1986*

Letter from Ensign Theodor Oppermann of the Münden Landwehr Battalion to his Parents.

Ensign Theodor Oppermann of the Münden Landwehr Battalion, a brother of the future son-in-law to the Coulons, participated in the action at Quatre Bras on 16 June and in the Battle of Waterloo on 18 June.

Bavay France, 23 June 1815

It has been a long time, dear parents, that I have let you wait for a response while I was in our cantonments; but now I take the first opportunity to write you about myself and all my comrades; how things happened to us all at once and so very unexpectedly. We had camped at Brussels in the deepest calm for more than 4 weeks and were thoroughly enjoying life in the big city. Without any idea of what was to happen, ourselves and the entire garrison had to march off early in the morning of the 16th. While resting at Waterloo towards noon, we heard that the French had advanced and were already fighting the Prussians. In the most oppressive heat, we then went by way of Genappe, where heavy artillery fire could already be heard, to Quatre Bras (1 hour from Genappe towards France, it consists of only 4 single houses). We there formed up behind a ridge and passed over it in line formation towards the fighting. Having been discomfited by the oppressive heat and the stressful march, I cannot deny that I went ahead feeling a bit uneasy. The Hanoverian artillery had already done good execution and had silenced the French immediately. A charge by the enemy cavalry upon our artillery stationed at Quatre Bras was completely thwarted by the Brunswick squares and our canister fire. While this happened, the right wing of our brigade took heavy fire and of the Verden Battalion 1 officer was killed, 1 man wounded and 3 taken prisoner. Our battalion came off [relatively] well in this action, and had only 1 man killed and a few wounded. The fighting ended towards evening, but neither party had been forced to yield. We camped on the field during the night. In the morning, about 3 o'clock, the French attacked again and there was heavy musketry, but no cannon shot was fired by either side. Our brigade was then in the third line and was left in peace and cooked its meat. During this time, I visited the battlefield where many dead of both parties were lying about. The groaning of the wounded, all of the dead, and the bustle of the living, all that dear parents, was terrible to hear and to behold. The Duke of Brunswick was wounded in this affair and died soon thereafter. He was mourned by all of our troops. Bonaparte had reportedly said: The death of the Duke gained him more than 10,000 enemy killed.

Towards noon, the small arms fire ceased and all of a sudden we had to retreat to Waterloo (3 hours from Brussels) because the Prussians had been driven back [from] near Fleurus. Here we had hardly taken up position on a height when the French tirailleurs showed up with a cannon. Our battery began its work and the French preferred to take to their heels. We set up our bivouac in the evening without being disturbed, but now it started to rain in sheets, and the downpour lasted until the next morning at 8 o'clock. I can assure you, dear parents, that never have I experienced a more terrible night. Lieutenant von Spitznas was struck by a severe bout of a cold fever, and several officers were unable to either walk or stand straight and the soldiers' yammerings was terrible. In short, nobody can have an actual idea about this night who was not there.

After we now had completely been soaked by the rain, the enemy attacked the right wing of the army. Fighting was getting heavier with every minute, and about 11 o'clock the left wing had to break camp (where we stood at the very end). Two brigades formed square immediately, with the cavalry on the left and the artillery on the right flank. The enemy dared an attack but was thrown back immediately by the artillery and the enfilading fire. The dragoons pursued them at once and did great execution. We thereupon formed line, and our battalion was unfortunately ordered to cover a battery. If we never had been under artillery fire, we now found out what it was like. Men were falling by files, particularly in our No. 4 Company. At this horrible place where one faces combat but cannot loose off a single shot we stayed until after 5 o'clock.

During this time, I took a look at the situation of our army and found that many changes had occurred. The right wing advanced vigorously, the cavalry made 3 charges and had completely thrown back the French cuirassiers. Everything turned out well when all of a sudden, Lord knows how it happened, the enemy moved up so heavily that there was a general yielding on the right wing and at the centre, and the artillery would almost have been lost if the cavalry had not cut it free. Suddenly, the brave Prussians appeared on the left wing, more to the rear of the enemy. They made a strong forward move at once and completely cut the French off. During these manoeuvres we came away from behind the battery and were posted closer to the centre, between 2 slight elevations and facing an enemy battery. Here we suffered quite badly again, and all of the company's officers were wounded except for myself. Now, however, the French pressed forward more heavily with every minute because they wanted to push through to Brussels, Bonaparte's main target, as they had been cut off at their rear. We retired a few paces and everybody believed that matters were turning for the worse. I then received a shot on the left side of the knee on my right leg. I had one of the men take me back right away because I did not know whether this was a serious wound or not. On getting closer to Waterloo I realised that the wound was only from a sharp grazing shot, but because walking became too painful and since I did not know the outcome of the battle, I spent the night at the village, otherwise I would have returned the same evening.

I greatly regret not having been able to witness the splendid outcome of the battle. Just as I had gone away, a strong formation of Prussian cavalry moved in on the French and overpowered everything, which then decided the battle. Everybody rejoiced and was happy, only this poor devil knew nothing about it. The army camped right on the battlefield and slept among the dead and wounded. On the next morning, the 19th June, I returned to the battalion, walking all by myself across the battlefield where the men lay in heaps. The wounded who had been there for 12 hours by now cried for water and something to eat. I arrived at the battalion towards midday at 11 o'clock. They were all very glad that I had come off as well as I did. Our line had advanced about a half hour's distance.

Theodor

2nd Netherlands Division of Lieutenant General Perponcher

No. 23 From La Belle Alliance

Pflugk-Harttung's letter no. 119
*Report of the 2nd Netherlands Division (Perponcher) on its actions from 15 to 19 June**

Headquarters at St Leu [la Foret] Taverny,† 25 October 1815

Events involving the 2nd Netherlands Division under the command of Lieutenant General von Perponcher in the Battles of Quatre Bras and La Belle Alliance‡

15 June
Headquarters at Nivelles;
First Brigade at the same place;
27th Jäger Battalion at the same place,
7th Line Battalion at Feluy, Arquennes and Petit-Roeux [lez Nivelles],
5th Militia Battalion at Obaix and Buzet,
7th Militia Battalion at Nivelles and Baulers,
8th Militia Battalion at Monstreux and Bornival.

* I have chosen to include this account from Colonel Pierre-Henri van Zuylen van Nyevelt, a Dutch officer, as it includes much on the Nassau troops, who although they were German, served with the Netherlands army.

† Three miles north of the centre of Paris.

‡ Pflugk-Harttung's footnote: See F. De Bas and T'Serclaes de Wommersom: *La Campagne de 1815 aux Pays Bas III*, pp. 289 ff.

Second Brigade at Houtain le Val;
1st Nassau Battalion-Usingen at the same place, at Vieux-Genappe and Loupoigne,
2nd Nassau Battalion-Usingen at Frasnes and Villers-Perwin,
3rd Nassau Battalion-Usingen at Baisy and Sart-Dames-Avelines,
1st Battalion Regiment No. 28 at Bousval, Thy and Glabais;*
2nd Battalion Regiment No. 28 at Genappe and Ways;
Volunteer Jäger at Thines.
Foot Battery at Nivelles.
Horse Battery at Frasnes.

In the morning, a number of cannon shots had already been heard. Since there was no ruling between armies to notify each other of their firing exercises, no particular attention had been paid to these shots. For several days now, every battalion assembled at its rallying place during the day and returned to its cantonments at night. As a result, the troops were formed by battalions at noon on the 15th when, at 4 o'clock, General von Perponcher received a dispatch from the commander of the 2nd Nassau Battalion that the firing was coming much closer from the direction of Gosselies and that small arms fire could be distinctly heard. The general immediately issued orders for the division to concentrate at the alarm stations at Nivelles and Quatre Bras. Before this order had reached Quatre Bras, the village of Frasnes, where the horse battery and half a battalion of the Nassauers were placed, was suddenly attacked by tirailleurs of the Imperial Guard.† Forced to act by the firing nearby, Major Normann of the 2nd Battalion, 2nd Nassau, had his troops stand to arms and had deployed some pickets. These were overrun by the French cavalry at 5 o'clock, after everything had been quiet since 1 o'clock. The 1st Flanqeur Company under Captain Müller and 80 volunteers under Lieutenant Hoelschen‡ were sent against the enemy and held him up.

Major Normann had earlier received general instructions to assemble his battalion at Frasnes in case of an attack, and not to abandon the artillery, for whatever reason. He now observed, however that most of the enemy approached from the wood at Villers-Perwin and from the side of Gosselies, also, that the artillery would be forced to retreat from its park in front of the village. He then gave the order to fall back, seeing that, otherwise, his left flank would be exposed to the enemy for half an

* Pflugk-Harttung's footnote: De Bas, p. 290, has placed the 1st Battalion at Genappe and Ways, the 2nd Battalion at Bousseval, Thy and Glabaix.

† Actually by the Light Garde Cavalry Division of General Lefebvre-Desnouettes consisting of the Chasseurs à Cheval and the Chevaux-légers lanciers regiments.

‡ He presumably means 1st Lieutenant Hoelzgen.

hour and he would be at risk to be cut off while on the way to join the brigade at Quatre Bras. The enemy immediately attacked upon becoming aware of this movement. Fortunately, the entire artillery park was already on the move through the foresight of Captain Bijleveld. While a reserve force was under way, Major Normann had the artillery take up a good position to the right of the highway and had it covered by four companies, while he posted the other companies on his flank. The enemy was held up for a short time by the artillery and small arms fire, but Major Normann was now pressed by superior numbers on his left flank that caused him to pull back and take up position in front of Quatre Bras at the farm near the Charleroi highway while keeping a strong force in the Bossu wood. This movement was executed under heavy fire; but a few well aimed cannon balls and the musketry fire kept the enemy at an appropriate distance.

Upon receipt of the order for the concentration of troops, the 2nd Brigade under Colonel the Prince of Saxe-Weimar was formed up in column on the highway, with its front towards Gosselies. The 1st Nassau Battalion stood alongside the road from Houtain le Val and had placed two companies on the right edge of the wood. Two companies of the 3rd Nassau Battalion, and the grenadiers and two companies of the 2nd Battalion, No. 28 Regiment, were sent to reinforce the position of the 2nd Battalion [Nassau]. The company of Volunteer Jäger, formed in four platoons, was told off to cover the wood. Two guns with infantry cover were placed in a forward position on the Namur highway, and a 6-pounder gun was stationed near the outpost on the Charleroi highway. At 7 o'clock, the Brigade Adjutant of the 2nd Brigade arrived [at Nivelles] and provided General von Perponcher with a report on the attack and the evacuation of Frasnes, as well as on the present disposition of the troops. His Excellency gave order that the position must be held as long as possible. A report of the attack was sent to the Prince of Orange, with a request for further instructions. Meanwhile, His Excellency dispatched the heavy baggage and all field equipment to Waterloo, there to await further orders. The 1st Brigade and the artillery [Captain Stievenart's foot battery] had now been assembled at Nivelles; the 27th Jäger Battalion was placed at the town of [Haine] St Paul,* and was later relieved by the 7th Battalion of the Line.

Until this time, no reliable intelligence had been received about the enemy. Neither was information available about the advance of the entire French army and about the outcome of the engagement near Charleroi and Gosselies, which led to the retreat of the Prussians to Fleurus. Not only was our left flank left uncovered, but so was also the main highway from Brussels to Waterloo. All that had become known about the enemy

* On the Mons to Nivelles road.

consisted of contradictory rumours spread by Prussian fugitives coming from Thuin and Lobbes, until the arrival of a French Adjutant Captain at division headquarters. Returning to the colours of his lawful allegiance he had deserted from the French army in peasant's clothes and brought the news of the outcome of the action against the Prussians. At the same time, he confirmed that Bonaparte was leading 150,000 men in their advance on Brussels.

At 9 o'clock [in the evening], the Prince of Saxe-Weimar sent word that the enemy was very numerous and that he feared he was not strong enough to duly resist a strong attack. General Perponcher commanded him to defend to the utmost the position at Quatre Bras; only if the enemy would attack in greatly superior numbers might he withdraw to Mont St Jean* where in that case he were to be joined by the 1st Brigade. Meanwhile, a company of Jäger and a line company were sent off to deploy along the road between Quatre Bras and Nivelles. The battalions stationed in front of this town despatched frequent patrols to secure information about any approaching enemy.

At around half past ten, an order was received from the Prince of Orange to concentrate the entire division at Nivelles, where it would be supported by the 3rd Division, while the cavalry was ordered to assemble on the high ground of Haine Sainte Pierre. The intention of this order was obviously not to oppose the enemy in small troop bodies but in a large mass; it was nevertheless General Perponcher's opinion that, being in Brussels, His Royal Highness was perhaps not adequately informed of the movements of the French and Prussian armies, and was apparently unaware that Charleroi had been evacuated and that the Prussians were rallying at Fleurus. Relying on all available information and all reports, the general realised the paramount importance, in order to protect Brussels, of closing the gap that had opened up between himself and the Prussians and of preventing the enemy from penetrating to the passage through the Bois de Soignes, which would have cut off all support. For that reason, General Perponcher felt that he could take it upon himself not to follow that order and, rather, to hold to the utmost the position at Quatre Bras, of which decision he informed His Royal Highness. At 12 o'clock, an officer of the General Staff arrived with a dispatch from the Quartermaster General that His Royal Highness had been informed of the enemy's movements, and that HRH might be expected any minute now on his return from Brussels. The troops bivouacked at their locations, and things remained unchanged at the position during the night.

* It is interesting that he confirms that the fall back position was Mont St Jean, where the Battle of Waterloo was fought – rather than the La Belle Alliance position.

16 June

At 2 o'clock in the morning, His Excellency left for Quatre Bras with the 27th Jäger Battalion and the 8th Militia Battalion. Immediately outside Nivelles, His Excellency encountered a detachment of 50 Prussian hussars from the 2nd Silesian Hussar Regiment,* commanded by Lieutenant Sellin,† who had become separated from their corps. Having no cavalry himself, the general made the suggestion that they stay with him, which was accepted. On the march, the general also had the detached companies join him, and arrived at Quatre Bras at about 4 o'clock. He reviewed the troop dispositions made by the Prince of Saxe-Weimar, which he approved, but extended the line in order to hide our weakness from the enemy and to strengthen the posts at the wood of Bossu. At 5 o'clock, the 27th Jäger Battalion was placed to the left of the Charleroi highway, and the two Flancqeur companies were stationed on the left wing to relieve the 3rd Nassau Battalion and to keep the enemy under better observation. The 8th Militia Battalion remained in reserve at the centre of the 2nd Brigade behind the houses of Quatre Bras.

The 2nd Nassau Battalion sent off some forward patrols and followed them later. A number of enemy horsemen that were encountered were chased off with a few musket shots. This battalion took up position on a ridge in the rear of Frasnes and had one company detached to keep this village under observation and two others to cover the tip of the wood; in this way, the battalion occupied almost all of the wood of Bossu and regained the terrain lost on the previous day. In the course of their reconnoitring, the Prussian hussars made a few splendid charges at the enemy cavalry which, however, drove them back and made them lose four men and thirteen horses. This detachment later received word from its corps and marched off to Sombreffe.

In the meantime, in order not to denude Nivelles entirely, General Perponcher had left General Bijlandt with three battalions and a battery at that place; but the Prince of Orange, who had passed through Nivelles at 6 o'clock, ordered two battalions of the 1st Brigade and the artillery to move to Quatre Bras, while the 7th Battalion of the Line was to remain at Nivelles until relieved by a battalion of the 3rd Division. From the left wing, two companies of the 27th Jäger Battalion were told off at 6 o'clock to seize a height, from which the enemy could closely observe all of our movements. They succeeded in taking the height, until their further advance was prevented by the approach of infantry reinforcements, whose heavy volley fire was reinforced by occasional cannon shots.

* Pflugk-Harttung's footnote: 1st Silesian Hussar Regiment.

† Pflugk-Harttung's footnote: It said 'Sioholm', which was crossed out and corrected to 'Sellin'. De Bas p 300 shows Zehelin.

This fire lasted until the arrival of the Prince of Orange in person, who then ordered the advance of additional troops, in a line parallel with the Charleroi highway and to extend our position far enough that our right wing was posted a short quarter of an hour from Frasnes, and that the wood of Bossu was occupied as far as its tip. The eight guns of the horse battery were placed in reserve under cover from the enemy fire.

During the march from Nivelles to Quatre Bras of the 5th and the 7th Militia Battalions and the Foot Battery, some enemy cavalry appeared on their right flank near Houtain le Val in the direction of Rêves. The chief of the General Staff* had the 7th Battalion halt in front of the wood of Haiby until all of the column had passed, which arrived unhindered at Quatre Bras at 9 o'clock and was placed on the highway in reserve. At 7 o'clock, the enemy reconnoitred our position and made a few cavalry charges, which were repulsed, with loss on his side. Since things had here remained quiet for one hour, HRH the Prince of Orange had the soldiers take a rest and cook their meals.

Until now, the enemy had not appeared in great strength; apart from some infantry of the line, the troops with whom we had been engaged had only consisted of chasseurs à cheval, lancers, and horse artillery, all belonging to the Guard, and were part of the corps of General Reille. Large numbers of enemy troops might be hidden by the forest of Villers Perwin and by the approach roads from Gosselies to Frasnes. But from the enemy's movements, one would have to conclude that his thrust against Quatre Bras was intended to mask another movement and that it would be limited to a reconaissance in strength. On the other hand, the heavy cannonade in the direction of Sombreffe would lead one to assume that the Prussians were attacked, who had been retreating that way, the more so since Napoleon's strength would not appear to be great enough to fight a battle on both of his wings.

Surprisingly, Napoleon did not make a greater effort to seize Quatre Bras after having gained substantial advantages over the Prussians. On our side, attention had been directed with good reason at the mistake of having placed the boundary between the allied English and Prussian troops along the line most favourable for the enemy's operation, should he intend to invade Belgium (there not being a single fortress in his path). If Napoleon had detached one or two divisions from his left wing for a similar movement in force towards Brussels by way of Nivelles, he could have by-passed in this way the Quatre Bras position before the arrival of our troops at Mont St Jean. To the very least, he could have been there at the same time and have secured the important route through the Forest of Soignes, thereby depriving the allies of all the advantages, which later

* Colonel van Zuylen van Nyevelt.

on in the Battle of Belle Alliance turned out to be of critical importance.

At 9 o'clock [a.m.] the Duke of Wellington arrived here; he inspected and approved the position taken so far, and then departed in the direction of Sombreffe. The 2nd Nassau Battalion, having been under fire since the previous day, was relieved by the 3rd Battalion and sent back to Quatre Bras to rest and cook its meals. In the meantime, the 3rd Division had arrived at Nivelles and had there relieved the battalion of our division which had been left for the protection of the town. That battalion arrived at Quatre Bras around 12 o'clock and was placed behind the wood in closed column. The entire division was thus assembled at Quatre Bras; its forces stood before and in the wood of Bossu, occupied the plain of Frasnes, had its left wing on the Charleroi highway, and kept the wood of Villers Perwin under observation.

Regarding the artillery, two 6-pounders and a howitzer of the horse battery were placed on the road to Frasnes, one 6-pounder and a howitzer to the right of it, and the three remaining guns of this battery on the Namur highway. The two howitzers and 4 guns of the 6-pounder foot battery were drawn up in front of the position at Quatre Bras with the troops of the second line; Lieutenant Winsinger was detached with the remaining two guns to the right wing of the first line. The remainder of the artillery and the train were placed behind Quatre Bras in reserve.

From the reports of an adjutant general who had deserted and from prisoners reliable information had been received that we were opposed by eight infantry divisions and four cavalry divisions under the command of Marshal Ney; they were General d'Erlon's 1st Corps, General Reille's 2nd Corps, two divisions of heavy cavalry under General Kellermann, one light cavalry division under General Piré, and one division of cavalry of the Guard, consisting of the Red Lancers under General Colbert and the Chasseurs à Cheval under General Lefebvre Desnouettes. By 1 o'clock, the enemy's movements made it obvious that he intended to advance in force on Brussels, by way of Quatre Bras and Waterloo. Two companies of the 27th Jäger Battalion were detached to the left, and skirmishers were posted in the wood of Villers Perwin for a better observation of the enemy; another company was told off to cover the foot battery in its forward position. In the meantime, a large number of troops began to appear on the enemy's side, and a heavy skirmishing fire erupted all along the entire line which was to mask a movement of his left flank to the right.

Towards 2 o'clock, the 7th Line Battalion still stood in closed column on the plain but, soon afterwards, was at first ordered to move behind the wood, and then to take position to the right of the wood. The 7th Militia Battalion followed this movement and crossed the wood which just then was attacked in force by the enemy. As a safeguard, the 5th Militia Battalion was posted more to the left on the Charleroi highway to cover a farm next to it [Gémioncourt]. The 1st Battalion of the 28th Regiment [Orange Nassau] and the 8th Militia Battalion formed the extreme right wing and deployed in line, but were ordered a short time later to retire and take up position to the rear of the wood of Bossu.

The 1st Nassau Battalion was posted in front of the wood. The two companies of Captains Werneck and Trittler,* deployed as skirmishers, were charged several times by the lancers of the Guard, but, led by HRH in person, repulsed these attacks with great sangfroid. As the enemy advanced in greater strength, the battalion was no longer able to hold its position on the plain and received the order to withdraw to the edge of the wood of Bossu. The eight cannon of the horse battery and two 6-pounders of the foot battery were placed with the troops of the first line, and the other guns of the foot battery with those of the second line.

In this position, the division was entirely on its own and without cavalry. The cannonade and the small arms fire were very violent and were only interrupted from time to time by cavalry charges. We had already suffered significant losses when, at half past three, the enemy energetically attacked our entire line from all sides with shouts of '*Vive l'Empereur!*' Our cavalry was expected every moment, and did arrive a short time later; but the English, Scottish and Brunswick troops could not be expected very soon since they had moved out of the Brussels area only during the night from the 15th to the 16th. Supported by a most violent cannonade, the enemy eventually forced our troops back from their position in front of the wood and took possession of most of it. On falling back, some of the troops took up their stand on the north side of the wood, while others crossed the highway and deployed on the commanding height to its left.

As the enemy was pressing in an oblique line from the wood of Villers Perwin against our left wing, the general of the division ordered the 27th Jäger Battalion to advance some 100 paces to cover the left wing of the 5th Militia Battalion. The companies which had been sent forward were attacked and driven back before they were able to reform, and then rallied behind the battalion. The enemy took advantage of his success by placing a battery in front of this battalion, which was then forced to fall back. This movement was executed in column by divisions at platoon distance, in order to be able to form square at any time.

In the meantime, the enemy, having driven back the 7th Line Battalion, made rapid progress in the wood [of Bossu], from where the 8th Militia

* He was made an officer of the Légion d'honneur by Napoleon in 1808 during the emperor's Spanish War.

Battalion had been expelled by a heavy cannonade. The 1st Battalion of the 28th Regiment and the 7th Militia Battalion remained in reserve to the right of the wood, while the two retreating battalions reformed on the high ground to its rear. HRH had the 2nd Nassau Battalion move up, whose flank was covered by the 2nd Battalion, 28th Regiment. But the first line was pressed back by the enemy's great superiority, by his well sustained cannonade and musketry, and by continuous cavalry charges. Led by HRH in person and General von Perponcher, this retreat was executed without hurry and in good order while under the continuous fire from both sides. The troops and the two guns of the foot battery came for the greater part through the wood and, from there, moved to the highway of Houtain le Val.

The Red Lancer Regiment of the Guard and the 6th Chasseurs à Cheval Regiment charged the 27th Jäger Battalion, which had not yet fully reformed, and dispersed it and inflicted great losses in wounded and prisoners; the greater part of the latter, however, returned during the night. As the enemy had thus succeeded in seizing most of the terrain in front of the position, he made every effort to force the centre and drive on through the Quatre Bras farm.

The brigade of light cavalry of General van Merlen had now arrived and had taken up position to the left of the main highway. The vanguard of the columns of the English division under General Picton and of the Brunswick troops arrived at the position around 3 o'clock and deployed on the left wing, which was then extended along the Sombreffe highway. As soon as the enemy became aware of our reinforcements, he redoubled his attacks on Quatre Bras, where the 5th Militia Battalion was posted [at the farm of Gémioncourt]. HRH commanded here in person and, waving his hat, rode at the head of the troops and led several charges by which the enemy was driven back and suffered losses. The artillery always advanced a few hundred paces, but was unable to remain a match against the superiority of the enemy artillery in both numbers and size of the pieces. The captain of the foot battery was killed; many officers and men were killed and the horses shot down so fast that it was hardly possible to keep up firing with the guns.

The 5th Militia Battalion, led by the brave Lieutenant Colonel Westenberg, and inspired by the example of HRH, performed miracles of bravery, but hardly had one assault been repulsed, when another occurred, with more and fresh troops. The light cavalry received orders to advance, but, carried away by their courage, they fell upon the enemy's 8th and 11th Cuirassier Regiments and had to yield to the enemy's superior force. On their retreat (in disorder), many of our cavalrymen pulled the artillery and infantry along. As the enemy cavalry drove forward between the houses of Quatre Bras, it was received by the fire of the troops still holding the position. The 1st Brigade [of Perponcher's Division], placed on the right side of the road, attacked the enemy's left flank, and the 2nd Brigade, stationed on the left side of the road together with a regiment of Scotsmen, struck at his right flank, forcing him to retreat while under canister fire from the artillery and thus losing many men.

In the meantime, the enemy had gained possession of the wood [of Bossu]. HRH ordered the 2nd Nassau Battalion and some Brunswick Jäger to retake it. They bravely attacked but failed because it was held by an enemy in superior strength. The Scottish and English troops on our left wing had charged at the enemy's right flank, and as our troops had been reforming, an attack was undertaken on Quatre Bras which had remained in the possession of the enemy.* At the same time, HRH gave orders to Colonel van Zuylen van Nyevelt, Chief of the General Staff, to retake the wood, using three battalions, and press on to the high ground where the 2nd Nassau Battalion had been standing in the morning. This battalion then attacked and was supported by the 1st Battalion, No. 28 Regiment, while the 7th Militia Battalion remained in reserve. The wood had been occupied in great strength by the French Guard; but after a heavy skirmishing fire our troops advanced to the high ground in question. As a major outcome of our well directed attacks on Quatre Bras [the farm of Gémioncourt] and in the wood, all the wounded and prisoners were regained, while the enemy only succeeded in carrying off one howitzer and two 6 pounders, which, however, were recaptured two days later.

Apart from the English division of General Picton and the Brunswick troops, the two divisions of the Guards and of General Alten had arrived, as well as the 1st Regiment [of the Duchy of] Nassau, several cavalry regiments, and numerous artillery pieces. The division was relieved at the points that it had held, and now occupied on the right that part of the wood that it had retaken, and the line of communication to the right at the highway to Houtain le Val. Certain movements of the enemy army, the detachment of the [French] 1st Corps against the Prussians, and the onset of darkness caused the fighting to end. Everybody remained wherever they had been fighting. The division bivouacked on the high ground to the rear of the wood of Bossu, the 1st Battalion, 28th Regiment, and the [2nd] Regiment Nassau on the right of the wood in column formation; the other troops formed two lines, with the English division to the right and the Brunswick troops to the left. The 5th Militia Battalion, which had suffered most, and the 8th Militia Battalion bivouacked behind the position, together with the artillery that had to restore its complement. The 27th Jäger Battalion had been ordered by HRH himself to return to

* The farm of Gémioncourt was obviously meant in this context.

Nivelles where it spent the night.

This had been a most glorious day for the Netherlands troops. The 2nd Division, of a strength of not more than 7,000 men, had alone withstood for several hours the persistent onslaughts of the enemy's left [wing], whose entire 2nd Corps had tried everything to seize Quatre Bras. The Prince of Orange's dispositions of troops over a wide expanse were greatly aided by the features of the terrain; the wood of Bossu masked all our movements and caused the enemy to believe that the troops posted there (who were our entire force) were the vanguards of several columns. However, the division could not have held on to its position much longer, the men were very tired, having been under fire the whole day. Due to the losses, some rest was needed to reform the corps. The artillery had lost three pieces, four had their barrels dismounted, and on several guns the barrels had cracked; it was deficient in officers and men so that there were very few left to service the guns. The vigorous firing on the left wing kept going well into the night, and judging by the sound, neither party had made any progress [a reference to the Prussians' battle at Ligny].

17 June

All remained calm during the night. At daybreak, the 27th Jäger Battalion returned from Nivelles, and all the corps were reunited. Only the artillery remained behind our left wing, protected by the 5th Militia Battalion, and was much in need of repairing its equipment. Several regiments of British cavalry were sent off to Houtain le Val on the right wing to keep the plain near that place under observation. After some time, the news arrived of the defeat at Ligny [of the Prussians] and the retreat towards Wavre. It was easy to see that the Duke of Wellington would shortly break camp and intended to fall back, in line with the Prussians; orders were therefore given to cook meals. At around 9 o'clock, the Prince of Orange arrived and ordered our retreat on the Brussels highway. Near La Baraque, the detached units rejoined the division, which then followed the 3rd English Division on the highway to Genappe. All of the army's baggage and equipment took the same road and collided with artillery and transport wagons and carts in the narrow thoroughfare of Genappe, causing much confusion. The general of the division ordered a search for an alternative route and, having found one, had the units move in double file at marched-off right formation and wade across the Dyle creek. The column was reformed on the far side of Genappe.

The division had been given orders to form up in parallel to the highway from Waterloo to Nivelles, with its left wing leaning on the village of Mont St Jean and with its right wing towards Braine l'Alleud. According to this order, the 3rd Division was to adjoin ours. The troops arrived at this position at about 1 o'clock and deployed in battle order, with the artillery behind the line and 2 guns and 2 light companies on the high ground, which covered the right wing and from where the area of Braine l'Alleud and the approaches to Nivelles could be kept under observation. It began to rain in the afternoon, and at 6 o'clock an order came to march off to the left wing and form the first line. The division then marched off in column by sections to the left and advanced to the left as far as the farm of [La] Haye Sainte. From there, it marched up to the left, and at the ridge of Mont St Jean it turned to the right and formed a battle line, with its right wing on the Brussels highway and the left towards Wavre, having the hollow way at its rear, which leads from that town to Braine l'Alleud. Six guns were emplaced well apart, on the right wing, to put the Genappe highway in their target range; the three remaining guns were placed on the left wing on the high ground, with the villages of Frichermont and Smohain in their range. A screen of 400 skirmishers was stationed 150 to 200 paces in front of the line.

The division stood on the forward slope of the Mont St Jean ridge. The ground on the right wing consisted of marshy terrain, that on the left wing of clayey soil, both soaked by the rain. Behind the line was the hollow way leading from Ohain to Braine l'Alleud, which was bordered by shrubs and hedges on both sides. English and Scottish divisions had here taken their position, which was well provided with 9 pounders. Before the front was a deeply cut ravine, and on the opposite side from the ridge of Mont St Jean, before the right wing, was the farmstead of La Haye Sainte, and before the left wing the hamlet of Smohain. From its left, a hollow way led to the Chateau Frichermont (owned by the Seigneur de Beaulieu), that was located on a height two musket shots distant from the hamlet.

The English cavalry had been driven back and passed through our lines, with the enemy in pursuit. The firing of the artillery came closer, and the noise of musketry could already be heard. The British rearguard made a stand in front of La Haye Sainte and the enemy ended his pursuit as darkness set in. He took up position on the heights opposite to us. Our screen of skirmishers was twice relieved before nightfall. It was a terrible night, the incessant rain and a strong wind from the east made the soldier's situation most uncomfortable; there was no straw to build a hut and no wood to make a fire, and we had to stand up to the ankle in water.

18 June

Towards 2 o'clock in the night, a false alarm was sounded and the division had to stand to arms. Even those who had found some protection from the weather were now thoroughly drenched. At daybreak, only a few enemy skirmishers could be observed on the heights facing us, but almost no troop bodies. During the night, only a few fires had been seen, perhaps due to the rain, or because the enemy had left his troops at Genappe.

At 6 o'clock, Brigade Major Coustoll reconnoitred the area of Smohain and Frichermont, whereupon four companies of the 1st Battalion, 28th Regiment, were posted at the two locations. Around 8 o'clock, His Royal Highness in person inspected the line and thanks to his untiring efforts some foodstuffs had arrived. The ammunition was replenished and the arms were made battle ready. At 9 o'clock, His Royal Highness ordered 800 men of the division to be sent to the right wing, for which the 1st Battalion, 2nd Light Regiment Nassau, was despatched. This battalion, under the command of Captain Büsgen, took possession of the farmstead of Hougoumont. It consisted of a large building within a garden, surrounded by a wall in which loopholes were made, as were also in the doors and roofs of the building. To the right of this farmstead was a small wood, in which three companies were stationed while the three remaining companies took position in the garden and buildings as time permitted.

The weather began to improve, and sunshine and rain were alternating for the rest of the day.

At around 10 o'clock, Bonaparte concentrated his forces on the heights opposite from us. At 11 o'clock, movements were observed in the enemy line, which seemed to indicate a reinforcement of his right wing, together with a massing of cannon in that area. The troop bodies seen on the heights were advancing and showed signs of attacking our left wing.

At 12 o'clock,* the entire 1st Brigade and the artillery on the right wing moved farther back to avoid interfering with the English artillery and to reduce their exposure to enemy fire. It crossed the hollow way and deployed on its northern side in the same order as before, adjoined to the right and left by English and Scottish troops. The 5th Militia Battalion moved into the second line, which consisted also of English and Scottish battalions.

The 2nd Brigade was deployed as follows: The 2nd Battalion, 28th Regiment, formed in square, and four companies of the 3rd Nassau Battalion, in column formation, were both in reserve behind the village, whereas the remainder of the troops were posted behind hedges and other features of the terrain in the direction of the village of Smohain. Four companies of the 1st Battalion, 28th Regiment, occupied Chateau Frichermont; one company of the 2nd Battalion of the same Regiment

---

* This confirms that prior to the battle Bijlandt's troops were ordered to retire behind the hedges and were not left on the forward slope exposed to the heavy French artillery fire.

guarded the hollow way leading from Smohain to the Seigneur de Beaulieu's manor. The guns attached to the left wing remained emplaced on the forward height and soon began firing at the enemy cavalry which showed itself on the plain of Frichermont. The enemy cannonade against our left wing had hardly begun (killing the brave Major Hegmann, commander of the 3rd Nassau Battalion) when it extended all along the line, in particular at Hougoumont and La Haye Sainte.

The attack on our left wing was actually only a reconnaissance in force to determine if we were in contact with the right wing of the Prussians, or whether a turning movement was possible around our left flank by way of Frichermont. In this first attack, only artillery was used and cavalry, which was repulsed and returned to its former position on the enemy's left wing.

In a vigorous attack, the French at first took the wood of Hougoumont. Our troops retreated into the farmstead, which General Reille now attacked with the 1st Corps [2nd Corps]. Towards 2 o'clock, after an extended and violent cannonade the attack on our centre commenced, to which Bonaparte had assigned the 1st Corps. Regiment upon regiment followed in the assault on La Haye Sainte. Every inch of terrain was conquered with blood; there were corpses everywhere; the position remained in our hands. In the meantime, three attack columns, led by Count d'Erlon, moved against our position, with the 103rd (or 105th) Regiment* at their head. The enemy crossed the ravine, protected from our fire, and drove back our skirmishers. Having approached to within fifty paces, no shot had yet been fired, but our soldiers could no longer be restrained. They began firing by ranks, but the enemy kept advancing bravely. In this attack, the brigade stood in two ranks, which caused the firing to be weak and poorly sustained. As a few of our files were overthrown, some gaps opened in the line through which the enemy column now advanced.† Everything before its front was forced to give away; however, the platoons on our flanks attached themselves with great sangfroid to our nearest troops.

After the enemy had passed through the first line, our second line now moved against him. An English cavalry regiment closed up, ready to attack as soon as he [the French] happened to retreat. The enemy now faced the troops that he had been unable to see from his position as they

* It was the 105th Ligne who were to lose their eagle.

† An interesting comment to an English reader used to reading of their native forces fighting in two ranks. European forces were more used to fighting in three ranks and it would appear from Nyvelt's comments that this was a new formation and one they were unused to and uncomfortable with. This may well have affected their morale and led to the subsequent disintegration of much of this division.

had lain down behind the hedges. He now attempted to reform [into line]; our second line pressed against his flanks and, thus protected, our troops of the first line were able to rally. The enemy was driven back past the hollow way and pursued with levelled bayonets [back] to his own position. At the same time, our cavalry fell upon him and did great execution.

The Netherlands troops had hurried forward well in advance of the English* and had already seized two cannon,† when the fleeing enemy unmasked his artillery and was forcing the attackers to retire to their former position. In this action, Lieutenant van Haren, of the General Staff, was killed; General Perponcher had two horses shot dead under him, Colonel [van] Zuylen van Nyevelt [the author] was wounded, and a large number of commanders and officers had also been wounded. Non commissioned officers and soldiers had been detached on escort duty with the prisoners; and it was thus necessary to reform the troops.

The attacks were continuing on the right wing. The enemy once succeeded in penetrating the garden [orchard] of Hougoumont but was immediately driven out again by a regiment of English Guards. Most of the attacks by his infantry did not succeed; his cavalry fought with changeable luck.

The enemy continued his attacks on La Haye Sainte, supported by heavy artillery fire, and thereby weakened our infantry. He was intent on conquering our position before the Prussians' arrival.

Contact had been made with the Prussians by way of Ohain, and definite information had been obtained that their arrival was delayed only by the poor roads and the narrow defile of St Lambert. The corps of Prince Blücher was to debouch from Jean Loo‡ while that of General Bülow would attack the right wing of the French from the east side of that wood.

At 6 o'clock, a heavy cannonade was heard on our left wing. General Perponcher had remained until then in our centre with the 1st Brigade; but assuming that his presence was now needed on the left wing, he and the Chief of the General Staff went to the village of Smohain. On becoming aware of the approach of the Prussians, the enemy [had] attacked vigorously and took possession of a few houses in Smohain and some outer buildings of Chateau Frichermont. From these, he was driven

---

* Apparently a reference to the 7th (Belgian) Line Battalion under Lieutenant Colonel F. C. Vandensande, which was the only battalion of the 1st Brigade that was not overrun by the French; cf. N. Vels Heijn, *Glorie zonder helden* (Amsterdam, 1974), pp. 195–6, citing also the 'Historicus van de divisie Picton'.

† An error in Pflugk-Harttung; it should read 'fanions', or pennants.

‡ Pflugk-Harttung's footnote: Genleau on modern maps [1 km west of Lasne].

Plate 1 Nassau square attacked by cuirassiers, detail from Dumoulin's *Panorama at Waterloo* (top)
Uniforms of Bremen Field Battalion 1814–15 by von Scriba (bottom)

Plate 2 KGL uniforms by Bernhard Schwertfeger, *Geschichte der Königlich Deutschen Legion, 1803–1816*: top, infantryman (left) and sharpshooter (right), middle, officer sharpshooter (left) and captain (right), Line Battalion; bottom, officer, 2nd Hussar Regiment (left) and officer, 1st Hussar Regiment (right)

Plate 3 KGL uniforms by Schwertfeger: top, private (left) and officer (right), 1st Light Battalion; middle, private (left) and officer (right), 2nd Light Battalion; bottom, Light Dragoon staff officer (Major or Lt Colonel) and captain (right), Foot Artillery

Plate 4 The Duke of Brunswick leads a cavalry charge

Plate 5 The death of the Duke of Brunswick by Heath

Plate 6 General Chasse leading the attack on the Imperial Guard by Hoynck van Papendrecht

Plate 7 The wounding of the Prince of Orange at Waterloo, contemporary Dutch print by Maaskamp

Plate 8 Sortie at La Haye Sainte by Knötel

out again, on one side by Major von Normann's 2nd Nassau Battalion and on the other side by Prussian skirmishers who came in great numbers from the wood between Jean Loo and Aywiers.[*] An unfortunate incident was caused by the similarity of the Nassau uniforms and those of the French, as the Prussians began to fire on our men. His Excellency ordered our skirmishers to retire, until the misunderstanding had been clarified; our men then joined the Prussians.

As Napoleon was faced with the Prussians' appearance on his right flank, he had no choice left but to either retreat or venture everything on a desperate attack, he chose the latter. Several batteries were brought into action against Hougoumont, which went up in flames. Its garrison was forced to leave the farm.[†] The wounded perished in the flames, among them Lieutenant Hardt.[‡]

Since Napoleon had now gained more terrain before his left wing, he now commenced a general attack again. His artillery was moved forward and caused us terrible losses. All our men were in the front line, and there were no reserves left.

The 5th Militia Battalion had returned to the first line, which moved forward about half way towards the ravine, in order to provide support to the troops who covered the left side of the farmstead of la Haye Sainte. The enemy had concentrated his entire artillery of the reserve and of the Guard on this spot. Apart from some cavalry charges on our right wing, there were no attacks on our line except for the centre. Here, he assaulted with great fury; entire battalions perished and were replaced by others; every foot of ground was tenaciously defended. At one time, the enemy succeeded in driving our troops out of La Haye Sainte, due to their having run out of ammunition; but it was soon retaken.[§] On this occasion, the Prince of Orange was wounded by a canister ball at the moment when he encouraged his troops in their attack against the enemy.

The 1st Brigade, stationed on the crest of the ridge, was exposed to the fiercest fire and, as it had no cartridges left, was withdrawn behind the line under command of Lieutenant Colonel de Jongh.

When, at 7 o'clock, Blücher's corps was approaching, Bonaparte gave the order for a renewed attack, which, however, was beaten back by the English troops. At the same time, Blücher attacked the enemy's right wing. An English cavalry division and von Ziethen's cavalry advanced

---

* Near Couture-Sainte-Germain.

† This is incorrect.

‡ Only some of the wounded perished in the flames. Lieutenant Hardt was actually the First Lieutenant Andreas Harth of the 1st Battalion, 2nd Duchy of Nassau Regiment.

§ This is an error; once lost it remained in French hands until they retreated.

and drove back the enemy cavalry. General von Bülow was already manoeuvring behind the enemy's right flank, which caused the French line to waver; Wellington used that moment to advance with his entire line. Within a short time, all of the enemy line was thrown into disorder. As the highway was blocked by wagons, the French fled along both sides of the roadway and were pursued by the Prussians and a part of our troops.

The enemy apparently intended to take a stand at Genappe, but was driven off by a few cannon shots. The Prussians took charge of the pursuit from here on. In the meantime, darkness had set in, and the troops moved to their camp grounds. The division bivouacked as follows:

On the right wing, the 1st Nassau Battalion at the farmstead of Hougoumont. In the centre, the 1st Brigade in front of the forest of Soignes and to the left of the Brussels highway. On the left wing, the Staff and the 2nd Brigade on the road from Ohain to Braine l'Alleud, where it is intersected by the road from Ransbeche* to Jean Loo. The four companies of the 1st Battalion, 28th Regiment, remained at Château Frichermont and in the village of Smohain.

A false alarm had caused some drivers of the train to take flight; they cut the traces and rode off on the highway to Brussels.

On these three days, the division had lost 90 officers and 2,090 men and 4 guns. The artillery had fired 1,600 rounds and the infantry 500,000 cartridges.

19 June

The troops remained in their bivouacs until 10 o'clock in the morning. The English troops then assembled near Nivelles, and the Netherlands troops on the heights of [Orphain] Bois-Seigneur-Isaac . . .

The Colonel in Chief of the General Staff Zuylen van Nyevelt

* Ransbeche is 1 km east of Waterloo village.

2nd Brigade Colonel Prince Bernard of Saxe-Weimar
1st Battalion, 2nd Duchy of Nassau Infantry Regiment

No. 24 Sergeant Andreas Buchsieb
From Memorabilia 1808–1815*

The Battle of Waterloo

'God is with us, the Fatherland is at stake!'
DUKE WILHELM VON BRUNSWICK

At Paris on 25 July 1815

After my service period had ended [in early 1815], I let my captain and the other officers talk me into joining them in entering the Netherlands army. Not much later the news arrived that Napoleon was again coming with a mighty army. We received live cartridges and prepared to march off.

On 31 March 1815, led by General Maass, we advanced to Charleroi by way of Liège and Namur and here formed advance posts for six days until we were relieved by the Prussians. Our Nassau regiment pulled back about five miles and joined the remainder of the army. The grandest preparations were undertaken because indications were that a decisive battle would be fought in this area.

On 15 June, we already heard firing by the Prussian advance posts. Our hornists and drummers sounded the alarm, and everybody moved with the utmost dispatch to the alarm post at Quatre Bras, which was at a distance of a quarter mile from us. On our arrival, the enemy balls already whistled past us. The army increased its forces more and more and took up its order of battle, our regiment formed the vanguard. I had taken up position with my men in a garden and we fired vigorously at the enemy who was coming closer all of the time. Napoleon eventually advanced with his entire army, and we had to fall back to avoid being cut down by the French. Fortunately, I have to say, in our direst need the English under Wellington came to our aid. It was at a cross roads, close to the wood near Quatre Bras, that Wellington beat back the enemy, and the fighting had to end for the day as night set in.†

---

* Written within six weeks of the battle by a non-commissioned officer with little access to more definite information, this account includes a number of errors as to date and time and troops involved. There are also brief fictitious tales concerning the main actors that apparently originated around the camp fire.

† Quatre Bras was attacked by Marshal Ney's wing of the French army, while Napoleon fought the Prussian army at Ligny with the major part of his army. On 15 June, only the 2nd Brigade of the 2nd Netherlands Division, consisting of Buchsieb's 2nd Duchy of Nassau Regiment, the Orange-Nassau Regiment, and a volunteer rifle company, was engaged with Marshal Ney's vanguard. Buchsieb here mentions

During the night from the 15th to the 16th, all the troops on our side were completely assembled. A large number of artillery pieces had been moved up, and everything was prepared for battle. But Napoleon had also gathered his troops and advanced against us early in the morning. The French were about 70,000 strong, ours about 60,000 men.* Napoleon,† who was wearing a blue coat, made fun of the English and their red coats, but Wellington said: 'Just you come on, and we will soon dye your coats red with your blood.'‡ The action began and within half an hour both armies were engaged in violent fighting. The enemy attacked with the utmost violence but was beaten back each time. When the French renewed their attack, three battalions of brave Scotsmen stormed against them at the double-quick with levelled bayonets and knocked down whole platoons of the enemy as if they were discarding rubbish. Napoleon eventually had his heavy cavalry charge us to cut us down. First came the armoured cuirassiers. When these approached, the English let them move up quite close and then fired a terrible hail of canister shot at them so that most of them, horse and rider, fell down and then forgot to rise again. The action continued until evening with the utmost vehemence, until the enemy finally retreated while our side remained in possession of the place. Everything was quiet during the night.

On the next morning, the 17th, Field Marshal Blücher all of a sudden arrived at the gallop with his blue hussars. Marshal Wellington was right there at the moment, and so the two leaders saluted each other, rode up to a hill and worked out their battle plan. It was decided to entice Napoleon to come to the ridge at Waterloo, and Blücher promised to support Wellington with his entire army. After the two gentlemen had shaken hands once more, Blücher rode back to his army.§ Marching orders were

---

events that occurred in the afternoon of the following day, when on 16 June Allied reinforcements began to arrive at about 3.00 p.m., and Wellington assumed command of the troops at Quatre Bras.

* He describes the battle of Quatre Bras, but greatly inflates the forces involved on both sides.

† Napoleon was not present at the battle of Quatre Bras, as he commanded at the battle of Ligny.

‡ The 2nd Netherlands Division was the only Allied formation that occupied and held the Quatre Bras area against Marshal Ney's advance between late afternoon of 15 June until about 3.00 p.m. of 16 June. Strength of the opposing forces before arrival of Allied reinforcements was about 7,000 men of the 2nd Netherlands Division and about 18,000 men of Marshal Ney's part of the French army.

§ This example of Buchsieb's fictitious tales had apparently at its core two actual events. A detachment of some 50 Prussian hussars, who had become separated from their unit, did, in fact, appear at Quatre Bras early on 16 June and returned to its main body later in the morning. And then there had been the well known meeting between Wellington and Blücher at Ligny on 16 June before the French army attacked in

now quietly issued, the meat that we had cooking on the fires now had to be taken down and be wrapped up together with the kettles.

Our Nassauers were the first ones to move up to the ridge near Waterloo; the Netherlanders came after us, and they were followed by the enemy. We took up position on the ridge in the most terrible rain storms and waited for the enemy until morning.

At first light of 18 June, that forever memorable day, we Nassauers – the No. 1 and No. 3 Companies of the 1st Battalion and the entire 3rd Battalion – as well as a battalion of English Guards and a battalion of Brunswickers, moved to the right wing and then forward to the Hougoumont Castle.* It was located in the middle between the two hostile armies, was surrounded by gardens and woods and everything had been prepared with loopholes for its defence. Every one of us four sergeants were assigned his position by the officers. On my part, I was posted with 8 men at a gate that had 4 loopholes, so that the lower corner of the house was in the range of our fire. No. 3 Company occupied the garden which was enclosed on its east side by a high wall, and which also had many loopholes.† We had hardly manned all of our posts when Jerome's Infantry Division made a very powerful attack upon us. They were resisted each time because many were felled before they came close to the house, and when they turned around they were struck from behind. The enemy eventually renewed his attack, and even though every one of us shot down an enemy, the remainder stormed forward to the gate, quickly chopped down some trees and crashed the gate by force. As they stormed into the courtyard, we had to take refuge in the house, and fired at them from windows, doors and roof that they toppled over each other; the rest were chased outside with the bayonet. The gate was blocked up again

earnest, both at Quatre Bras and Ligny.

* Buchsieb is peculiarly uninformed about the Nassau detachment at Hougoumont. It consisted of six companies of the 1st Battalion of the 2nd Nassaus. The 3rd Battalion fought as part of the Nassau force at Papelotte at the eastern end of the Allied Line. As to the British contingent, by about 10 a.m. of 18 June, it consisted only of the two Light Companies of the 2nd Guards Brigade. The Brunswick battalion that Buchsieb assumed to be part of the Hougoumont defence was in fact a Hanoverian detachment, a company of Feldjäger and 100 men, each, of the rifle armed Lüneburg and Grubenhagen Battalions of the 1st Hanoverian Brigade. It was not uncommon at the time that the Hanoverians were still called Brunswickers, even though their Electorate, later a British affiliated Kingdom, had split off from Brunswick some 100 years earlier.

† Buchsieb belonged to his Battalion's Grenadier Company that had been posted at the Gardener's house and the adjoining single storey buildings. He was stationed at the South Gate that closed off the archway under the Gardener's house. As to the garden, it was occupied by the no. 1 and no. 3 Companies; its high wall enclosed both the east and the south sides.

and barricaded.[*] A ferocious battle raged on all sides. Towards 2 o'clock in the afternoon, Bachelu and Foy Divisions also moved up against our little fortress. As we moved into the estate, we had our colours raised on the roof, but to avoid losing it in the fighting Lieutenant Colonel Hardt had it quickly taken down again. Since I and my men were still at our post at the gate, he turned the colours over to me. He hurriedly returned to the courtyard, and was hardly back there when he was shot in the head and was dead on the spot. We defended ourselves with the rage of desperation, and, with good luck, chased the rest of the enemies once more out of the yard that was covered with killed and wounded.[†] When the enemy realised that he could not conquer our little fortress in this way, he threw some shells at it so that the house and farm went up in flames. We had to seek refuge in the garden, and had to return from there to our main body.[‡] On our arrival with the colours, the English dragoons had just cut down an enemy square and brought back as prisoners those that were still alive, although covered with severe wounds.[§]

The enemy now tried with all his might to defeat or beat back our army. Napoleon all of a sudden stopped his white horse in alarm and asked: 'Who are those troops that attack our right flank?' The terrified general answered: 'These are Prussians!' 'Oh my God!' said Napoleon, beat his brow with his hand, and turned the command over to the general.

Blücher and his troops had debouched from the wood at the right time, one column after the next, like waves on the ocean, and at once had

---

* This describes the first (and famous) incursion of the French into the Hougoumont complex which occurred through the North Gate which led into the farmyard of the estate.

† The second intrusion was through a narrow side door between buildings on the west side. The Nassau officer killed was First Lieutenant Andreas Harth.

‡ The gardener's house remained untouched by the flames. After the garrison of Hougoumont was reinforced by some 700 British Guards, the Nassau Grenadiers handed the defence of the house over to the British and joined their comrades in the garden. They did not have to 'seek refuge in the garden'. W. Isenbart, *Geschichte des Herzoglich-Nassauischen 2. Infanterie Regiments* (Berlin, 1903), 158).

§ Buchsieb was the non-commissioned officer who, with his men, took the battalion Colours back to the protection of their main body. His testimony refutes a story by an author 'W', apparently a Guards officer, who claimed that at Hougoumont '. . . of the Nassau contingent . . . not a man was to be found on the ground after 1 o'clock, with the exception of one officer, who made his appearance about eight at night, after the action was over, for the purpose of asking a certificate of the loss of the colours of that corps by fire. This certificate was granted upon his representation of the fact, and no doubt at this moment forms a conspicuous proof and document of the hard services and gallantry of that distinguished body of troops.' 'W', 'More reminiscences of Waterloo: the defence of Hougoumont', *United Service Journal*, July 1836, ii, 354; italics as in original.

fallen on the enemy's right flank in a violent attack. The French made one more onslaught against Blücher but in vain. The Prussians' attack was so powerful that the enemy was forced to retreat. Now that the Prussians had joined in the battle at the decisive moment, Wellington had his entire line advance and we then drove the enemy, who fell into ever greater disorder, towards Belle Alliance. Several batteries emplaced near the buildings around this farm were seized in our first charge. The battalions of the French Guard had also been dispersed by repeated cavalry attacks, and a disorderly large mass, unable to resist, moved on and beside the road to Genappe, and the retreat of the French soon turned into a terror filled rout. Blücher had the enemy pursued until late at night, which made the French lose the greatest part of their cannon and powder wagons.

But the brilliant outcome of this battle, the complete dissolution of the defeated army, had been bought with not inconsiderable losses. Those of the Duke of Wellington's army numbered about 14,000 killed and wounded, 15 generals among them and more than 800 other officers. The Prussians lost about 8,000 men. The losses of the French army, on the other hand, were 25,000 killed and 6,000 prisoners.

The Battle of Waterloo had thus been decided! Still, it had taken the combined arms of all of Europe to overthrow the imperial colossus of a Napoleon and to free Germany of his rule and to open the road towards a much yearned for peace!!!

It is from Paris, which we entered on 7 July, that I send my mother the glad tidings of my good fortune of soon being able to return to my beloved homeland; dated on the day of the big parade before the Emperor of Russia, the Emperor of Austria, the King of Prussia, the Prince of Holland, Field Marshal Blücher and the Duke of Wellington. Be God with those who have consummated the sacred contest!

2nd Battalion, 2nd Nassau Regiment

No. 25 Captain Louis Wirths

Nassovia, *bimonthly journal, Wiesbaden, vol. 6, no. 12, 1905, pp. 142–4*

Born in 1787, the son of a mining official, Louis Wirths became a cadet in 1802 in the Dutch subsidised military establishment of the German principality of Waldeck (by 1815 a part of the State of Westphalia), and was advanced to second lieutenant in 1803. His unit was involved in defending the Dutch possessions at the Cape of Good Hope against the British in 1805–6. In 1809, Wirths joined the 1st Duchy of Nassau Light Infantry Regiment, by then part of Napoleon's troops of the Confederation of the Rhine, and saw action in the Austrian campaign that year and, from 1810 to 1813, in the Spanish War.

The Duchy of Nassau's military joined the Allied side upon the Emperor's demise, and after Napoleon's return from Elba contributed some 5,500 soldiers in two regiments to Wellington's army. Wirths transferred to the 2nd Duchy of Nassau Regiment, which by August 1814 had become part of the Netherlands army. In the Waterloo campaign his regiment, together with the Orange Nassau Regiment and a volunteer Jäger Company, formed Prince Bernhard of Saxe-Weimar's 2nd Brigade of the 2nd Netherlands Division.

Promoted to captain and company commander in February 1815, Wirths witnessed the beginning of the Anglo-Allied Waterloo campaign on 15 June 1815 when his 2nd Battalion 2nd Nassau clashed as the first unit in Wellington's army with the vanguard of Napoleon's left wing at Frasnes and Quatre Bras. At the Battle of Waterloo on 18 June, his No. 8 Company was heavily engaged in open order fighting with tirailleurs of Durutte's Division in the Ter la Haye area at the extreme left flank of the Anglo-Allied army.

For the rest of his military career, Wirths was no longer involved in armed conflict; promoted to major in 1841 and made Commandant of the Marksburg fortress high above the Rhine River, he and his garrison consisting of a company of partly disabled war veterans which kept guard over some of the Duchy's armoury and over its central powder magazine. He passed away in 1853, one year short of his retirement.

Notes on the Battle of Waterloo

15 June 1815

The 2nd Battalion, 2nd Regiment Nassau, had its Staff and 3 companies - the Grenadier, No. 2, and No. 4 Companies – quartered in Frasnes, together with a battery of Netherlands horse artillery, while the remaining 3 companies – the No. 6, No. 8, and Flanqueur companies – were quartered in Villers Perwin.* In accordance with orders, for several days the battalion had to assemble and take up position in front of Frasnes before daybreak every morning. While remaining there until the arrival of full daylight, patrols were sent out to search the surrounding area; if nothing suspicious was observed, the troops were ordered to return to their quarters. The battalion was thus also on 15th June 1815 in position in front of Frasnes and kept the chaussee to Charleroi under observation.

After there was full daylight and the patrols had returned without

* In a Nassau Regiment the line companies of the 2nd battalion were even-numbered as shown in the text. The Grenadier, no. 2 and no. 4 Companies formed the battalion's right wing, and the no. 6, no. 8, and the Flanqueur (Light) Companies its left wing. In a regiment's 1st Battalion, the line companies were odd-numbered.

reporting anything unusual, the battalion continued its exercises until its commander Major Philipp von Normann* ordered the men back to their quarters. They were in the process of doing so when distant artillery fire was heard coming from the Ligny direction, which gradually increased. Since this aroused our suspicion it was decided to keep the battalion under arms and to wait until the nature of this firing could be determined. We remained therefore at this position in column formation, but noticed that the gunfire became heavier and closer. One could eventually distinguish infantry volleys and the popping fire of tirailleurs, and was able to observe thick clouds of powder smoke rise behind the woods in front of us.

Because the battalion was under orders in the event of an attack not to hold the Frasnes position but to retire to Quatre Bras, which was ½ hour away, it marched back through Frasnes and placed itself outside on an area surrounded by tall hedges where the artillery battery had also halted and which allowed easy access to the road to Quatre Bras. An observation post was left at the previous position, manned by 1 sergeant, 1 corporal and 12 soldiers. Major von Normann then sent a mounted gunner to Colonel von Goedecke† at Houtain le Val with the information about the suspicious firing noise and a request for further instructions.

It was in the afternoon around 2 o'clock that the mounted gunner returned from Houtain le Val with the order from our colonel for our battalion to return to quarters because the firing was due to manoeuvring by the Prussians which involved gunfire. At the very moment of our beginning to comply with this order, a Prussian hussar, covered with wounds and blood and without his weapons, broke through the hedge near where the battalion stood. He reported that the French were already quite close and would probably debouch right where the battalion's picket had been posted.

Hardly had this been said when our picket, visible from this place (as was also part of the chaussee to Charleroi), was observed taking up arms

---

* Major Philipp von Normann (1785–1863) began his military career 1801 as a cadet in Austrian service, joined the Duchy of Nassau military in 1803 and advanced through the ranks to that of major in August 1814 in the 2nd Duchy of Nassau Regiment. After participation in Napoleon's Prussian campaign in 1806–7 and in the Spanish War 1808–13, his regiment went over to the allied side to become part of the Netherlands army and, in the Waterloo Campaign, part of Prince Bernhard of Saxe-Weimar's 2nd Brigade, 2nd Netherlands Division.

† Wirths was unaware that Colonel Friedrich Wilhelm von Goedecke (1770–1857) had yielded command of 2nd Brigade, 2nd Netherlands Division, to Colonel Prince Bernhard of Saxe-Weimar who until then had been commander of the Orange-Nassau Regiment. On 12 June the horse of one Major von Steprodt had kicked von Goedecke so severely that he had to pass command of the brigade on to Prince Bernhard.

and trying to halt a column of cavalry in red uniforms, whom we could clearly perceive. At the same moment we also noticed that our picket gave fire, was charged by the cavalry and dispersed; the men scattered into the protection of garden hedges, from where they later returned to the battalion one by one.

Our battalion and the artillery gave up the present position and started to retreat towards Quatre Bras on the main highway, which formed a sunken road at some distance from Frasnes. The artillery covered the highway, and the battalion slowly moved on both sides of the roadway in closed columns of equal size towards Quatre Bras. We had hardly proceeded on our way for a short distance when groups of French Gardes lancers* came galloping towards us from all directions and made charges at us, whereupon the battalion halted and with levelled bayonets repelled every one of their attacks.

We thus moved very slowly without accident or losses along the road from Frasnes to Quatre Bras, a distance usually covered in half an hour. On arrival at the well-known wood [Bois de Bossu], as many pickets as possible were then posted, and the battalion took up a favourable position. The enemy failed to undertake any action against the position, either for the rest of the day or during the following night, while our army gradually began to concentrate around Quatre Bras.

16 June 1815

Of this day, there is very little to report, either because my memory fails me, or because nothing exceptional happened. After the major action began, my company and I were in that wood on a skirmishing assignment for the greater part of the afternoon, putting a stop to the enemy's penetrating it and driving him out again.

On second thoughts I remember the following: after the battalion had occupied the previously mentioned position in the wood during the night from the 15th to the 16th, it still remained there the morning of the 16th, having stationed pickets in the high wheat in front as protection from the enemy, and thereby formed the extreme right wing of the troops gathered there so far.

At around 10 o'clock in the morning the battalion was relieved and stationed at Quatre Bras near the tavern to cook its meal since it had not had anything to eat [since] the day before. But before the meal was ready it had to take up position in closed column between the wood and the Nivelles road, where it suffered some losses from enemy artillery fire. It was from here that my own, No. 4 and the Flanqueur companies of the

* The Chevaux-Légers Lanciers, part of the cavalry of the Garde Imperiale, reconnoitred in advance of Marshal Ney's left wing of Napoleon's army.

battalion were ordered into the wood to skirmish, as I mentioned earlier. After the enemy had thus been driven out of the wood, I had my company hold the edge of the wood where we faced the enemy position at a hillside farm. This I did until ordered back to the battalion which I reached, at the far side of the Nivelles road behind the Quatre Bras tavern, returning through the wood. My company again took up its place in the closed column formation of the battalion, which stood with its left wing leaning on the Brussels chaussee. I have no recollection of anything noteworthy happening for the rest of the day. In the evening, the 2nd Regiment rallied on the field in the rear of Quatre Bras between the wood and the Nivelles road and bivouacked there during the night.

18 June 1815

The 2nd Regiment passed the night from the 17th to the 18th with a most terrible rain on the army's left wing near the Wavre road. On the morning of the 18th it was posted as follows:

The 1st Battalion, commanded by its senior Captain Büsgen,* was ordered to defend the important Goumont position, on the extreme right wing of the army.

The 2nd Battalion, 2nd Regiment Nassau, was assigned the position in the rear of, and facing, the [Ter] la Haye Farm, on an elevation which gradually descends towards the farm. Drawn up in closed column, it formed the extreme left wing of the army. Later on, a regiment of English Light Dragoons† deployed to the rear of the battalion. The 3rd Battalion was sent down towards the Papelotte farm.

While the 2nd Battalion was thus deployed, an enemy battery took up an enfilading position on the opposing side. At the beginning of the battle that battery fired several 8-pound balls at the 2nd Battalion which killed and wounded several men.

Immediately at the start of the affair, the 2nd Flanqueur Company, at the time commanded by First Lieutenant Fuchs,‡ was ordered forward to the la Haye farm, to operate against the tirailleurs on the enemy's

---

* Captain Moritz Büsgen was put in charge of 1st Battalion after Major Johann Friedrich Sattler, its commander, took over the command of 1st Regiment upon Col. von Goedecke's disabling accident. Besides being Brigadier, von Goedecke had also commanded the 1st Regiment. See Büsgen's own account, *Waterloo Archive,* vol. II, letter no. 43. Goumont was the original name of Château Hougoumont.

† Major General Sir John O. Vandeleur's 4th British Cavalry Brigade.

‡ First Lieutenant Heinrich Fuchs (1794–1863) had joined the Nassau military as a cadet in 1810 and had seen action in Napoleon's Spanish War. After the Emperor's demise and Nassau's joining the Allied forces, Fuchs took part in 1814 in the build-up of 2nd Regiment Nassau under Netherlands command and was wounded at Waterloo. He afterwards remained in Duchy of Nassau service and eventually attained the rank of Lieutenant Colonel before his retirement in 1851.

right flank and to prevent their advance towards our left flank. After a few hours, around 3 o'clock in the afternoon, Sergeant Lind of that company reported that his company's 3 lieutenants had been disabled (its Captain Joseph Muller* had already been wounded on the 16th): First Lieutenant Fuchs and Second Lieutenant Cramer had been wounded, and Second Lieutenant von Trott had been killed.† Our battalion commander von Normann then ordered me and my No. 8 Company to move to the support of the Flanqueur Company. That company had already suffered severely in the preceding fire fights with enemy tirailleurs. When I met its men, part were at the la Haye farm, and part in the adjoining gardens.

The increase in our fire power from my company caused the enemy tirailleurs to retreat towards their right wing. I then drew up my company beyond the farm, in an open field on the opposite side of the narrow grassy valley that extends towards Smohain, with a supporting detachment left in my rear. I posted my men by a turning movement in a skirmish line on the enemy's flank that was protected, however, by two batteries and a battalion of the Middle Guard.‡

My course of action was to alternately advance and retire, depending on circumstances, until I chose a hollow way as a defensive position, which ran in the rear of and parallel to, my front line. Thus well covered, I repelled the enemy's attacks with vigorous musketry fire, and was able to maintain this position until the end. The company lost many men in this action, but I do not recall anymore their exact number. Also wounded were the two second lieutenants, Leiter and Wagner,§ the former in one of his legs and the latter in his head. I myself was badly hit in my lower left leg by a ricochet ball, but this did not make me leave the field.

At around 6 o'clock in the evening, Prussian skirmishers debouched in our rear from the direction of Smohain. It so happened that for a brief

---

* Captain Franz Joseph Muller (1790–1868), after becoming a cadet in the Nassau military in 1806, had seen field service similar to that of other officers of the 2nd Nassau by the time he had been wounded on 16 June at Quatre Bras. He transferred to the Prussian army in 1816.

† Both Second Lieutenants Franz Ferdinand Cramer (1793–?) and Friedrich von Trott (1798–1815) had entered Nassau service as cadets in December 1813 and received their promotion to second lieutenant in January 1814. As noted by Wirths, von Trott was killed at Waterloo.

‡ Wirth is in error regarding the opposing troop body. In the Papelotte/Ter la Haye area, Prince Bernhard's Brigade faced the 85th and 95th Ligne regiments of General Brue's 2nd Brigade of General Durutte's 4th French Division. H. Lachouque, *Le Secret de Waterloo*, Paris, 1952.

§ Second Lieutenant Mathias Leiter (1791–?) entered Nassau service in 1812 and left in 1816. Second Lieutenant Heinrich Wilhelm Wagner (1795–?) joined the Nassau Military in December 1813, was wounded at Waterloo and promoted to First Lieutenant in 1818, but in 1820 left for employment in the Civil Service.

period they fired at my company, assuming that we were French, an error which was soon corrected. In the meantime, the Prussians had also advanced from the direction of Wavre, and there now occurred a general attack against the enemy positions which, as is well known, ended with the most brilliant victory.

I and my company then joined my battalion in rear of the la Haye farm. We marched together with the 3rd Battalion and two Orange Nassau battalions to the Soignes forest where we bivouacked for the night. On the following morning we joined the 1st Battalion on the road to Nivelles and began our march towards France.

Nassau Reserve of Major General Kruse

No. 26 From La Belle Alliance

Pflugk Harttung's letter no 85

Letter of Colonel Prince Bernhard of Saxe-Weimar to his father regarding the action at Quatre Bras and the battle of La Belle Alliance[*]

Bivouac near Waterloo, in the forest between Brussels and Genappe, 19 June 1815[†]

Dear father!

Thank God I am still alive and healthy after having gone through two bloody battles. The first one was on 16th June, and the second one yesterday. In reading this, I ask you to have the Ferraris map at hand.[‡] I and the Orange Nassau Regiment, whose colonel I am, were quartered in Genappe for four weeks. On the 15th this month, I was appointed Brigadier of the 2nd Brigade of the Perponcher Division; my predecessor had the misfortune of having broken a leg. In addition to my two Orange Nassau battalions I also now commanded three battalions of Duchy of Nassau troops. My brigade then had a strength of 4,000 men; today I have hardly 1,200 left. On the aforementioned 15th June, the French fell upon the Prussian army and pushed it hard. My brigade was cantoned at the left wing of the Netherlands army, which had it headquarters at Braine-le-Comte. My

---

* Details in R. Starkloff, *Das Leben des Herzogs Bernhard von Sachsen-Weimar-Eisenach I*, 138pp.

† At the date of this letter, Prince Bernhard would have been unable to give accurate estimates. The French force at Quatre Bras consisted of General Reille's 2nd Corps, including the 5th, 6th and 9th Infantry Divisions, about 19,200 men; also General Pire's 2nd Cavalry Division, and in addition, a brigade of Cuirassiers commanded by General Kellermann, for a total of 2,700 horse. They were backed by 30 guns.

Before the arrival of Allied reinforcements at around 3 p.m., the Quatre Bras position was held by General Perponcher's 2nd Netherlands Division of about 8,200 men (10 Battalions) and 16 guns.

‡ The maps of Ferraris and Capitaine were produced in 1797.

division commander was located at Nivelles. There was a Nassau battalion and a battery of Dutch horse artillery at Frasnes. Upon the retreat of the Prussians towards Fleurus, our advance post at Frasnes was attacked and was forced back. The infantry took position in the wood to the right, and the artillery conducted a fighting retreat to the area of Quatre Bras (les Quatre Bras is the name of some houses at the crossing of the highways from Brussels to Charleroi and from Nivelles to Namur). I had assembled my brigade at this important location and from there contained the enemy and succeeded in holding him off. I maintained this post through the night; towards morning on the 16th, I was reinforced by a battalion of Dutch Jägers and one of militia troops. Shortly thereafter my division commander and the Prince of Orange arrived. With the latter I reviewed our pickets, and on his order I started reconnoitring with a battalion and two guns.

Towards the afternoon, the enemy drew up a strong force and began a cannonade of our position. It was said that on this day he had brought three army corps into the battle against us. We were able to field only five battalions against him, of which three were given me for the defence to the last, of the edge of the wood. The Duke of Wellington had been present during the beginning of the fighting. I held off an enemy force that was three times stronger than my own, and for my defence I had only two Belgian guns. The enemy took a narrow section of the wood in front of me and bothered me on my left flank. I promptly gathered volunteers and two Dutch Militia companies and retook that part of the wood with levelled bayonets; I led the attacking force myself and had the honour of being one of the first in storming the wood. On trying to cut down some branches I hurt my right leg slightly with my sabre; I was not for a moment hors de combat. The wound is not even worth mentioning; I refer to it here only in order to keep you and dear mother from becoming upset by exaggerated and wild stories. While I stubbornly defended our wood, the enemy had been driving our left wing back to Quatre Bras. On that occasion the brave Duke of Brunswick was killed by a ball through his chest. Strong infantry columns turned my right flank; I requested instructions on what move to take but received none. Upon seeing myself surrounded on all sides, and my men having run out of ammunition, I retreated in good order. The Hanoverian Division of [General] Alten supported me and retook the wood, but lost it again. It was eventually reoccupied by the English at great loss, and was then kept in our hands through the night. I bivouacked that night at the wood. The Prussians had retreated to Wavre on this day, and because of this retreat we had to withdraw to a position near Mont St Jean between Genappe and Brussels. This happened on the 17th. We were exposed to terrible rains and were forced to bivouac on very muddy terrain. The decisive battle began yesterday at about 10 o'clock in the morning,* which ended in the evening in Wellington's total victory over Napoleon himself. Sixty guns were the gains of this bloody victory.† I was in command on the left wing, being in charge of defending a village and an adjoining position. This I succeeded to do, although with considerable loss of men. Victory was still in doubt when at about 4 o'clock the Prussians under Generals Bülow and Ziethen arrived on our left flank and decided the outcome of the battle. The Prussians who were to support me in my village saw my Nassauer's, good Germans that they were, in their French style uniforms, mistook them to be French and opened up a most terrible fire on them. They fell in to rout, and I reassembled them again at a quarter hour distance from the battlefield. The commander of my division is with me; his 1st Brigade is a total wreck. I must end because just now I have received an order to march towards Nivelles in pursuit of the enemy.

All the best, dear father, greetings to my mother, my sister-in-law, my brother, to all my friends and particularly to Count Edling, and be assured that I will do everything to be worthy of you.

Colonel and Brigadier Bernhard Prince of Saxe-Weimar

No. 27 From La Belle Alliance.

Pflugk-Harttung's letter no. 86
Response of the officers of the 2nd Regiment Nassau to the letter of Prince Bernhard of Saxe-Weimar‡

Correction

In no. 192 of the Frankfurt O. P. newspaper an article has appeared with the title: Weimar, 5 July. *Letter of the Prince of Saxe Weimar to his father, the Royal Highness.*

This letter contains the following relation concerning the Duchy of Nassau 2nd Infantry Regiment, which attacks its honour and dearly attained good reputation, and we therefore cannot leave it unanswered. At the end of his letter, the Prince states as fact:

'The Prussians who were to support me in my village unfortunately saw my Nassauers, good Germans that they were, in their French style uniforms, mistook them to be French, and opened up on them a most terrible fire. They fell in to rout, and I reassembled them again at a quarter hour distance from the battlefield.'

We, however, will now report the unvarnished truth about what

* Pflugk-Harttung's footnote: This time indicated, which also exists in the Prince's diary, deviates from that of other sources by 1½ hours

† Pflugk-Harttung's footnote: The more brilliant results of the pursuit could not have known on the morning of the 19th.

‡ Original in Hessisches Hauptstaatsarchiv Wiesbaden, file no. 202/532.

happened: On the morning of 18th June, the regiment was posted as part of the 2nd Division of the Netherlands army on the left wing of the army of the Duke of Wellington. At 9 o'clock, the 1st Battalion, commanded by Captain Busgen, was ordered to march towards the centre and to occupy the Hougoumont farm, which was located in front of the army. This battalion and 200 men of the English Guards steadfastly held on to this post throughout the battle, repulsed the repeated attacks of a furious enemy, defied the fire of the burning buildings, of which many of our wounded men became victims, and, while encircled by the advancing French army, proved German steadiness throughout eight hours.*

The 2nd and 3rd Battalions of our regiment on this day remained by themselves under the direct command of our brigadier, His Highness the Prince of Saxe-Weimar. They represented, with the Orange Nassau Regiment, the extreme left wing of the army, near the village of la Haye, which was crossed by a road from Wavre towards the highway between Brussels and Charleroi. Five companies of our regiment under the command of Captain von Rettberg were posted at this village; several companies of the Orange Nassau Regiment occupied the chateau of Frichermont, while the remainder of our two battalions stood in column formation in support behind la Haye and never left this position throughout the battle until the general attack. Our five companies in charge of la Haye were attacked by the enemy at 11 o'clock whose attacks with musketry lasted until the end of the battle. At 6 o'clock, the Royal Prussian Army Corps of von Bülow and Ziethen moved forward on the road from Wavre towards la Haye; their skirmishers, advancing towards the flank both of the enemy and of our own, fired at them and at us. Having remained ignorant of the arrival of Prussian troops, our companies returned their fire, until after some time the error was discovered. Captain von Rettberg and a few men went to the Prussians and convinced them of the error, whereupon the firing was ended on both sides, and was then jointly directed against the enemy until the evening.

This is the rout that His Highness the Prince of Saxe-Weimar has seen and has claimed to have reassembled at a quarter hour distance behind the battlefield. But here is our story that we solemnly and publicly urge the

* At the time of the writing of this undated letter (apparently in mid-July 1815), Captain Büsgen, commander of the 1st Battalion at Hougoumont, lacked information about the important role of the British Foot Guards in keeping the strongpoint in Allied hands. As at the beginning of the fighting, he had been in contact with the two light companies of the Coldstream and Third Guards who then were the only Guards force at Hougoumont. Twenty years later, he acknowledged in his battle report the presence of the battalion of the Coldstream Regiment, stating, however, that he was unable to make out any other supporting forces 'due to the ongoing fighting, and obstruction to my observations from trees, hedges, and walls'.

prince and anybody present then and there, to refute. The public, that we call on to be our judge, may then decide whether we fulfilled our duty or whether we disgraced our name.

In the name of all officers of the Duchy of Nassau 2nd Regiment,

Sattler Major and present commander, Frensdorf most senior captain, Wittlich most senior lieutenant

No. 28 From La Belle Alliance

Pflugk-Harttung's letter no. 87
*Letter of Colonel Prince Bernhard of Saxe-Weimar to Major Sattler in regard to the letter of 19 June**

St Leu [La Foret] Taverny, 31 July 1815

My dear Herr Major!
Due to an incomprehensible indiscretion, a private letter from me to my father has been published in the Frankfurt *Oberpostamtszeitung*. Since a statement therein, meant strictly for my father's eyes, can be misconstrued, as was confirmed in a letter from Major General Kruse, I hurry off to you the declaration included herein.

I authorise you to have published the same in the aforementioned newspaper. If it had been my intention to harm the good name of the regiment, you, my dear major, would be the best judge of all that I have done on its behalf. Should you need a better proof for what I have just said you may wish to remember the written reply from the Duke of Nassau to my letter to him that was communicated to you by Major Vigelius. I have received just yesterday an assurance from the Prince of Orange that all the decorations had been granted that I had proposed. It is with pleasure that I am able to assure you that your name was the very first on my list of proposed decorations. I would not have mentioned this in consideration of your personal modesty, had this not become necessary to prove the esteem in which I have held you and the regiment. I ask you to communicate to your officers whatever you deem appropriate of the contents of this letter.

Allow me, my dear dear major, to assure you of my fullest and sincerest regard.

Bernhard Prince of Saxe-Weimar, Colonel and Brigadier

* Pflugk-Harttung's footnote: Details in Starkloff, i, 212ff. The declaration no longer exists, which must have been included with the letter.

No. 29 From La Belle Alliance

Pflugk-Harttung's letter no. 88

Letter of Colonel Prince Bernhard of Saxe-Weimar to the reigning Duke of Nassau about the days from 16 June to 18 June.

Bivouac in the forest of Mormal, between Le Quesnoy and Landrecies, 23 June 1815

I have been appointed Brigadier of the 2nd Brigade of the Perponcher Division by His Royal Highness the Prince of Orange, after Colonel von Goedecke had the misfortune of having broken one of his legs. Your Serene Ducal Highness's 2nd Infantry Regiment has thus been placed under my command. It was on the memorable 16th and 18th of this month that I had the distinctive honour to lead this regiment into battle and to stay with it throughout the affair. Major Sattler will already have given Your Serene Highness a detailed report about the battle and how brilliantly the 2nd Regiment has defended the left wing of our position on 18 June. I can therefore omit these details and limit myself to express to Your Serene Highness my profound satisfaction in having the Duchy of Nassau troops under my command . . .

Your Serene Highness's 2nd Regiment has a reputation in the Royal Netherlands army of being its bravest corps. It also has a most outstanding name regarding its soldierly discipline and orderliness. Lieutenant General von Perponcher as well as myself will make every effort to retain it under our command.*

Bernhard Prince of Saxe-Weimar
Royal Netherlands Colonel and Brigadier

No. 30 From La Belle Alliance

Pflugk-Harttung's letter nos 17 and 73

Sent to Captain the Honourable L. Benne - Report of Major General August von Kruse on the participation of the Duchy of Nassau Troops in the Waterloo campaign†

Wiesbaden, 7 January 1836

In response to your honour's kind letter of 25 November of last year, it pleases me to inform you in the following of the role of the Duchy of Nassau troops in the actions on 15 and 16 June, as well as in the Battle of Waterloo on 18 June 1815, with the request to kindly forward these notes to the British General Staff in London.

---

* The concern of the two commanders was caused by the fact that, as of 23 June, the 2nd Regiment had been removed from Netherlands to British command, to form, with the 1st Nassau Regiment, the Nassau Division in Lord Hill's 2nd British Corps on the march to Paris.

† Original in Hessisches Hauptstaatsarchiv Wiesbaden, file no. 202/1015.

The Ducal Nassau Brigade consisting of two infantry regiments was not a combined force during 15,16,17, and 18 June 1815. The 2nd Regiment was in Royal Netherlands service since 1814.

The 1st Regiment, representing the Duchy's actual contingent, which had arrived only a few days before, had not yet been attached to any army corps and was stationed until 16 June in widely spread quarters between Brussels and Laeken and had the following formation and strength on 15 June, which I need to qualify in that the brigade was not united in those days, but that the 2nd Regiment had been an auxiliary corps of the Royal Netherlands army, and marched off as part of this army from its Maastricht garrison on 30 March 1815.

The 1st Regiment consisted of 3 battalions, each battalion of 6 companies, to whit, 1 Grenadier, 4 Jäger, and 1 Flanqueur company. The first [of these] stood on the right flank and the last [named] on the left flank. As to its strength, each company had 3 officers and 160 NCOs and soldiers. A battalion thus consisted of 18 officers and 960 NCOs and soldiers, and the [Regimental] Staff of 13 officers and 46* NCOs and soldiers.

This regiment, which formed a brigade of its own, marched from its quarters early on 16 June towards Quatre Bras, where it arrived in the evening, after the action had ended. On 18 June, without being attached to a division, it became part of the 1st Corps, commanded by HRH The Prince of Orange.

This regiment had been put on a war footing in April 1815 at battalion strength, and therefore had to be supplemented by more than 3/4 [of its strength] with recruits. It arrived at Brussels on 7 June 1815.

On 18 June 1815 the regiment was under my command, and was attached to the 1st Corps under the supreme command of HRH The Prince of Orange.

The 2nd Regiment consisted of 3 battalions, each battalion had 6 companies; 1 Grenadier, 4 Jäger and 1 Flanqueur company. Each company had 4 officers and 150 NCOs and soldiers; the battalion thus consisted of 24 officers and 900 NCOs and soldiers. The [Regimental] Staff numbered 12 officers and 33 NCOs and soldiers.

This regiment and the Orange-Nassau Regiment formed the 2nd Brigade of the 2nd Royal Netherlands Division, the former commanded by Prince Bernhard of Saxe-Weimar, the latter by Lieutenant General von Perponcher.

Uniforms

The grenadier companies had round busbies, all other companies had shakos. The uniforms of both regiments were dark green with black

* Pflugk Harttung says 46 but the original manuscript copy in Siborne says 40.

collars and facings, in front with a set of yellow buttons and [in back] with short coat-tails, the uniform as well as the side pockets with yellow piping; dark green fabric pantalons, trimmed with yellow cords; black fabric leggings. Belt and bandoliers, as well as the backpack straps, of light yellow leather. The officers' headgear and uniform was the same as that of the rank and file with the exception of the length of the coats, and that they wore grey instead of green pantalons. All officers had epaulets, which signified their rank, and orange coloured sashes, except that the length of the latters [coats] was equal to an arm's length, and they also had tight-fitting grey overalls. All subaltern officers carried swords attached to belts worn underneath their uniforms.

The regimental and battalion commanders as well as the six mounted Adjutant Majors wore round busbies; only the major general and his Staff, which consisted of four officers, had bicorns with plumes of hanging white feathers. All mounted officers had sabres. All officers without exception wore golden epaulets, the mounted staff officers spurs, and also orange coloured sashes.

The colours – each battalion had one – were made of light yellow silk, in the centre the ducal coat of arms embroidered in blue silk, with gilt pike-heads at the top of the poles, to which two gold tassels had been fastened.

It is true that at the Battle of Waterloo the shakos and cartridge pouches of the men of the 1st Regiment had white covers, which I ordered removed around 3 p.m. since these became excellent targets for the enemy artillery. The rank and file of the 2nd Regiment had similar covers of black oilcloth.

During the battle, none of the commanders or Staff officers were mounted on horses of a conspicuous colour, only I rode a pale dun-coloured horse ['*nur ich ritt einen Falben*'].

15 June 1815

The 1st Regiment was stationed near Brussels in widely spread quarters.

The 2nd Regiment stood in the most advanced outposts of the army and was quartered along the road from Brussels to Charleroi as follows:

Regimental Staff and 1st Battalion Houtain le Val

2nd Battalion Frasnes and Villers Perwin; a Netherlands horse battery was also quartered at Frasnes [les Gosseliez]

3rd Battalion Baisy[Thy], Sart [Dames] Mavelines and Quatre Bras.

This [latter] was the assembly point in the event of an attack.

Early in the morning, a heavy firing of artillery could be heard in the direction of Charleroi. Since no notice had been received of an enemy's approach, this firing was believed to be that of Prussian artillery, which had conducted practice firing quite often.

The cannon fire was heard ever more distinctly in the afternoon but the arrival of a wounded Prussian soldier left no doubt about the enemy's approach. The commander of the battalion stationed in Frasnes, Major von Normann, then took position with his battalion and the [horse] battery in the rear of Frasnes on the road to Quatre Bras and placed an observation post in front of Frasnes. At the same time, a mounted gunner was sent to the regimental command post with information about these occurrences. From there, the regimental adjutant took the report immediately to the commander of the division, General von Perponcher, at Nivelles.

During this time, at about 5 o'clock, the observation post was attacked and dispersed by enemy cavalry (lancers in red uniform). Immediately thereafter, the battalion itself was attacked by the same cavalry, which was received with such well conducted musketry and case shot that it retreated out of range of the fire. Frasnes was kept occupied by the enemy; he received strong infantry columns towards evening and set up pickets in front of Frasnes.

Faced with this superior force, the 2nd Battalion retreated towards a wood, located in front of Quatre Bras and on the right of the chaussee to Frasnes, where it bivouacked during the night. The 2nd Battalion bivouacked at the tip of the wood which had the name Bois de Bossu.

Upon its advance towards Quatre Bras, the 1st Battalion detached two companies as liaison to the 2nd Battalion; the remaining 4 companies of this battalion as well as the 3rd Battalion bivouacked at Quatre Bras.

16 June 1815

The 1st Regiment marched off to Brussels in the morning, and from there to Quatre Bras, where it arrived as late as 7 o'clock, due to various hindrances.

Early on 16 June, on orders from the Duke of Wellington, two companies of the 2nd Battalion, 2nd Regiment, attacked the enemy pickets, pushed them back to the heights of Frasnes, where they had to halt because of the reinforcements received by the enemy. The 2nd Battalion engaged in continuous musketry with the enemy until noon, when, having run out of ammunition, it was replaced by the 3rd Battalion. This and the 1st Battalion kept on firing. As the enemy attacks became more heavy in the afternoon, all 3 battalions took over the defence of the Bois de Bossu, where they repulsed several attacks by enemy infantry and cavalry (cuirassiers).

Also taking part in the defence of the wood were the Orange Regiment, a detachment of Brunswickers, and a battalion of Scotsmen. The 2nd Regiment bivouacked at the fringe of the wood from 16 to 17 June.

The 1st Regiment was not able to arrive at Quatre Bras until evening, due to its widely spread quarters and the fact that the road from Brussels was packed with all types of troops. It bivouacked near this point.

Losses of the 2nd Regiment on 16 June 1815:

Killed 14 NCOs and soldiers, wounded 3 Officers 91 NCOs and soldiers.

17 June 1815
The 1st and 2nd Regiments moved into their positions described below, the former by itself, the latter with the division of Perponcher, where they bivouacked until 18 June.

18 June 1815
The position which the 1st Regiment occupied at noon of 17 June and retained on the battlefield on 18 June was located on the plateau between the roads from Brussels to Nivelles and from Brussels to Quatre Bras, that is, at the centre of the army. The 1st Battalion was in first line and the 2nd and the Landwehr [3rd] Battalions in second line. The regiment had English and Hanoverian troops on its left and English battalions to its right, and English artillery in its front. This position was held by the regiment throughout the battle, except that at 6 o'clock it retreated about 100 paces due to the intense fire of enemy artillery directed towards the plateau as also at the attack of the Prince of Orange, described below.

Throughout this period, that is, between 2 and 6 o'clock in the afternoon, this regiment, as well as all the other troops posted on the plateau behind la Haye Sainte, had to endure several enemy attacks. Those of the enemy cuirassiers and lancers were all the more threatening, as the infantry was limited to its own strength and had little support, neither from the cavalry nor from the artillery, which had run out of ammunition. The enemy's most heavy attacks were those of General d'Erlon's Corps on [La] Haye Sainte, where a battalion of the King's German Legion and two flanqueur companies of the 1st Regiment Nassau* had been posted.

The enemy's attacks were as follows:

Around 2 o'clock vigorous attacks by tirailleurs, supported by cuirassiers and lancers. Towards 5 o'clock heavy infantry attacks of the French Guard, intermixed with charges by the cuirassiers, which continued incessantly until 7 o'clock.

Shortly after 7 o'clock, the Prince of Orange ordered a bayonet attack on the enemy Imperial Guard, which in the meantime had been approaching. I undertook this attack in attack column with the 2nd Battalion and the severely weakened 1st Battalion, although without success. The prince, at the head of the column, was wounded,† and both

* Only a single company was sent to La Haye Sainte. According to the War Diary of the 1 st Regiment Nassau, 'around 4 o'clock, the Flanqueur Company of the 2nd Battalion was told off to reinforce the battalion of the German Legion at La Haye Sainte'. During its advance it lost its commander, Captain von Weitershausen.

† General von Kruse led this detachment and the Prince rode at the side and there fell wounded off his horse. H. von Gagern's, 'Waterloo Letter', Nassauische Heimatblätter, no. 1, 1956, p. 24, *Waterloo Archive* vol. II, letter no. 56.

battalions were forced to retreat to their original position at great loss.

Towards 8 o'clock, the regiment advanced together with the entire army and bivouacked near Maison du Roi.

Losses of the 1st Regiment on 18 June 1815:
Killed 5 Officers 249 NCOs and soldiers, wounded 19 Officers, 370 NCOs and soldiers.

On the evening of 17 June, the Perponcher Division, which included the 2nd Regiment Nassau under the command of Major Sattler, took up position at the extreme left flank of the army.

On the morning of 18 June at about half past nine, the regiment's 1st Battalion of 800 men, commanded by Captain Busgen, was ordered to occupy the Hougoumont farm in front of the centre of the right wing. A company of Brunswick Jägers* had been posted at the edge of the wood of that farm, and a battalion of the 2nd English [Coldstream] Guards Regiment behind the orchards.

At 11 o'clock of the morning, the division of Jerome Napoleon attacked the wood and occupied the same.

At about 1 o'clock, the enemy renewed his attacks on the gardens and buildings, which, however, were repulsed.

Between 2 and 3 o'clock the buildings were set on fire by the enemy who made a third desperate attack. However, the farm was held until the end of the battle, although the musketry firing continued incessantly. The battalion bivouacked here during the night.

The story spread by the Spanish General Alava and repeated by several writers that the Nassau Battalion had abandoned the Hougoumont farm is not true. It apparently originated from the fact that the battalion had returned its colours at the beginning of the action because its commander felt that they could not be properly protected in the expected dispersed order of fighting.

The 2nd and 3rd Battalions of this regiment moved to their battle positions at 11 o'clock in the morning. To their right they had Hanoverians, to their left the 1st Battalion of the Regiment Orange Nassau and to their rear a formation of light cavalry of the Hanoverian Legion.

Papelotte was occupied by the Flanqueur Company of the 3rd Battalion, 2nd Nassau Regiment. After this company was pressed back

* The rifle-armed units detached to Hougoumont were Hanoverians: 130 Feldjägers and 100 men, each, of the Lunenburg and Grubenhagen Light Battalions of Kielmannsegge's 1st Hanoverian Brigade. Although Hanover had split off from Brunswick more than a century ago, in common usage Hanoverians were still called Brunswickers. Around 1810, even some London papers still had a habit of referring to the Royals as the House of Brunswick.

by a superior force of tirailleurs, its commander, Captain von Rettberg, received a reinforcement of 4 more companies. He then retook Papelotte and held it until the end of the battle* although the enemy's tirailleurs renewed their attacks several times. An attack against the enemy positions could not be carried forward from Papelotte because the enemy was supported by artillery, which the Nassau Regiment did not have.

Between 12 and 1 o'clock this company was pressed back by a superior force as enemy tirailleurs advanced towards Papelotte. At first, the Flanqueur Company of the 3rd Battalion was sent to repel them. It drove the enemy tirailleurs back beyond Papelotte. Between 3 and 4 o'clock, a strong line of tirailleurs attacked which was supported by infantry columns. The company retreated towards Papelotte, but then received 4 companies in support. The enemy was driven back to his former position in a bayonet attack, but heavy enemy firing of case shot limited further advances.

Towards 6 o'clock, the enemy renewed his attacks on Papelotte from Smohain and La Haye with unsupported tirailleurs, who were repulsed.

After 7 o'clock, the enemy suddenly retreated, while at the same time numerous tirailleurs of the Prussian army appeared, followed by columns of infantry. These advanced from Smohain and Plançenoit and fired at the Nassau troops who returned the fire, since they had not been informed of the arrival of the Prussians. This fire fight lasted for about 10 minutes; there were killed and wounded on both sides. The error was soon recognised and the firing was ended.

Our troops left Papelotte and advanced jointly with the Prussians. This movement was followed by the 2nd Battalion, which had held its position throughout the battle, but had been exposed all the time to enemy artillery fire.

Losses of the 2nd Regiment on 18 June 1815:
Killed 4 Officers 69 NCOs and soldiers, wounded 20 Officers 153 NCOs and soldiers. Two of my staff officers had been wounded.

Yours most respectfully
[No signature]

---

* According to the report of Major C. F. von Rettberg, dated 28 December 1835, *Waterloo Archive,* vol. II, letter no. 46, the Papelotte farm building itself never fell into enemy hands. The French apparently managed to occupy temporarily some workers houses on the farm grounds, but were later driven out. Many historians have relied on the report of General Durutte, published in *Sentinelle de l'Armée* (1838), who claims that his troops had driven the Nassauers out of Papelotte. The French historian H. Houssaye has found that Durutte's account of the battle varied from the facts in several respects.

1st Battalion, 1st Nassau Regiment

No. 31 From La Belle Alliance

Pflugk-Harttung's letter no. 72
Report of the 1st Regiment Nassau on its participation
in [the action at Quatre Bras and in] the Battle of La Belle Alliance

Malplaquet, 21 June 1815.

Relation of the events of 15, 16, and 17 June, and also of the battle on the 18th at Mont St Jean

Napoleon had gathered a large army at the Belgian border and had arrived in person at Maubeuge on the 13th. On the 15th, he attacked the Prussian advance posts and those of the left flank of Wellington's army and drove the latter back as far as Genappe [Quatre Bras].

On the 16th, our army was put in motion; however, only Perponcher's [2nd Netherlands] and von Alten's [3rd British] Divisions, the Brussels garrison and the troops in cantonments around this city, including the Duchy of Nassau 1st Regiment, could be assembled successively, a total of about 40,000 men. While the enemy had been pressed back somewhat by the Perponcher Division in the morning of the said day, he drew up in full force at 2 o'clock in the afternoon. The ensuing violent action lasted from then on until the evening, with varying results and with the two armies having held their positions by nightfall, although at considerable losses to both. On this day, the 1st Regiment was unable to take part in the action because it did not arrive until half past eight in the evening, due to various hindrances. The 3rd Battalion of the 2nd Regiment had been fortunate in having had a splendid engagement witnessed by His Highness, the Hereditary Prince [Prince Wilhelm of Nassau-Weilburg]. In the evening, the 1st Battalion of the same regiment also made a glorious attack that I observed with my own eyes. While the enemy's left flank engaged part of Wellington's army, his major force on the right attacked Field Marshal Prince Blücher. By 9 o'clock in the evening, the French cavalry succeeded in defeating the Prussian cavalry; it broke through the infantry and forced the army to retreat. All in all, [the Prussian] losses were about 14,000 men and a number of cannon. In addition, alarm spread to Brussels where a good number of refugees had arrived.

The enemy was expected to attack our army on the 17th in its position at Quatre Bras; however, all that he fielded were a few skirmishers. Upon arrival of the news of the Prussians' misfortune, the army was forced to retire and, without being pursued, took up position near Mont St Jean. In a cavalry engagement in the afternoon, the English cavalry had the worst of it.* In the evening, the enemy showed up, apparently for the purpose of reconnoitring our position. The uninterrupted heavy rains had made it impossible for the enemy to move up his numerous and heavy artillery before noon of the 18th. It was therefore as late as at the stroke of 12 that the first cannon shot was fired, which announced one of the most important and solemn events of our time, so rich in great deeds.

The enemy position on both sides of the highway from Brussels to Charleroi was so crowded that the line, on which 70,000 to 80,000 men were to fight, was barely half an hour's [ride] long. It was highly tenable because it occupied the dominant ridges. The allied position was equally well chosen in that there was a wide plateau in its centre to the right of the highway which dominated the position and masked any movements from one flank to the other.

The enemy began his movements against our right flank, where he was opposed by 40 artillery pieces and several battalions; this action, engaged in without great ardour, lasted for about one hour. By that time, the French artillery had arrived and began a most violent cannonade with its well served very heavy guns. This vigorous artillery fire was mainly directed against the plateau described earlier, being the key of our position. On this plateau stood four or five Hanoverian battalions, two English battalions, and the Ducal 1st Regiment, with its 1st Battalion in the first line, the other two in the second line. The entire cavalry of the army was deployed in several lines on the plain to the rear of these infantry lines. After the enemy artillery had caused havoc in the various battalions, and in the 1st Battalion of the Ducal 1st Regiment in particular, and after our artillery was for the most part demolished or out of ammunition, masses of enemy cavalry moved up. Covered by their artillery, they attacked our infantry continuously for over an hour. Without a single cannon and only weakly supported by our cavalry, our men were left to depend on their own bravery. It [the enemy cavalry] eventually halted 100 paces in front of our first line and very bravely defied its fire.

At this moment, the devastation in the 1st Battalion from the canister fire finally caused it to waver. The cuirassiers, waiting nearby, charged and took a number of prisoners, among them the brave Captains Schüler and Weiz.† Much weakened by this noteworthy action, the French cavalry

* This refers to the defeat of the 7th Hussars at Genappe, but does not mention the subsequent success of the Life Guards.

† Friedrich August Weiz; in his own report, he describes how his inept battalion commander had his men charge at two enemy guns. After the battalion advanced about 50 paces from the position, the two leading companies were overwhelmed by the cuirassiers waiting nearby. The remnants of the two companies and the rest of the battalion returned to their position. See the reports of Weiz, *Waterloo Archive*, vol. II, letter nos 51 and 52.

retreated, and the élite infantry, Napoleon's Guard moved up instead. It took possession of the plateau, from which our infantry withdrew, but only for 100 paces. A heavy small arms fire now broke out. The Crown Prince [Prince of Orange], who had commanded on the plateau throughout the battle and had displayed much courage and judgment, now attempted to end it with a bayonet charge and bestowed this honour upon the Nassauers. I then brought up the 2nd Battalion and advanced with it in column, it was joined by the remainder of the 1st Battalion. This attack was undertaken with much courage. I already observed a flank of the French Guard's square beginning to waver. Caused perhaps by the fall of the wounded Crown Prince, our young men panicked at the moment of their most splendid victory; the battalion fell into disorder and retreated. The remaining battalions of the first line soon followed, and the plateau was then held on both sides only by small bodies of brave men. I joined them with the Landwehr Battalion and the remainder of the 2nd Battalion, in a position that the enemy fire could have little effect on them.

While this happened, the enemy's right flank had advanced and occupied the rear of our centre [the ridge line near La Haye Sainte]. The Duke hereupon had the cavalry move against it, which then cut down [the French] infantry in a brilliant charge. From this moment on, the battle took a turn for the better. The Marshal [Wellington] had all the infantry on the right flank move to the centre. The Prussian army, much awaited for a very long time, now also appeared on the enemy's right flank. An all out attack then occurred, and in less than half an hour a most brilliant victory had been won over an enemy who had believed they were the victors and that with good reason. Nightfall prevented the total defeat of the French army, which fled in the greatest disorder, leaving behind its entire artillery.

The courage and the steadfastness of the regiment was much to be admired, of which its losses in killed and wounded bore ample testimony. Regrettably, it was well proven here that in critical moments courage alone will not suffice and that unskilled troops will become victims of their inexperience.* I am convinced that, if both regiments had been united,† their defeat of Napoleon's Guard on this important day would have brought immortal glory to the Nassau troops. The officers' conduct was faultless; many distinguished themselves, among them in particular Lieutenant Colonel von Hagen, Captains Schüler, Weiz, von Preen, Ahlefeld, Des Barres, the Lieutenants Rückert, Bickel and Gemmer, and more, whose death ended their service. I cannot fail to praise the conduct of all the officers of my Staff; Major von Breidbach and Captain v. Boose

* A rare and refreshingly honest assessment of his troops' abilities.

† The 2nd Nassaus were under Netherlands command.

were wounded, and Lieutenant Count Walterdorf had lost a horse. I am unable to provide an accurate listing of the regiment's losses as, due to the disorder which prevailed for some time at the rear of the army, many men had gone back with the wounded as far as Brussels. The list of killed and wounded officers is attached; Captains Schüler and Weiz, taken prisoner, freed themselves by evening, Captain Schüler has been terribly cut up and may not survive.

Kruse, Major General

No. 32 Private Peter Henninger, Grenadier Company

From 'Private Henninger's Experiences in and after the Battle of Waterloo: Recorded by his son', *Nassovia, Wiesbaden 1915, vol. 16, pp. 90–1*

After the massed French cavalry attacks and the enemy's capture of the farm of La Haye Sainte, the French moved artillery pieces to within 200 to 300 yards of the allied line and opened fire with canister shots at the battalions in the first line. Cavalry formations stood by to exploit any resulting disarray in the allied ranks.

The 1st Battalion, 1st Nassaus, posted between the Hanoverian 1st Brigade and C. Halkett's 5th British Brigade, was formed in attack column with a two company frontage [not in square as claimed by the original author]. Henninger's Grenadier Company, commanded by Captain Schüler, and No. 1 Company were those in front.

As their battalion suffered grievously from the French artillery fire, its commander, Major von Weyhers, decided to have his battalion rush at the French guns and disable them. Captain Schüler, the battalion's most senior officer, strenuously advised against this move because of the close threat of the enemy cavalry. Weyhers insisted in his decision and gave the order to attack.

After the battalion had advanced some 50 yards, it received additional canister shots which felled Weyhers and many soldiers. The battalion was ordered back to its former position by one of Wellington's aides de camp and the four rearmost companies did so. But the Grenadier and No. 1 Companies already found themselves surrounded and attacked by French cuirassiers. Although fighting with the courage of desperation, these Nassauers were eventually overwhelmed.

The following is Henninger's account:

Towards 5 o'clock in the afternoon* we were overrun by cuirassiers and lancers. Captain Schüler, who had halted at the right hand corner of the

* Most probably later, after La Haye Sainte had yielded to the French.

square, received three cuts on his head and a stab in the left hand by a French major. Our captain would certainly have been killed if I and two comrades had not brought down the French officer's horse. He came to lie under the horse and was killed by a shot in the head from one of my comrades.

When our regiment had withdrawn [to the rear], our captain found himself in a half sitting, half lying position on the ground because of his wounds. He called: 'You Grenadiers! Who of you can help me to move off?' I answered: 'I will, as best as I can, although I am wounded myself!' As it was, I myself had received three lighter stab wounds. The captain then said: 'Look at me, Henninger!' I then took hold of his right arm, raised him, and asked: 'Captain, Sir! Where do you want us to go?' He said: 'In that direction (while pointing at a farm); because if we go back we will be completely cut to pieces.' So we were going for a bit when Grenadier Reinhard Zahn came running after us, shouting: 'Captain, Sir! Are you also wounded?' whereupon the captain said to him: 'Yes indeed, Zahn! I see you are still well and up on your feet, come here and guide me along a bit!' whereupon Zahn took the captain's other arm. We had hardly gone a short stretch when some French cuirassiers came galloping past us, and I received a stab in my right side and I let go of the captain's arm and sank down, almost a dead man. On the captain's order, Zahn came back and said to me: 'Henninger, Henninger, come on! Get up!' and was going to help me move off. But that was no longer possible for me and I told him: 'Zahn, just let me lie here, it is over with me anyway! See to it that you can save our captain!' Zahn then returned to the captain and both went off.

I was lying there during the night, the following day (19th June) and also the next night in a condition that nobody can imagine who has not gone through this himself. My shako was cut this and that way. Blood was sticking to everything. Whenever I became conscious again, my thoughts went to my family far away who later claimed that I had thus 'left a message'. And now at night to hear the groaning and moaning of thousands and thousands of wounded and dying in the languages of all the nationalities who drenched the battlefield with their blood!

On the second day, two Frenchmen (Alsatians) came to me, who I believed, were plundering the wounded and dead. They asked me: 'Comrade, are you German?' When I affirmed this, they then asked: 'Do you have any money?' I affirmed this also and revealed to them that I had eight Spanish dollars sewn into my underwear (since I believed I would no longer have any use for them). They bent over me to try to undress me but then so much blood was spurting at them that they gave up and said: 'Comrade, keep your money, perhaps you may still need it!' I do not know if my painful moaning during their visit contributed to their compassion. To their credit I must add that, when I asked, they most readily let me drink from their canteen (cider), which I had noticed. This was the first time I had a refreshing drink on the battlefield.

Finally in the morning of the third day (20th June), five Englishmen carried me on a cuirassier's coat to the farm next to the highway [La Haye Sainte]. Towards 9 o'clock in the same morning I received a dressing from a Dutch surgeon. Here a Nassau voltigeur came to me, who visited the farm which had been taken by the French during the battle and whose interiors had been completely shot up and burned down. I cannot remember any more what caused him to come here; I asked him to help me get out of the place. He at once began taking care of me and asked my name. When I answered Peter Henninger from Schlossborn, he then exclaimed joyfully: 'How now? Are you not the brother of the teacher at Schwanheim?' Upon my answer in the affirmative, he then cried: 'Brother, I will not leave you, even if it will cost me my life!' He looked around at once and got me on a wagon, on which there were already 12 to 14 wounded. He made place for me by forcing an unwounded soldier off the rear end of the wagon. So it was that I arrived in Brussels at 10 o'clock in the evening and was brought to a church where there were already many wounded. I had the good luck that several comrades from my company came visiting me every day. Eight days later I was transferred to the Louise Hospital, where I remained until my complete recovery. [In the meantime, Henninger had been officially declared dead upon testimony from Captain Schüler and Grenadier Zahn. But he was able to notify his family that he still was alive, and his death certificate was then annulled] Having my wounds fairly well cured, I returned to my regiment which was stationed in reserve at Paris, and with which I returned to my fatherland after an absence of eight years. I also had the good fortune to see my captain again whose life had been saved with my help. For what was my duty as a soldier and fellow man in the hours of greatest peril I was decorated with the Medal of Merit in Silver.

2nd Battalion, 1st Nassau Regiment

No. 33 From La Belle Alliance

Pflugk-Harttung's letter no. 82
Letter of an anonymous officer of the [2nd Battalion] 1st Regiment Nassau regarding the battle of Belle Alliance

Brussels, 19 June 1815

The army gave battle for three days now; yesterday, the regiment suffered enormous losses. From 10 o'clock in the morning until 7 o'clock in the evening, we stood exposed to a continuous cannonade, which was terrible. The French cuirassiers charged us two times but were thrown back each time; in the end, the artillery and the infantry were out of ammunition. Both armies are worn out and no longer able to continue fighting. As to the regiment's losses, nothing definite is as yet known. Majors von Weyhers, Nauendorff and Preen are wounded severely, and at least half of the officers are dead or wounded. The Hereditary Prince [Wilhelm of Nassau-Weilburg] was also wounded, as were Breidbach and Boose.* I have never yet experienced the kind of fierce obstinacy with which the army was fighting yesterday. In the end, on the battlefield the artillery on both sides was out of ammunition and without horses and men. The French army is retreating.

I was hit on my chest by a ball, which occurred at 7 o'clock in the evening. But this will not keep me from being able to ride today. I had the sash slung over my shoulder and a wet coat on top, which prevented the ball from penetrating. Captain Goedecke† had a hand lightly wounded. Captain Schnelle is one of those killed,‡ and Captain Waldschmidt had a leg taken off.§

* Briedbach is in the lists as Braubach commanding 8th Company 2nd Battalion 1st Nassau Regiment. I have been unable to identify Boose.

† Captain Goedecke was in the 2nd Battalion 1st Nassau Regiment.

‡ Schnelle commanded the 4th company 2nd Battalion 1st Nassau Regiment at Waterloo.

§ Commanding the Flanker company 1st Battalion 1st Nassau Regiment.

Brunswick Contingent

No. 34 Lieutenant General August von Herzberg

From British Library MS Add. 34706, fo 23
*'Detailed Report on the Corps of Troops of His Serene Highness the Duke of Brunswick from the 15th to and including the 18th June of 1815 with two plans.'**

Memorandum
This narrative has been furnished by Lieutenant General Augustus von Herzberg of the Brunswick Service late Lieutenant Colonel and commanding the Light Infantry of the Duke of Brunswick Oels's Corps when the same was in the British service.
L. Benne.

The Corps of Troops detached to the Allied army by His Serene Highness the reigning Duke Friedrich Wilhelm of Brunswick and commanded by His Highness in person consisted of an independent Division under the command of Colonel Olfermann.

Its organisation was as follows:

Avantgarde Battalion
Major von Rauschenplatt, Commander,
consisting of:
2 Companies of Jäger }
2 Companies of Light Infantry } 672 men

Cavalry
a. Hussar Regiment of 6 Squadrons 690 Men Major von Cramm, Commander
b. Uhlans 2 Squadrons 232 Men Lieutenant Colonel Pott, Commander

Infantry
A. Light Infantry Brigade Lieutenant Colonel von Buttlar, Commander, consisting of:
Leib Battalion, Major von Pröstler, Commander 672 men
1st Light Battalion, Major von Hollstein, Commander 672 men
2nd Light Battalion, Major von Brandenstein, Commander 672 men
3rd Light Battalion, Major Ebeling, Commander 672 men

* The plans are missing. References to these in the original text have therefore been omitted in this transcription.

B. Line Infantry Brigade Lieutenant Colonel von Specht, Commander, consisting of:

1st Line Battalion, Major Metzner, Commander 672 men
2nd Line Battalion, Major von Strombeck, Commander 672 men
3rd Line Battalion, Major von Normann, Commander 672 men

Artillery

2 Batteries of 16 guns, Major Mahn, Commander
Horse Battery, Captain von Heinemann, Commander } 460 men
Foot Battery, Major Moll, Commander }
Train and Baggage, Captain Warnecke, Commander 50 Men

Military Police

Detachment of Police Hussars 12 men
Total 6,820 Men

After adding the General Staff and all officers, the corps then numbers 7,000 men.

Lieutenant-Colonel von Heinemann was Quartermaster General and Major von Wachholz Chief of Staff.

Aides de Camp

Captains von Lübeck and Bause Aide de Camp to His Serene Highness\
Captains Morgenstern and von Zweifel Corps Aide de Camps.

Attached to Headquarters

Colonel von Herzberg
Major von Grone
Major von Mahrenholz

The Brunswick Corps formed an independent division, as mentioned earlier. During the days of battle it was assigned to the centre of the Order of Battle.

The uniforms of the Ducal Corps in 1815 were as follows:

I Information on the clothing of the late Duke Friedrick Wilhelm

According partly to my own recollection, partly to the accoutrements preserved in the museum, the duke's dress was usually as follows, even on the days of battle:

a) A round cap of black saffian leather (he wore his shako only on parades and during major social events).
b) A silken black neckerchief with, above, a narrow white rim showing of the white scarf tied underneath. (No forward turned shirt collar).
c) A simple vest of black cloth with black buttons.
d) A kurtka [tailless jacket] of black cloth with black braids and a turned down collar of black velvet cloth.
(To my knowledge, he never wore the order of the Black Eagle on his kurtka but only on his pelisse; I may have to concede, however, that that might indeed have been where it was attached. Earlier (1809) when, as an English regiment it was completely dressed in kurtkas, the duke has been wearing one of these with a blue upright collar, trimmed with a black cord, and also added to that the order).
e) A yellow silver-interwoven sash with two long cords and tassels with cantilles.
f) A cavalry sabre with iron basket guard, black hilt, iron scabbard. Belt of black leather, with yellow lion heads. (This sabre is notable in that it was a gift of Princess Charlotte, having a lock of her hair in a small capsule near the top of the hilt). A silver and yellow interwoven fabric belt.
g) Overalls a bit wide, of black cloth with light blue piping down to the ankles; brown straps.
h) Boots without spurs.

The duke rode a light brown gelding at his death. Black furniture, Hungarian saddle on a black shabraque, decorated with two rows of viper heads (*Otterköpfe*) around its edges, skull and crossed bones device at its tips, likewise of viper heads, and black tassels. The bridle was also ornamented with viper heads.

The staff officer, who was present at the duke's death, wore the same kind of kurtka and overalls; a black cap decorated with golden lace and a black leather pouch with the yellow initials F W, yellow straps. A similar sash.

II Uniform of the Troops
The corps commanders, the quartermaster and brigade Staffs, and the aide de camps: black dolmans with black braid, light blue collars and facings, pouch and sabretache of black leather with initials and yellow straps as already described. Hats with black horizontal feather, and silver sashes.

1 Avantgarde Battalion
a) 2 Jäger Companies
Tyrolean hats with green borders and a green feather, on the upturned

brim the Brunswick horse in white metal, grey coats with a row of white buttons, green collars and facings; grey trousers with green piping creases in front (Cossack trousers). Black leather accoutrements. Rifle and sword bayonet (*Hirschfänger*). Officers similarly, pouch with white accoutrements; and sash as above.

b) 2 Light Infantry Companies
Black dolmans with black braids and green collar. Tyrolean hats as above. Black leather accoutrements. Bayonets instead of small sabres; French muskets. Black canvas knapsack with the rolled overcoat and small kettle attached. Officer pouch and sash as above.

2 Hussars
Black dolmans with light blue collar and facings, black braids. Shakos with black horsehair plume, death's head badge and yellow chin straps. Pouch and sabretache of black leather and yellow accoutrements. Iron sabres, blue and yellow sashes. Black trousers with two blue stripes, leather along inner seam. Officers have silver and yellow sashes.

3 Uhlans
Black kolletts with blue piping and light blue collar, facings, cuffs and turnback facings. Black fabric belt with light blue borders 1 inch wide. Light blue czapkas with black piping, head fitting and peak of black leather, yellow chin straps. Pouch and sabretache of black leather with yellow accoutrements. Iron sabres. Lance pennons yellow and blue. Overalls similar to hussars. Officers' epaulettes with blue base and yellow half moons. Pouch with golden border. Silver sashes similar to infantry.

4 Leib Battalion
Black dolmans with light-blue collar, black braids. *Shako with death's head* and horsehair plume; black accoutrements, no side arm, French muskets. Black canvas knapsacks black leggings and loosely overhanging black trousers. Officers' sashes as before.

5 The 3 Light Battalions
Black dolmans with black braids.
Colour of collars: 1st Light – chamois [yellowish brown],
2nd Light – yellow,
3rd Light – orange.
Shako with pompon, 4 inches high, bottom inch blue, yellow above; white hunting horn badge in front, black chin straps. Remainder same as the Leib Battalion.

Officers had short yellow plumes with blue tips.

6 The 3 Line Battalions
Black dolmans, as before.
Colour of collars: 1st Line – red,
2nd Line – green,
3rd Line – white.
Shako with white plate in front, showing the running horse and the motto *Nunquam retrorsum* [never backwards]; a pompon yellow, and blue at the top, as at 5. Remainder same as the Leib Battalion.

Officers had short blue plumes with yellow tips.

7 Horse Artillery
Black collettes with short tails; braids as on dolmans, black collars with yellow piping, facings, and facings on tails. Shakos with horsehair plume and death's head, yellow chin straps, black pouch and sabretache and yellow accoutrements, same as the hussars.

The train drivers had grey jackets with black collars, one row of black buttons, grey riding trousers faced with leather.

8 Foot Artillery
Same as the Horse Artillery. Shakos with yellow pompons and plate; black leather accoutrements.

9 Police Hussars
Black dolmans with red collars and facings; shakos with white horsehair plume. Remainder same as the Hussars (at 2)

10 The Band of the Line Infantry
Black uniform with red collar, facings, and facings on tails, with gold piping; red 'swallow's nest' wings faced with gold and braids in gold on the dolmans instead of wool.

***

Of the entire infantry, only the three Line Battalions had 2 colours, each; exact drawings are here reproduced [missing from the document].

Description of the horses of the commanders on the days of battle.

1) His Serene Highness the Duke rode at his death the horse already described at the end of Paragraph I.
2) Colonel Olfermann – a yellow pollack [Polish horse].
3) Lieutenant Colonel von Heinemann – a chestnut pollack.
4) Lieutenant Colonel von Specht – a chestnut gelding.
5) Lieutenant Colonel von Buttlar – same.
6) Major von Wachholz – a chestnut pollack.
7) Major von Rauschenplatt, Commander of the Avantgarde – a grey gelding.
8) Major von Cramm, Commander of the Hussars – a grey pollack (at Quatre-bras).
9) Major von Oeynhausen, 2nd Commander of the Hussars – a chestnut pollack (at Waterloo).
10) Major von Pröstler, Commander of the Leib Battalion – a brown-checkered pollack.
11) Major von Hollstein, Commander of the 1st Light Battalion – a chestnut gelding.
12) Major von Brandenstein, Commander of the 2nd Light Battalion – a dark-checkered pollack.
13) Major Ebeling, Commander of the 3rd Light Battalion – a black Spanish gelding.
14) Major Metzner, Commander of the 1st Line Battalion – a black English mare.
15) Major von Strombeck, Commander of the 2nd Line Battalion – a brown pollack.
16) Major von Normann, Commander of the 3rd Line Battalion – a chestnut pollack with long tail.
17) Lieutenant Colonel Pott, Commander of the Uhlans – a gelding, brown with white spots.
18) Major Mahn, Commander of the Artillery – a chestnut gelding.

Relation

The experiences and movements of the Corps of Troops of the Duke of Brunswick in the period from the 15th to, and including, 18 June 1815.

The Corps of the Duke of Brunswick had gradually moved into its assigned cantonments since 13 May, at which date its first column had arrived near Brussels. These were located within the northern semi circle of the outskirts of this city, its widest diameter measuring more than 4 hours [travel]. The duke's headquarters was at Laeken.

When the Duke of Wellington received information about the action at Frasnes on the evening of the 15th, he ordered the allied army to break camp. This order arrived at Laeken at 10 o'clock in the evening and specified: that the corps was to form up at daybreak on the Allee Verte near Brussels, ready to march off. The required orders were sent out at 11 o'clock in the evening and were carried by courier hussars to the detachments. The night was extremely dark; the roads were in poor condition and difficult to find as the terrain was broken up, like everywhere in the Netherlands, these hussars were thus unable to ride fast. The distance to the detachments located farthest away amounted to [rides of] 2 to 3 hours, as for example the artillery in and near Assche, the Hussar Regiment in Cobbeghem, the 3rd Light Battalion in Grimberghem, etc. Most of these could not receive their orders to break camp until a later hour than they were already ordered to be present at Brussels. It so happened therefore that the corps was not yet fully assembled at 6 o'clock on the morning of the 16th; still missing were the Uhlan squadrons, the two artillery batteries, the 1st and the 3rd Light and the 2nd Line Battalions.

Since the duke had received an order from the Duke of Wellington to have his corps pass through Brussels, to march on the Charleroi road to Waterloo and there await further instructions, he ordered the available troops to march off immediately. He had several officers remain behind and given follow up directions for the missing detachments upon their arrival. On his part, he [Duke of Brunswick] rode to Brussels and accompanied the Duke of Wellington, who was about to leave for Quatre Bras in order to reconnoitre the enemy's situation. The road to Genappe, five Brabant leagues or as many hours, was covered in 2 hours. Upon receipt of news at that place of strong movements by the enemy and of the great likelihood of his attack, officers were immediately sent back to order the Brunswick Corps, as well as the 5th English Division under the command of Lieutenant General Sir Thomas Picton, which used the same road, and the Nassau Corps, to continue their march to Genappe.

After a short rest near Waterloo, the Brunswick Corps then resumed its march and arrived in front of Genappe towards noon, where it halted and watered the horses. By that time, the Uhlan squadrons and 2nd Light Battalion had now also joined the corps; still missing were the artillery and the 1st and 3rd Light Battalions. The Duke had returned in the meantime and had a quarter hour's sleep while sitting peacefully on an earthen berm. During this time, the 5th English Division and the Nassau troops passed through Genappe and kept marching on.

It seems it was about 2 o'clock that the corps received the order to advance quickly to Quatre Bras, which it then did at once.

In the meantime, the enemy under Marshal Ney, Duke of Elchingen, had taken up position near Frasnes with 3 divisions of the 2nd Corps of infantry (Reille) and the cavalry under Count Valmy (Kellermann). He was opposed by the Prince of Orange who, in the morning, had already assembled the 7,000 men of the 2nd Netherlands Division, Perponcher, by reinforcing the brigade of Prince Bernhard of Weimar, which had already seen action near Frasnes on the 15th, with the brigade of Major General Count Bijlandt. They were positioned as follows:

The brigade of Prince Bernhard of Weimar occupied the wood of Bossu; that of Major General Count Bijlandt was placed to the rear of the farmstead of Gemioncourt. An engagement of skirmishers had already started until midday when, towards 2 o'clock, the French commenced their attack. Supported by cavalry, the French Bachelu Division had forced Gemioncourt, and, after a short but fierce action, had driven the Netherlands Bijlandt Brigade from its position, which then had to withdraw to Quatre Bras.

The French division of Foy was already in possession of Pierrepont, and the French light cavalry division of Piré and a cuirassier brigade were about to advance upon Quatre Bras.

According to the reports, this was the situation of the engagement when the corps arrived at Quatre Bras at 3 o'clock in the afternoon. In order to cover the left wing, the 2nd Light Battalion was detached to the left towards Pireaumont and to occupy the wood nearby and drive out any enemy troops posted there. The two Jäger companies were sent to the wood of the name Bois de Bossu to cover the right wing, and a few cavalry pickets farther to the right for the observation from there of enemy movements. Upon advancing in the wood, the two Jäger companies met the Netherlands Brigade, which had been forced back and was leaving the wood. The companies therefore had to take up position farther to the rear at the border of the wood; in rear of them were two battalions of Nassauers who had also been forced to retreat. The remainder of the troops moved off the road, forward of Quatre Bras, and formed line facing the road.

This first position of the corps thus formed the 2nd Line behind the English Division of Picton (consisting of English troops and troops of the English German Legion and Hanoverians), which stood on the road itself, and the Netherlands Brigade that had retired from the line of fire, all of them having some light troops before their front.*

* Picton's Division did not include troops of the King's German Legion. The only KGL units involved in the action at Quatre Bras were the 2nd KGL Horse Battery, attached to Cooke's 1st Guards Division and the 4th KGL Foot Battery, attached to von Alten's 3rd Division.

The enemy had taken up position on the height of Gemioncourt on both sides of the road, in part formed in line, part in column, and made some movements, which seemed to point more at a defensive stance than at preparations for an attack.

Hardly had the lines been formed when the Belgian cavalry, having dared to attack but then having been repulsed, returned in disorder and rushed towards the troops. The infantry therefore formed square, and the Hussar Regiment, just having arrived, was ordered to charge the pursuing enemy cavalry, which, however, considered it unwise to approach too close to our infantry and fell back. The squares were then opened up.

A short time later, the Duke of Wellington communicated his wish to the duke to have some of his troops posted in a more forward position on the Charleroi road so as to better discern the enemy's intentions. This was taken care of immediately; the Leib Battalion, the 1st Line Battalion and the two light companies of the Avantgarde were posted on that road, between the sheep farm and the Bois de Bossu, in closed column to be able to form square quickly in case of a cavalry attack. A skirmish line was deployed between them and the Bois de Bossu to the right, where it was to make contact with the Jäger located there. Behind these troops, in rear of the elevation, stood the hussars and uhlans. The 2nd and 3rd Line Battalions were given orders to position themselves in and outside Quatre Bras so as to be able, in the event of an enemy attack and a retreat by our side, to receive our troops and to defend these key points to the utmost, whereupon they placed themselves in the houses as a fall back screen.

The enemy could not fail to become aware of these movements; he immediately moved up a battery opposite us near Gemioncourt and opened a heavy fire with balls, shells and canister upon our troops who had little or no cover. This, as well as uninterrupted musketry fire from tirailleurs close by, which within a short time caused us considerable losses that included the death of Major von Cramm and the wounding of Major von Rauschenplatt. The Hussar Regiment in particular suffered much at this location, as it was formed in line and often received a whole canister charge at a time. The duke himself remained at this place, and even though many a ball struck close to him, he kept casually smoking his pipe, and calmly issued any necessary orders, this to instil courage and fearlessness in his inexperienced young warriors through his own example.

After one hour had thus passed and the enemy's fire had not eased up, the duke asked the Duke of Wellington to send him some English cannon since his own artillery had not yet arrived. This request was immediately granted, and the four pieces sent accordingly were placed to the right of the infantry. They had hardly fired off several shots when the enemy's rate of fire seemed to redouble; two of the guns were soon demolished, and several horses were shot dead. At the same time, two French columns (the division of Prince Jérôme, of Reille's 2nd Infantry Corps), each apparently 2,000 to 3,000 men strong, were observed at a distance, advancing towards us, one after the other, along the edge of the Bois de Bossu and apparently intending to attack us. In front of the first one was an infantry battalion formed in line and some artillery; the second one included cavalry. A large formation of cavalry was also advancing on the Charleroi highway. Soon, those columns had come up to the right wing of our skirmish line and, owing to their superior strength, had driven it back, and also the troops holding the wood.

The duke then ordered the Hussar Regiment to withdraw to the highway on the other side of Quatre Bras, since with the wood in its rear it was unable to move freely, and there to await further developments; as to the Uhlans, he ordered them to charge the advancing infantry and led them himself in person. The enemy's strength and posture caused this attack to fail, and they also fell back to the rear of Quatre Bras. In view of the enemy's strength, our infantry posted at the highway was also directed by the duke to retire to the main line, which it then did. The 1st Line Battalion moved back on the highway; the duke and the Leib Battalion, however, retired by the side of the road. Major von Pröstler tried to have this movement performed in as slow and compact a manner as was possible. But the hot pursuit of the emboldened enemy, the column being struck by several cannon balls and the approach of a French cuirassier regiment, resulted inevitably in some disorder among the inexperienced troops. The duke* was attempting to restore order when he was hit by a shot that struck him off his horse. By chance, almost none of the officers

* Friedrich Wilhelm of Brunswick (1771–1815) inherited the Duchy of Brunswick upon the death of his father, Duke Karl Wilhelm Ferdinand, in 1806. As Brunswick had been allied with Prussia in the ill-fated campaign of 1806 against Napoleon, the emperor made the duchy a part of his brother Jérôme's Kingdom of Westphalia. The new Duke Friedrich Wilhelm went into exile in Austria and from there raised an army in his former possessions that was to become known as the 'Black Corps' from its black uniforms. After joining Austria in the campaign against Napoleon of 1809, Duke Friedrich Wilhelm did not surrender after Austria's defeat at Wagram but led his corps through Germany to the North Sea coast where it boarded British ships. It became part of the British army, not least because of dynastic ties – the British royals of the time were variously known as the House of Hanover or of Brunswick. The corps fought in the Peninsular War, and was dissolved after the defeat of Napoleon in 1814. Upon the emperor's return to France, Duke Friedrich Wilhelm reformed his army and put it at the disposition of the Duke of Wellington when invited to do so early in 1815.

of his Staff happened to be nearby except for Major von Wachholz. He immediately had some men of the Leib Battalion, who had already picked up the Duke to carry him across the road and to the rear of the line. He was put down at that location to allow removal of his sash and sabre which obviously had caused him some discomfort while being carried, and was then placed on a blanket that had just been found. No surgeon could be called on in a hurry, despite all efforts by several officers. The deathly pallor of his face and his half closed eyes made one fear the worst. He opened his eyes one more time, recognised those around him, and asked to see Colonel Olfermann. He also asked for some water which, however, could not be obtained at the moment.

Since the situation seemed to become more perilous to the point that he might fall into the enemy's hands should the troops need to retreat, he was taken up again and carried in the blanket up the highway to the nearest houses of a locality named la Baraque. Staff Surgeon Dr Pockels happened to be at that place; he examined the duke's wound and then pronounced him dead. The shot that had killed him was apparently a musket ball which had pierced his right wrist, had penetrated his lower right abdomen, had passed through it, and left it on his left side.

These were the last moments of a hero who, when everybody bowed down before the force of circumstances, was the first to face events with defiantly raised head; who first spoke up courageously on what then were only emotions and thoughts in the German's mind, and who later was to save the fatherland; who ranked it higher to be just a man instead of a ruler, to be, first a father rather than a prince.

Let us now return to the battlefield. The moment of decision had arrived, and never had our side been in greater peril. The enemy's infantry and cavalry made several violent attacks upon our troops in and near Quatre Bras, but were thrown back each time. However, two events now occurred which determined the outcome. The first one: when Ney ordered his reserves (3 divisions of the 1st Infantry Corps, under d'Erlon) to support the attack, in which case our situation would have become very critical due to his great superiority, these were already directed by Napoleon to move against the Prussians and were thus not available. The second one: at this moment our artillery arrived, which had covered part of the journey at the trot. The two light battalions had also come up and were immediately used as a reinforcement of the line battalions at Quatre Bras. The artillery was placed on the left where it opened a very effective fire in conjunction with the English artillery. The results could soon be seen; the enemy cannon, drawn up far in front of their line, was silenced and the infantry showed signs of retiring. This moment was used to have several English and Netherlands battalions, as well as our Leib and 2nd

Line Battalions, advance and make a bayonet charge against the enemy who was posted between the sheep farm and the wood. There was some violent fighting; many were its victims, including Major von Strombeck and Captain von Bülow. The enemy yielded in the end. All our points were adequately reinforced by freshly arriving troops, and the enemy was soon forced to abandon the battlefield completely and retire to his former position. Of the recently arrived English troops, the 3rd Division, von Alten, had moved into the battle line on the left wing towards Pireaumont, and the Hanoverian Halkett Brigade of the 2nd Division (Clinton) cleared the enemy from the Bois de Bossu, of which it took possession. Von Dörnberg's Cavalry Brigade had also arrived and formed up behind the left wing of Picton's Division. The battle ended when it was already quite dark, and the troops were assigned their bivouac locations. The Uhlan squadrons took up picket positions to the right of the Bois de Bossu and had two Nassau battalions posted to its rear. As already mentioned, the wood had been occupied by the Hanoverian Halkett Brigade;* another English brigade and the 1st Light Battalion. Behind it in the ditch and at the edge of the wood the 2nd and 3rd and Leib Battalions were posted. Farther to the left were English and Netherlands troops. The artillery, the hussars, and the rest of the infantry of the corps had their bivouacs near Quatre Bras on both sides of the Brussels highway. The 3rd Light Battalion, two cannon, and a detachment of hussars were sent to reinforce the 2nd Light Battalion, which, as mentioned earlier, had been detached to cover the left flank towards the wood near Pireaumont. Together with other troops (a regiment of Scottish Highlanders, joined later by the English 95th Regiment and the Hanoverian Lüneburg Jäger Battalion), it had here been engaged since the beginning of the action and had suffered significant losses.

The troops were extremely exhausted after 17 hours spent on the march and in the action, not having had anything to eat but dry biscuits, and just sank down totally fatigued, not even feeling the lack of food.

---

* The 'Hanoverian Halkett Brigade', that is, the 4th Hanoverian Landwehr Brigade under Colonel Hugh Halkett, did not participate in the fighting at Quatre Bras. Instead, it was Major General Sir Colin Halkett's 5th British Brigade that was involved in that action. Later in the afternoon, the Bois de Bossu was cleared of the enemy by the troops of Cooke's 1st Guards Division. Major General von Dörnberg's 3rd British Cavalry Brigade arrived in the evening of the 16th after the fighting had ended and bivouacked between Genappe and Quatre Bras.

The Losses of the Corps on this Day:

	Killed		*Wounded*		
	Officers	*Rank & File*	*Officers*	*Rank & File*	*Horses*
General Staff	1				
Hussar Regiment	2	15	2	27	68
Uhlan Squadrons	—	4	—	10	8
Horse Battery	—	—	—	—	2
Foot Battery	—	—	—	—	—
Avantgarde	—	9	4	43	—
Leib Battalion	—	15	5	106	—
1st Light Battalion	—	—	—	3	—
2nd Light Battalion	—	18	3	49	—
3rd Light Battalion	—	—	—	—	—
1st Line Battalion	1	16	2	86	—
2nd Line Battalion	2	23	4	162	—
3rd Line Battalion	—	4	1	19	—
Total	6	104	21	505	78

In addition, 10 men were taken prisoner and about 200 were missing so that the over all losses amounted to 27 officers and 819 men.

Everything remained quiet on the morning of the 17th except on the left wing, where the skirmishers of the 3rd Light Battalion became engaged. The enemy conducted major movements and large troop formations were assembled on the heights of Frasnes. Dispositions were made to repulse an eventual attack. Some foodstuffs and forage had arrived and were distributed, and meals were cooked. Two hussar squadrons had to dismount to carry the wounded back to Waterloo,* where they rejoined their regiment in the evening.

The defeat of the Prussians near Ligny and their retreat in the direction of Gembloux necessitated taking other measures, and we therefore had to commence our retreat around 11 o'clock and move off, unseen to the extent [that was] possible. To cover this retrograde movement, the English cavalry and the 3rd English Division under the command of Lieutenant General Baron von Alten, as well as the 2nd and 3rd Light Battalions, remained behind. The Avantgarde also had to keep holding the Bois de Bossu, and only after some time was it allowed to follow. Meanwhile, the corps marched off on the Brussels highway past Genappe, and at Belle Alliance it turned left off the road. So far, the march had been cumbersome

* An interesting comment and not one that the editor has come across before.

due to the oppressive heat, but now the skies became covered with clouds and we were drenched by cold downpours.

The allied army took the following positions: The right wing under Lord Hill was leaning on the hamlet of Braine l'Alleud. The centre under the Prince of Orange was posted in two lines from the Charleroi highway to the right wing, in between crossing the Nivelles highway. The cavalry stood in the third line in front of the village of Mont St Jean. The left wing, under the command of General Picton, extended from the Charleroi highway along the road, which leads from Braine l'Alleud to Louvain and is bordered by hedges. Our corps was assigned a position in the second line of the centre. The right flank adjoined Merbe Braine and the left flank the Nivelles highway. Only the Avantgarde was posted on the far side of Merbe Braine on the right flank. Towards evening, artillery fire was heard and was getting closer all the time, announcing the arrival of the rearguard. Upon becoming aware of our retiring, the enemy on his part, had the 1st Infantry Corps under Count d'Erlon and Jacquinot's Cavalry Division take off and pursue us on the major highway to Brussels. Napoleon reinforced them with 12 cannon of the horse artillery of the Garde, and followed himself with the entire army. Milhaud's Cavalry Corps advanced cross country on the flanks of the columns. General von Alten's Division and the English cavalry covered the retreat of the allied army. The cavalry had already been engaged in front of Genappe, where the English cavalry blocked the advance of the French cavalry to give General von Alten time to pass through Genappe on his slow, fighting retreat. The heavy rains obstructed the enemy's advance with slippery roads and the soft soil of the fields, and thus helped us greatly on our retreat.

The 2nd Light Battalion was part of the rearguard and lost only one man wounded. The 3rd Light Battalion, however, had lost one man killed and 2 officers and 26 rank and file wounded during its engagement in the morning. When General von Alten arrived before our position at 8 o'clock in the evening, the entire army stood to arms, whereupon the enemy ended his pursuit and set up camp opposite from us on the heights of Belle Alliance. As darkness had set in, we also set up bivouacs on our side. The rains continued throughout the night, causing the troops great discomfort and made them yearn for the morning.

The Battle of Waterloo

The memorable 18 June dawned, the skies started to clear a little and sustenance of the troops and horses was taken care of to the extent possible, although falling very much short of their needs. Everything was prepared for a great event to happen, but it was only at 10 o'clock that movements on the enemy's side could be observed. At some points, a cannonade commenced, and at 11 o'clock the army stood to arms. The corps remained at the place it had taken the previous evening without suffering losses from the artillery fire to which it was exposed. The 2nd and 3rd Light Battalions joined us here; they had bivouacked with General von Alten's troops during the night.

Towards 1 o'clock, the corps eventually received orders to march off left and take position in the first line. The farmstead of Hougoumont, located in front of the right wing of our army, would have greatly facilitated an attack on our position, had it been in the enemy's hands. It was attacked by the enemy's 2nd Infantry Corps, and specifically by Prince Jérôme Napoleon's Division as early as 12 o'clock.

The corps was posted on the crest of the plateau behind the farm, and the Avantgarde was immediately detached to its garden [orchard] in support of an English regiment of Guards of Byng's Brigade which defended it. The Leib and 1st Light Battalions were posted close to its rear on an elevation, to cover it and serve as a reserve; in front of the former was the horse battery. The other battalions of the corps formed up alongside and behind the country road which ran along the plateau, with the left flank adjoining the English battalions of the centre. The English artillery was emplaced before the entire line and kept up a vigorous cannonading duel with that of the enemy. The Hussar Regiment and the two Uhlan squadrons were placed in reserve, together with the 1st and 2nd Light Dragoons and the 3rd Hussar Regiment of the English German Legion, as was the foot battery. The enemy artillery moved forward and attacked us with a heavy cannonade. Our troops were somewhat protected by the height in front of them, but the charges of the well directed projectiles frequently struck the columns and caused significant losses. During this time, the Avantgarde was strongly engaged in the defence of Hougoumont where it defended the park of the chateau most tenaciously and repulsed the enemy's attack.*

From 2 to 4 o'clock

This was the battle situation, until after 2 o'clock. The enemy sent the 3rd Cavalry Corps under Count Valmy [Kellermann] forward of the three

* References to the 'Park' of Hougoumont in this context and elsewhere in the Brunswick Report are misleading. The park (or formal garden) as such adjoined the east side of the buildings and was enclosed by a high brick wall on its south and east side and by an impenetrable high hedge on the north side. It was accessible only from an inside courtyard. At the height of the fighting, the garrison inside of the complex, buildings and the park, consisted solely of about 800 men of the British Foot Guards, 400 Nassauers, and some Hanoverian sharpshooters. No other troops are mentioned in the descriptions of eyewitnesses as being part of the inside garrison.

divisions of Girard, Foy, and Bachelu that were deployed in line, and before the 2nd Infantry Corps (Reille),* in order to attack and attempt to break through our line. As soon as the Duke of Wellington observed this, he had our battalions move farther up towards the crest of the plateau; they immediately formed squares. At that moment, the enemy cavalry had already advanced and was between the guns in front of us (our foot battery had also joined them in the meantime), whose crews and train had sought refuge behind the line. But here they became exposed to well directed small arms fire that made them stop short. But before our cavalry had saddled up, the infantry squares made a bayonet charge against the wavering enemy who retreated immediately and was vigorously pursued by our cavalry. He nevertheless rallied soon under the cover of his reserves and drove our cavalry back behind our lines. In this way, the attacks were repeated several times, but were always repulsed by the infantry which pursued him with the bayonet. But this always resulted in great losses; as soon as the infantry had advanced to where it was no longer protected by the height, it was exposed to a murderous fire of canister, which forced it to retreat.

Two extraordinary feats need to be mentioned, which occurred during this part of the battle:

1. Bombardier Johann Gottlieb Büchner of the Foot battery was in command of the No. 2 howitzer. When the French cuirassiers had overrun the Foot battery in their first charge from the left flank, Captain Orges – still among the guns – found himself between two cuirassiers. From all appearances, he seemed lost if Bombardier Büchner had not killed one of the cuirassiers with his small sabre and thus had helped free his captain. Büchner was awarded an Honorary Ducat (replaced at the present time with the Distinguished Service Cross 2nd Class of the Order of Henry the Lion).

2. Gunner Johann Dietrich Rietz distinguished himself when, felled by a wound on his foot, he crawled on the ground and attached the prolonge rope† to his gun, thus making it possible to pull it back to the squares. For that he received the Honorary Medal of the Guelphic Order.

---

* Girard's Division was not at Waterloo; it had been left at Fleurus after its severe losses in the Battle of Ligny on the 16th. The author apparently intended to refer to Prince Jérôme's Division. This, Foy's and Bachelu's Divisions, together with Piré's 2nd Cavalry Division and an artillery complement, made up Reille's 2nd Corps.

† The 'prolonge rope' was attached to a gun to manoeuvre it by hand rather than having to attach the horses and limber.

From 4 to 7 o'clock
The enemy now had Foy's and Bachelu's infantry divisions advance in columns in order to support the attack to be commenced upon Hougoumont and to give time to the cavalry to reform. While present at our corps, the Duke of Wellington ordered the 44th* and 95th Regiments, and the 2nd and 3rd Light Battalions and the 2nd Line Battalion to move down the height against the enemy. These advancing columns came under heavy canister and small arms fire; entire files were mown down in no time at all. The enemy had observed the effectiveness of his fire and now repeated his cavalry attacks with the support of horse artillery. The battalions, that had advanced, repulsed all attacks but were forced to retire onto the plateau having suffered severe losses. The Duke of Wellington again gave the order to advance; the three just mentioned battalions, having the two English regiments to their left, again passed over the height and descended down the forward slope. But this time, after having repulsed the cavalry attacks, they were again forced to withdraw to their former location due to the most violent fire from the enemy. This point they always held, although at this position a large part of the artillery had been completely demolished. In support of the advancing infantry, the cavalry of the [Brunswick] Corps and the three cavalry regiments of the English German Legion mentioned earlier moved forward, after attacks had been repulsed, and pursued the enemy. Always yielding before a renewed and stronger enemy charge, our cavalry reformed each time behind our squares, from where they counter attacked and thereby continued the action. During this phase of the battle Colonel Olfermann, Commander of the corps, was wounded by a shot in his right hand and had to leave the battlefield, and command of the corps passed on to the Quartermaster General Lieutenant Colonel von Heinemann. Majors von Brandenstein and Ebeling were here also severely wounded.

On this occasion, two extraordinary feats are to be mentioned:

1. Cavalry Sergeant Eggeling of the Hussar Regiment, a brave soldier, full of fighting ardour, was always one of the first against the enemy and was a shining example to his comrades. He is now a retired lieutenant and holder of the Guelphic Medal and of the Distinguished Service Cross, 2nd Class, of the Order of Henry the Lion.

2. Uhlan Lindemann wounded the commander of the French cuirassiers while close before their front, but was himself wounded by a shot through

* The 44th (East Essex) Regiment, at Waterloo with its 2nd Battalion, was part of Pack's 9th British Brigade in Picton's 5th Division on the left wing of Wellington's army, and not in the 2nd Allied Corps on the right wing as is indicated here.

his neck. He was awarded the Guelphic Medal and the just mentioned 2nd Class of the Distinguished Service Cross.

At the same time, the enemy had the division of Prince Jérôme Napoleon repeat its attack upon Hougoumont, supported by artillery and Piré's light cavalry division. The buildings were set on fire with incendiary fire, and the garrison was driven out into the park which was defended step by step by the English regiment of Guards together with our Avantgarde who eventually had to yield to the enemy's superior numbers.* On Lord Hill's orders, the Leib Battalion was sent to the park when it was already too late, because the dispersed English and Brunswickers, driven out of the park, hardly had time to form up and defend themselves against the enemy's light cavalry. After this attack had been repulsed, the Leib Battalion moved forward and took up position in part of the park, while the English Guards Regiment formed up again, and advanced to the right of Hougoumont and there took its stand. Next to it, the Avantgarde Battalion also had formed up.

At the same time, the 1st Light Battalion was detached to move into the park; having the Leib Battalion on its left flank, it maintained liaison with it by a line of skirmishers, whereupon the enemy infantry was driven out of the park. The two battalions formed in columns after they arrived in the open on the far side of Hougoumont.

It was in this action that Major von Bülow, second commander of the Avantgarde, was wounded.

From 7 to 8 o'clock

The moment of decision was approaching; Napoleon believed that he could still launch a decisive thrust against the centre of the allied army, although he was pressed hard by the Prussians on his right flank. He therefore had set his Guard in motion. Four battalions of the Middle Guard and 4 batteries advanced upon La Haye Sainte, followed by the 8

---

* Contrary to this account, the garrison was never driven out of its positions in the buildings and the enclosed garden After 2 p.m. the garden, erroneously referred to as the park, was mainly defended by a battalion of the British Third Guards Regiment. Out of some 700 men, its losses were 4 officers and 67 rank and file killed, and 9 officers and 188 rank and file wounded. On the other hand, the losses of the Brunswick Avantgarde, out of some 600 men at Waterloo, were 7 rank and file killed and 1 officer and 20 rank and file wounded. This would indicate that the contribution of the Avantgarde to the defence of Hougoumont may not have been as substantial as might appear from this and earlier references. The involvement and movements of the troops of the 2nd or Coldstream Guards and the Third Guards Regiments at Hougoumont differs from this description, but a clarification would exceed the limits of this note.

battalions of the Old Guard.* On our side, masses of troops and artillery were marshalled at this decisive point against the desparate attack of the most seasoned and valiant warriors of the French army. Our corps was also ordered to quickly move there. The battalions closest to the centre (4.5.6.7.8.)† at once marched off by the left. That movement was soon followed by the battalions at the Hougoumont position (1.2.3.)‡ and by our cavalry.

The corps, after arriving at the decisive point, had hardly begun to deploy and form at the proper distances when the enemy skirmishers had already climbed up the steep slope and were only a few paces away from the troops. Their unexpected nearness, the all enveloping dense clouds of powder smoke, the men's exhaustion, the partial disorder of the still incomplete deployment, and, lastly, the powerful thrust of the attack caused several battalions to hesitate at first and fall back a little. However, the 3rd Line Battalion under Major von Normann quickly formed up again, took a stand against the enemy and received him with such well directed fire that he ceased his advance. By virtue of the officers' strong efforts, the other battalions had fallen in again, closed up, and, together with the Netherlands Aubremé Brigade§ and the Nassau Brigade, advanced upon the enemy.

This as well as the murderous fire of the English artillery, a few splendid charges by the English cavalry under Lord Uxbridge, and the powerful forward pressing of the Prussians forced the enemy to retreat. This turned into a total rout, as the army now moved forward at all points,

The corps was to deplore the loss of its Quartermaster General Lieutenant Colonel von Heinemann in this last attack. He was a highly esteemed, capable and energetic officer. At this time, Major von Wolffradt, interim commander of the brigade of the line, and Captain von Schwartz Koppen, who commanded the 2nd Line Battalion, were wounded, the latter so severely that he died soon afterwards.

From 8 to 9 o'clock

The corps advanced on the Charleroi highway, met the Prussian troops

* The final attack of the Imperial Guard was not directed towards La Haye Sainte but, rather, upon the Allied line between La Haye Sainte and a point north-east of Hougoumont, where two battalions of the British First Guards Brigade were stationed. The first wave consisted of four battalions of the Guard, with a second wave of six battalions of the Guard.

† The numbers refer to the 2nd and 3rd Light, and 1st, 2nd, and 3rd Line Battalions.

‡ The numbers signify the Avantgarde and the Leib and 1st Light Battalions.

§ It was Col. Detmer's 3rd Brigade of the 3rd Netherlands Division that was involved in the counter attack against the French Guard, and not Aubremé's 4th Brigade which remained in the second line. N. Vels Hejn, *Glorie zonder helden: De slag bij Waterloo, waarheid en legende*, Amsterdam 1974, pp. 206–7.

near Belle Alliance, and eventually, towards 10 o'clock, set up its bivouac to the right of the road near the village of Maison du Roi. The cavalry here rejoined the corps; but the artillery, much damaged in the action, moved to Brussels to make the necessary repairs.

The losses of the corps on this day are shown in the appendix attached to this relation.

No. 35 Colonel Olfermann

British Library Add MS 34706 fo. 23

Report of Colonel and Brigadier Olfermann to the Princely Privy Council at Brunswick. In the night from the 16th to the 17th June 1815, at the bivouack near Quatre Bras.

At the bivouac near Braine l'Alleud, 9 o'clock in the morning of 18 June

In the evening of the 15th at 11 o'clock we had received marching orders, we took off on the 16th towards Quatre Bras, [a distance of] some 10 to 11 hours from the cantonments of the corps. One of the bloodiest battles happened there, in which our much loved duke was struck by a musket ball, after he had involved himself most actively in all command decisions with his inborn intrepidity and courage. [That ball] had smashed his hand and pierced his abdomen and liver. This tragic incident occurred at about 6 o'clock in the afternoon. His Highness was personally leading 2 battalions against a strong enemy column which was threatening our entire right flank, and held it back for a long time despite its immense superiority, but was finally forced to fall back to the second line. The only words that the duke said before his death were to Major von Wachholz, and were, 'Oh, my dear Wachholz, where is Olfermannn?' Captain Bause went at once in search for him [Olfermann], but sudden death kept the duke's last wishes from being fulfilled.

Apart from this irreplaceable loss, we regret the deaths of Majors von Strombeck and Cramm. Major von Rauschenplatt has been severely wounded. All three were by my side, either when they were killed or were wounded. As soon as more detailed information is available on all those killed, wounded or missing of the corps, which now is impossible to provide due to the ongoing operations, I shall report to the Princely Privy Council the particulars immediately and in detail. Most of the losses were suffered by that part of our corps which operated at the right flank of our army, from a heavy cannonade lasting for three hours. We had no artillery [with which] to respond because the artillery of our corps had not yet arrived due to its remote cantonments. The cavalry suffered in particular at this point. However, it refilled with great sang-froid the ranks from time to time that had been taken out by howitzer or canister fire, as also did the infantry battalions near there. The duke was here, also, almost during the whole time that the heavy cannonade lasted, and by his presence instilled the utmost intrepidity and calmness in his soldiers.

Of particular distinction was the conduct of the 2nd Line Battalion, the 2nd Light Battalion, and the Leib-Battalion. The first of these had formed square and completely threw back with great steadiness and sang-froid the repeated charges of enemy cuirassiers, and hindered the enemy's advance, inflicting a considerable loss in killed. The last two battalions contended with the enemy for the possession of a wood, which was lost three times and regained just as many times. The battalions eventually remained masters [of the wood]. All in all, these mostly young troops have conducted themselves in the bravest manner, and even more so as they were led by the duke himself against the enemy and by his presence were filled with unlimited confidence. I cannot praise enough the performance of the officers of the General Staff, Lieutenant Colonel von Heinemann, Majors von Wachholz, von Grone, and von Mahrenholz, the Captains von Lübeck and Bause, as well as of my aide de camps, Captains von Morgenstern and von Zweifel. All of them displayed the strongest initiative and most outstanding bravery, and their support was of particular help to me after the command of the corps was handed to me upon the duke's unfortunate demise. Majors von Grone and von Mahrenholz were in charge of the duke's corpse.

The Duke of Wellington's army has been victorious, notwithstanding the enemy's superiority. His advance posts are positioned one hour beyond the line that the French had held before the beginning of the battle. We are facing another battle tomorrow. Prisoners claim that Napoleon and Ney under him had been in command of the enemy army.

After a night spent in the bivouac in heavy rain, we are still at the same position as on the day before, 17 June, when a withdrawal movement had been made without anything of importance having occurred. I hasten to despatch this, in order to assure that this information arrive at Brunswick at the earliest.

Signed Olfermann

No. 36 By the Same

Laeken, 19 June 1815

When I attempted to continue my last letter, the army was suddenly attacked and we were forced to break camp. At first, the Brunswick Corps stood in the 3rd Line; however, after 2 hours I received an order to have the corps advance to the 1st line. This movement was promptly executed, and the infantry battalions formed attack columns on the [rear] slope of a ridge, on which English and Hanoverian artillery had been emplaced and, for 2 hours, traded fire with the enemy cannon. Until then, only a few balls had struck our battalions, and there were only minor losses. During this cannonade, the enemy had formed up considerable masses of cavalry, which soon launched the most violent charges against the allied artillery, although always without success. A short time later, one of these masses debouched from the corn fields at our side. This cavalry, perhaps consisting of four to five cuirassier regiments, was apparently emboldened by not being fired at and, possibly, did not expect squares ready to fire on the other side of the ridge. They crossed the plateau and were about to charge the battalion squares at full gallop, but this heavy attack was repulsed, and entire ranks of this cavalry were shot down.

Since this moment, the Duke of Wellington stayed for quite some time with the infantry squares of our corps, while these were attacked in renewed cavalry charges. But to those the same happened as to the earlier one; they were always forced to turn back with heavy losses. A short time later, the Duke of Wellington ordered me to have 3 battalion squares advance and move over the ridge. This movement was calmly commenced by the battalions, although it was on everybody's mind that heavy canister and infantry fire was awaiting us on the other side of the ridge. That expectation unfortunately turned out to be true enough. Hardly had we passed the ridge when entire ranks of the battalions were shot down in quick succession. The enemy soon became aware of the effectiveness of his fire, and began to support the cavalry attacks with his horse artillery. It was impossible to hold out here any longer.

I gave the order to return to our earlier position. Soon thereafter, we were here also most violently attacked, but at no gain to the enemy. The 2nd and 3rd Jäger Battalions and the 3rd Line Battalion stood like rocks. The Duke of Wellington was still near us, and again sent orders to advance. An attempt was made, but the enemy moved up with a stronger force, particularly in artillery, and the losses in our infantry battalions became ever greater. The three just mentioned battalions nevertheless occupied repeatedly the slope on the far side of the ridge, but were forced to return each time to the former position. This we held despite the continuous enemy attacks, even though the allied artillery had almost totally been demolished. During one of these attacks, several of my fingers were smashed and the right hand shattered; these wounds forced me to go to the rear. I handed the command over to Lieutenant Colonel von Heinemann towards 7 o'clock in the evening. Lieutenant Colonel von Buttlar had suffered a contusion and had to leave the battlefield. Around 9 o'clock, the greatest victory was won in conjunction with the Prussian Army Corps. 100 cannon and 15,000 prisoners were captured. The enemy is in full retreat.

The losses suffered by these three battalions is quite considerable. They made an essential contribution to the army through their steadfastness and outstandingly good conduct. The severely wounded commanders of the brave 2nd and 3rd Jäger Battalions, Majors von Brandenstein and Ebeling, and also Captain Häusler and Major von Normann, have excelled in a most brilliant manner. Captain Häusler had led a skirmish line and, with great bravery, had done considerable damage to the enemy. The aide de camps of the late Duke, Captains von Lübeck and Bause, as well as my aide de camps, Captains von Zweiffel and Morgenstern, have greatly distinguished themselves. Through their activities they contributed outstandingly to the performance of the corps, and repeatedly gave proof of their intrepidity and their competency in the military field.

Olfermann

(by Captain Bause, the colonel being unable to write due to his wound)

Losses of the Brunswick Corps on 16 June at Quatre Bras*

	Killed		*Wounded*		
	Officers	*Rank & File*	*Officers*	*Rank & File*	*Horses*
General Staff	1				
Hussar Regiment	2	15	2	27	68
Uhlan Squadrons	—	4	—	10	8
Horse Battery	—	—	—	—	2
Foot Battery	—	—	—	—	—
Avantgarde	—	9	4	43	—
Leib Battalion	—	15	5	106	—
1st Light Battalion	—	—	—	3	—
2nd Light Battalion	—	18	3	49	—
3rd Light Battalion	—	—	—	—	—
1st Line Battalion	1	16	2	86	—

* These figures are identical to those supplies by Lieutenant General Herzberg above.

2nd Line Battalion	2	23	4	162	—
3rd Line Battalion	—	4	1	9	—
Total	6	104	21	505	78

In addition, 10 men were taken prisoner and about 200 were missing so that the overall losses amounted to 27 officers and 819 men.

The Hussar Regiment lost 68 horses, the Uhlans 8, and the Horse Battery 2 horses.

Listing by name of the Officers of the Brunswick Corps killed in the action at Quatre Bras:

1 His Serene Highness the Reigning Duke Fredrick Wilhelm.
2 Major von Cramm, Commander of the Hussar Regiment.
3 Captain von Pavel, Hussar Regiment.
4 Ensign Hersche, 1st Line Battalion.
5 Major von Strombeck, Commander of the 2nd Line Battalion.
6 Captain von Bülow, 2nd Line Battalion.

***

Losses on 17 June 1815 in the action near Liermont[?] and during the retreat to Waterloo:

2nd Light Battalion	0 killed	1 wounded
3rd Light Battalion	1 killed	28 wounded
Total	1 killed	29 wounded

The wounded include Lieutenant von Specht and Ensign Seeliger, both of the 3rd Light Battalion

Losses of the Brunswick Corps in the Battle of Waterloo on 18 June

	Killed		*Wounded*	
	Officers	*Rank & File*	*Officers*	*Rank & File*
General Staff	1	—	4	—
Hussar Regiment	1	27	5	45
Uhlan Squadrons	—	—	2	13
Horse Battery	1	2	—	6
Foot Battery	—	—	—	18
Avantgarde	—	7	1	20
Leib Battalion	—	14	1	36
1st Light Battalion	—	4	3	41

	Killed		Wounded	
	Officers	*Rank & File*	*Officers*	*Rank & File*
2nd Light Battalion	2	37	2	73
3rd Light Battalion	1	35	5	75
1st Line Battalion	—	9	—	46
2nd Line Battalion	1	2	1	6
3rd Line Battalion	—	10	2	51
Total	7	147	26	430

The total losses, including 50 missing, thus amounted to 33 officers, 627 rank and file, and 77 horses.

Listing by name of the officers of the Brunswick Corps killed in the Battle of Waterloo:

1 Lieutenant Colonel von Heinemann,General Staff.
2 Lieutenant Lambrecht, Hussar Regiment.
3 Lieutenant Diedrichs, Horse Battery.
4 Ensign Bruns, 2nd Light Battalion.
5 Ensign Sensemann, 2nd Light Battalion.
6 Captain von Braun,3rd Light Battalion.
7 Ensign von Vechelde,2nd Line Battalion.

Supplementary listing of names of those who had received the Honorary Ducat in recognition of meritorious service on the days of battle that now has been exchanged for the Distinguished Service Cross 2nd Class of the Order of Henry the Lion:

1 Sergeant Kinkel, on 16 June received a severe wound in his face and was shot in the leg on the 18th.

2 Sergeant Müller, requested permission to step in front of the square upon the approach of enemy cavalry in order to drive back the skirmishers, and shot down 2 French officers.

3 Sergeant Fuhr, carried one of the battalion colours; was lightly wounded on the 16th, but after receiving several severe wounds he shouted 'Will somebody take the colours to keep them from becoming lost.'

4 Sergeant Fischer, distinguished himself on 16 and 18 June by his bravery and good conduct, in particular while skirmishing, and by inspiring his men.

5 Private Heilemann, always was the first to volunteer on advancing and, although stunned by a head injury, kept fighting until the end of the affair.

PRUSSIAN ARMY

6th Uhlan Regiment*

No. 37 Volunteer Henri Nieman

'The journal of Henri Nieman, of the Sixth Prussian Uhlans',
English Historical Review *vol. III, 1888, pp. 539–45*

On the last day of April the new troops left Bremen, accompanied by a numerous escort of friends, and arrived at Bassum, where, having emptied the wine casks, our friends departed.

From Bassum the line of march was to Diepholz, where the troops rested two days, Osnabrück was reached on 4 May. In the beautiful garden of the castle at Munster the troops were regaled on the 7th with a splendid dinner and plenty of Rhenish [wine]. Here they remained three days. Passing through Werne, Witten, Ronsdorf, and Elberfeld, they reached Dusseldorf on 15 May. On the following day they crossed the Rhine with a tremendous hurrah, marching toward Neuss and Gatswester,† where there was an arrest and a duel. Aix-la-Chapelle‡ was reached on the 19th. On the 21st Rech, the first French village was passed, and on the following day the troops entered Liege. Marshal Blücher received the regiment on 25 May, at Namur, in the twilight of the day. Three days later at Charleroi, General Ziethen and Major von Lützow formally received and reviewed the volunteers and after this the troops were distributed amongst the large and elegant farms near Thuin, on the frontier of France, where, writes

* The original article in the *English Historical Review* states that Nieman served in the 6th Hussars. However, this is clearly an error, made possibly because Nieman may have referred to his unit as hussars. His regiment had only recently been formed partly out of Lützow's Freikorps which wore hussar style uniforms. However Nieman states that his regiment was in von Lützow's Brigade in Ziethen's Corps and he also mentions that his men had lances. Therefore he must have belonged to the 6th Uhlan Regiment. I have therefore taken the liberty of converting all mention of hussars to uhlans in his statement to avoid perpetuating this confusion.

† I have been unable to identify this town.

‡ Modern Aachen.

Nieman, 'We had at last Napoleon before our noses.' While at these farms the troopers had a very pleasant time in spite of reconnoitring day and night to watch Napoleon's movements along the line.

I found it very unpleasant to sit on my horse in a dark night facing the enemy and watching every sound. My horse was of a restless disposition, like its master, and I had trouble to keep him quiet to enable me to end in passing my two hours' post. One night in particular I was as a young soldier in trouble. I was ordered to ride along the line of our vedettes on a dark night for several miles. I struck on a Prussian sentinel. Coming within speaking distance, I asked, 'Who is there?' 'A sentinel.' 'The word,' I replied. Answer, 'I forget it.' According to military custom, having my pistol in my hand I should have shot *him* down, but being convinced he was one of my own regiment, I only put him in arrest. After remaining in this locality for some five weeks the Prussian uhlans were relieved by a dragoon regiment and marched back six leagues.

On 15 June it was made known to the army under Blücher that the first three shots of heavy ordnance would be a signal of hostilities commenced, and the troopers were ordered not to undress.

I was lying on a bundle of straw when, early in the morning of 15 June, I heard those three shots. This was 3 o'clock in the morning, and about three hours after we marched towards the frontier again. We passed through Gilly and took position on the other side of it. Napoleon came nearer with his army; firing began. My heart began to beat, but I soon forgot I might be shot. By command of General Ziethen we engaged the French; but it was nothing but a pretension; they retreated before us. Not having yet removed our wounded from the field, they renewed the fight with a stronger force. Fighting, we slowly retired. We were obliged to cover our retreat, and the hail of balls in covering our artillery from the enemy's attack was not very pleasant. However it was of no use to make long faces; we lost in all about three thousand men. Towards evening of that day our brigade, of four regiments of cavalry,* reached Fleurus; we bivouacked before the city, but an order came to break up [camp]. We marched through Fleurus and bivouacked on the other side that night. I would have paid five francs for a glass of water. On the right of the road was a windmill.

On the morning of the 16th we were ordered to change our position. It was a beautiful morning. Blücher's favourable position was turned later. Looking down the line at sunrise as far as the eye could reach it appeared like silver mountains, regiments of muskets, artillery, and cuirassiers. About 10 o'clock I was ordered to procure food in the city

* Von Lützow's Brigade consisted of 6th Uhlans, Westphalian Landwehr cavalry and 1st and 2nd Kurmark Landwehr Cavalry regiments.

for the men and horses of my regiment. In attempting this, the French marched in at the other gate, and of course I said 'Good-bye' for the present. Immediately our 80,000 men were ordered to fall back at a slow pace, and thus Blücher's beautiful position had to be changed, and this day's dreadful slaughter commenced. No quarter given; Napoleon determined to crush Blücher first, because he feared him, and then finish Wellington, and therefore he attacked Blücher's corps with his whole army and 240 pieces of artillery. Every foot was disputed. The village St Amand I have seen taken and retaken seven times. At 9 o'clock my light hussar regiment was ordered to break a French square, but we were received with such a rain of balls that we became separated. Lützow was taken prisoner.* Blücher's fine charger was here killed under him, and an officer of my regiment, Schneider, gave Blücher his own horse and saved himself. The French cuirassiers drove us before them, but we soon rallied and drove them back. At this moment Blücher was yet lying under his horse. Nastich, his aide de camp, had covered *him* with his cloak; after the French, driven before us, had passed, Nastich sprang forward, took the first horse by the bridle, and Blücher was saved. After 11 o'clock we left the field of this great battle and halted half an hour's distance from it. Exhausted, thirsty and hungry, I sucked clover flowers, halting in a large clover field. The French bivouac fires were before our eyes; neither party was conquered. Napoleon estimated our loss in the French bulletin [at]15,000 men killed; since no quarter was given on either side we were not troubled with many prisoners. Several of our brave generals fell here wounded.

The next morning, early on the 17th, we moved toward Wavre, ten miles from Genappe, where we bivouacked. The rain all night fell in torrents. In the afternoon we heard a brisk cannonade toward Quatre Bras. The English forces being posted in that neighbourhood, it was supposed that nobody could be engaged by Napoleon except them. To guard, however, lest my brigade might come between two fires, I was commanded to reconnoitre in that direction and make a report to General Treskow.† I took three picked men of our lancers, with a French guide, and rode in a dreadful storm in the direction of the thunder of the cannon. I fortunately struck the desired point. After inquiry of an English officer, at a picket, how the battle went, he informed me that the English army was obliged to retreat. This was good news for us.‡ After several hours I arrived safe

---

* Lützow was twice wounded and captured at Ligny but escaped after Waterloo.

† Major General von Treskow commanded the 1st Cavalry Brigade of the 1st Prussian Corps.

‡ Presumably this was good news because the armies could continue to coordinate their movements, as they were to such stunning effect at Waterloo.

at our bivouac and made my report to the old general, who was also glad to hear this news. He thanked me and I turned upon my heels.

At 2 o'clock in the morning of 18 June we broke up and marched towards Wavre, where Blücher's army concentrated itself. After a long and dreadfully hard march the whole day, in spite of the great battle of the 16th, and only one day rest, and privation for men and horses, we arrived at last in full trot at the field of battle at Mont St Jean towards 4 o'clock. Our brigade of four regiments of cavalry was commanded by the brave Major General von Folgersberg, Lützow having been taken prisoner on the 16th. Hard work for the Prussian army again. Wellington was almost beaten when we arrived, and we decided that great day. Had we arrived an hour later Napoleon would have had Wellington surrounded and defeated. At about 9 o'clock in the evening the battlefield was almost cleared of the French army. It was an evening no pen is able to picture: the surrounding villages yet in flames, the lamentations of the wounded of both armies, the singing for joy; no one is able to describe nor find a name to give to those horrible scenes. During the whole night we followed the enemy, and no one can form an idea of the quantity of cannon, baggage wagons, which were lying on the road along which the French retreated. Brandy, rice, chocolate, etc., in abundance fell into our hands. We also took Napoleon's carriage and amused ourselves with it. Among other things found in it we found Napoleon's proclamation in which he said, 'to dine at Brussels on the 18th' so certain he was to beat Wellington, not expecting old Blücher at Waterloo, on account of the dreadful conflict of the 16th.

At sunrise on the 19th we passed Genappe, and afterwards Quatre Bras, where Wellington was beaten on the 17th. Six miles beyond Quatre Bras, to the right of the road, we rested till afternoon. The heat was very severe. We marched forward again, and crossed the road between Fleurus and Gilly. The old grumbler General Treskow commanded our vanguard.

On the 20th we marched to Charleroi, and passed Chatelet, and crossed the river Sambre. There we went to the right and crossed the frontier of France.

On the morning of the 28th Prince William's dragoons* took two pieces of ordnance from the French near Crecy. Our first corps concentrated here, and our cavalry attacked Grouchy on the heights. Grouchy was beaten, and left the rest of the artillery in our hands; we followed them up as far as Nanteuil, where we bivouacked. My regiment of uhlans was put under the command of General Steinmetz†.

---

* Prince William of Russia.

† Major General Karl von Steinmetz.

The 29th, to Gran Drousie,* twelve miles from Paris, six miles from Montmartre. Ruined Chateau of St Denis; beautiful view to Paris. The next day was Ruhetag;† very hot and nothing to praise.

On 2 July we were relieved by the English and left to the right of St Denis, which was yet in the hands of the French, and proceeded to St Germain through Argenteuil, where I sold four horses. Here our army passed the river Seine On the 3rd to Meudon; bivouac in the vineyard; charming bivouac. At our arrival at Sèvres the French soon quit the bridge, which was still defended by them. The immense number of bivouac fires was a sight which no one can truly picture.

7 July. After a campaign of twenty-three days, in action continually, we entered Paris. My brigade, which always led the van during the numerous actions, was the first that entered Paris. Although the inhabitants hated the sight of the Prussians, it was astonishing to see the waving of white handkerchiefs at the windows in every street we passed. The following was the march into Paris: We arrived from Issy [les-Moulineaux] through the gate of the military school; crossed the Champ de Mars, over the Bridge of Jena to the Champs Élysées, Place de la Concorde, Quai des Tuileries, Quai du Louvre, Quai d'École, Quai de la Greve, Quai St Paul, Quai Marlanie, Quai Delertion, to the Place de la Bastille, to the Boulevard St Antoine, where we had to bivouac and rest on the pavement, with nothing to eat or drink.

On the 8th several of us, by permission, visited several places of note, the Garden of Plants, Museum of Anatomy, Museum of Natural History, the Palace of the Luxembourg, the Louvre, the picture galleries 1,400 feet long; to the Palais Royal, to the garden of the Tuileries and back. We witnessed the entrance of King Louis XVIII, an immensity of people; we joked in the Hotel de Nîmes.

The following day was Sunday, and after field church the Prussian troops were ordered into barracks. On the 10th the King of Prussia arrived. There was a dreadful fuss; on account of the unfriendly commotions in the capital on this occasion our cavalry had to patrol the streets all night.

On the 11th to the theatre; on the 18th to the very great opera *Castor and Pollux*. On the 14th to the Fabrique de Gobelins,‡ then to the Palais Luxembourg, the Pantheon, and the Catacombs with 2,400,000 bodies; the church of Notre Dame; the looking glass factory; Observatory; Hotel des Invalides, with 4,800 invalids; the Panorama; the Palais du Corps Legislatif, and back to the barracks.

---

* I cannot identify this village, but Siborne states that the 1st Corps was centred around Aulnay on 29 June.

† Rest day.

‡ The famous tapestry works on the Faubourg St Marcel.

On the 16th great parade, and after this field church. On the 22nd we had to leave Paris, to our great regret; but the soldier has to obey orders. We marched to Versailles: castle; splendid garden; orangery, Great and Small Trianon.

The 23rd to the village of Bazemont; *mittelmassige Qwartiere*.* The 24th to Bouafles on the Seine, and so on to Normandy, near Caen, towards the sea. Here we had first-rate quarters among the farmers, but only enjoyed them for two weeks, and then were ordered to Picardy, a poor country and poor people. Here we remained until the army was ordered home. I had better luck than others of my fellow officers, being commanded by Major General von Lützow, and worked in his bureau for two months, and had fine living, but had to write day and night. When we arrived, on our march home, near Versailles, I was ordered there with an officer to receive at this fortress, provision and forage for our troops. My quarter was in the hotel at the great docks. Here I made the acquaintance of a Dutch captain, with whom I spent many pleasant hours. Plenty of pleasure here, birthdays, punch parties and amusements of various kinds.

[Nieman returned to Bremen in early 1816.]

* Headquarters.

THE MEDICAL SERVICES

No. 38 From La Belle Alliance

Pflugk-Harttung's letter no. 96
Excerpt from the Brigade Orders of Colonel von Vincke about the conduct of the surgeons of the 5th Hanoverian Brigade at La Belle Alliance

Excerpts from the Brigade Orders

Arnonville, 4 July 1815

Every surgeon of the brigade will immediately report in writing:

a) Where he was during the battle on 18th June;
b) If he has been ordered by somebody to retreat, and if so, where to;
c) On what day he has returned to the brigade;
d) What has kept him from returning earlier.

As soon as these reports are received, the inquiry ordered by the general commander will be conducted.

St Denis, 12 July 1815

The surgeons will immediately submit through the brigade surgeon their explanatory report concerning their absence from the brigade since 16 June.

St Denis, 18 July 1815

The surgeons and assistant surgeons, who have not turned in until tomorrow morning at 9 o'clock their twice ordered explanation for their absence on 16th, 17th and 18th June, are to be placed under arrest and sent here by their commander.
E. Vincke, Colonel and Brigadier

No. 39 From La Belle Alliance

Pflugk-Harttung's letter no. 97

Report of the Brigade Surgeon Dr Lauprecht (Vincke's Brigade) about his conduct during and after the Battle of La Belle Alliance

In accordance with the Brigade Order of 4 July which ordered the surgeons of the brigade to answer in writing the following questions:

1 Where they had been during the battle on 18th June,
2 If they had been ordered by somebody to retreat, and if so, where to,
3 On what day they had returned to the brigade,
4 What has kept them from returning earlier.

I have the honour to properly respond with a simple and truthful account of my conduct from the beginning of the battle at 12 noon until the hour I was compelled to go from the battlefield to Brussels

(8 o'clock in the evening)

In regard to 1: At the beginning of the battle, I selected a small house in front of a small wood, next to a windmill and to the left of that place above Waterloo, a quarter hour behind the brigade, as the station where the wounded were to be sent. Colonel and Brigadier von Vincke gave his agreement when I informed him of this. I assigned Assistant Surgeon Adler to stay with the brigade on the battlefield to take care of transporting the wounded. The Assistant Surgeons Behrens, Oppermann, and Schröder I ordered to be at the dressing station; on my part, I planned to be alternately at the dressing station and the brigade, in order to properly oversee everything. What prompted me in particular to select the said location, which was hardly a quarter hour behind the brigade and protected from the fire of heavy artillery, according to my observations at the beginning of the battle, was that Brigade Surgeon Schulz of Best's Brigade had also set up his dressing station here, so that the surgeons of both brigades could mutually assist and help each other.

Shortly after I had made these arrangements which seemed the best to me, since I had no orders from the divisional surgeon and had no other instructions, when an Orange Nassau soldier came to the brigade and asked for help for a wounded officer of his regiment.* With the approval of Colonel and Brigadier von Vincke, I hurried through a rain of cannonballs to the wounded man and assured that he was placed on

* Apparently Major G. Hegmann, commander of the 3rd Battalion, 2nd Duchy of Nassau Regiment; early in the battle a cannon ball had smashed one of his legs. He died after unsuccessful amputation.

an available mattress. I then ordered the men transporting the wounded [officer] to carry him as gently as possible to the house selected as a dressing station. Since amputation of his lower leg would be necessary, I was unable to do this where I was, as neither he nor myself would be safe from the incoming cannon balls.

I then returned dutifully to the brigade on the assumption that there I would also find wounded men needing to be taken to the designated place. Since this was not the case, and most of the cannon balls were falling in the space between the just mentioned wounded officer and the brigade's battalions, I hurried on to the place designated for the wounded and instructed Assistant Surgeon Behrens to make sure of the careful transportation of the wounded [officer]. On arrival at the location to where the surgeons and medical pack horses had been ordered, I found neither surgeons nor medical pack horses, and not even the wounded officer. This was around 3 o'clock. In the opinion, that the surgeons and horses had moved nearer [to the brigade], I took the road the brigade had taken.* On the way, I spent time in dressing the wounds of some English and Scottish soldiers who were lying about. I then met Major von Rheden,† who was going to the brigade, and I joined him, together with Assistant Surgeon Adler, who had also helped some of the wounded on the battlefield and had joined me. He affirmed to me that he also had searched in vain for the medical containers.

The brigade was now located on an elevation and had formed in square [only the Hameln and Gifhorn Battalions, 5th Brigade]. Since the cannon balls passed over it and caused no casualties, Assistant Surgeon Adler and I rode to the rear in order to find the medical pack horses. After we had spent about a quarter of an hour at the square (until about half past four). As we were unable to locate the pack horses despite all our searching, Mr Adler and I returned to the brigade that still stood on the same elevation where we last had left it. There were no wounded to be treated. Since there was no use for us to remain behind the brigade at a dangerous location hit by many cannon balls, we went to a locality, to the side of the brigade and above Waterloo. On the way, we met Assistant Surgeon Behrens. Here in a small house, we were dressing the incoming wounded, mostly British, who were unable to find their own surgeons. After having taken care of these wounded who were moving on, we went to the wood near Waterloo. I was leading my horse who was limping with two legs

* The 5th Hanoverian Brigade had been ordered to a position near the Brussels highway from its original one at the extreme left flank.

† Commander of the Hildesheim Battalion, that, together with the Peine Battalion, 5th Hanoverian Brigade, had been marched back from the battlefield by Major Count von Westphalen, Commander of the Peine Battalion, due to a misunderstood order.

from having a spent cannon ball pass through between his legs, and in the pressing crowds I soon lost the Assistant Surgeons Adler and Behrens. Again, I now wanted to join the brigade which, according to what one of the wounded told me, was now located in rear of Waterloo, but I was prevented from doing so, being pushed back by the retiring cavalry and fast moving artillery wagons. The best I could do now, I believed, was to await the wounded, and remained until 8 o'clock on the road that leads from Waterloo to Brussels through the wood. Here, I put dressings on the wounded that were arriving and those already lying there.

In regard to 2: I did not receive an order from anybody to go to the rear; I did this on my own initiative because I thought this to be the best I could do. I had not received any instructions from a higher ranking military surgeon. Despite all my inquiries, I was unable to learn where the senior surgeon of the division was located whom I was to join according to my instructions. There was nothing I could do without instruments and medical supplies, which I hoped to find again in Brussels.

What prompted me primarily to go to Brussels, was the following: When I proceeded in a gap between masses of a disorderly mass of retiring cavalry and infantry (the crowding was getting worse from the artillery wagons), there was some shouting that French cavalry had cut them off and was pursuing them. This clamouring from the rearmost fugitives was to urge the more forward ones to move faster. At this moment, wounded Captain Bertrap came by on a wagon and shouted at me to hurry to the rear, confirming the assertions of the wounded and fugitives. Not being of any use, I thought it made no sense for me to remain and be made a prisoner or be maltreated. This retiring was so bad that several men were pushed down to the ground.

In regard to 3 and 4: I arrived at Brussels sick and with my legs swollen up to my knees, which can be verified by impartial witnesses. The swelling of my legs was caused by a severe cold and wetting while in bivouac, and partly also because from Waterloo onward I had to lead my horse, that limped with two legs, on the bad road and thus had to wade through the mud and was often kicked by the fugitives. On arrival in Brussels, unable to move any further from exhaustion and weakness, I sank down next to a house on Meibom Street, where I had my horse taken away by force by a Highland Scotsman. On the 20th I drove to Antwerp to pick up another horse because it was impossible for me to join the brigade by walking. On the 21st, I went to Waterloo to look for the brigade, but since it had left without trace, I went to Brussels where I was advised to follow the road to Mons because that was where the brigade was said to have gone. I wandered about from Mons until the 25th, when I finally found the brigade again at a village, as it was about

to break camp in the morning.
Lauprecht, Dr, Brigade Surgeon

No. 40 From La Belle Alliance

Pflugk-Harttung's letter no. 98
Official Questions addressed to Brigade Surgeon Dr Lauprecht about his conduct on 18 and 19 June

St Denis, 20 July 1815

The following questions were presented to Doctor and Brigade Surgeon Lauprecht.

a To whom has he reported or has made known his absence, after the brigade had on 18th June left its first position, and consequently a new location for dressing the wounded would have to be selected and be made known to the brigadier.

b Why has he instructed Junior Assistant Surgeon Thiele, Hameln Battalion, to await information in Brussels on the whereabouts of the brigade, instead of ordering him to immediately follow the brigade.

E. Vincke, Colonel and Brigadier

No. 41 From La Belle Alliance

Pflugk-Harttung's letter no. 99
Brigade Surgeon Dr Lauprecht to Colonel von Vincke about his conduct during the battle of La Belle Alliance

St Denis, 20 July 1815

To His Excellency Colonel and Brigadier von Vincke

In response to Your Excellency's questions addressed to me today, I have the honour to answer most obediently:

The originally designated location was also still suitable for dressing [the wounded], after the brigade had changed from the first position and had formed a square on an elevation. I therefore did not consider it necessary to select a new dressing station, and obediently report this to the brigadier. That I, in fact, had visited the square twice, together with Assistant Surgeon Adler, is well known both to Major von Rheden, as well as to Lieutenant Wundenberg and other officers of the brigade. I did not report my presence because there was no reason to do so that I knew of, and I did not notice anyone wounded. By the way, the fact that the medical containers and surgeons were not at the designated place was made known with a loud voice by Assistant Surgeon Adler and also by myself.

I did not send Junior Assistant Surgeon Thiele immediately back to the battalion, because I believed I would receive certain information on the whereabouts of the brigade, and did not want to send this young man out into the wide world without specific instructions. I was also firmly convinced that he would reach the battalion sooner upon the receipt of correct information than without it, as he happened to be in a country where he was unfamiliar with the area. Moreover, Mr Thiele claimed that he was weak and unable to walk, of which I convinced myself, this being the reason for my telling him to alternately ride and walk with me on the way to the brigade.

Dr Lauprecht, Brigade Surgeon

No. 42 From La Belle Alliance

Pflugk-Harttung's letter no. 100

Report of the Assistant Surgeon Behrens of the Hanoverian Peine Battalion about his conduct during and after the battle of La Belle Alliance

Arnoville, 6 July 1815

In the battle of 18 June, I stayed with the battalion until the beginning of the firing at the square; I then went to the place designated as a dressing station. After ordering the orderly to wait for me here with the medical supplies, I returned to the battalion to make the place known where the wounded were to be dressed. Having done that, Brigade Surgeon Doctor Lauprecht ordered me to search for a severely wounded Nassau major and to transport him to the field hospital. I was unable to find that major after a lengthy search and, after reporting this to Brigade Surgeon Doctor Lauprecht, I returned to the dressing station but found the place deserted.* Assuming that the men with the medical supplies had retired to Waterloo, I stayed here with Assistant Surgeon Adler of the Gifhorn Battalion to handle the dressing of the wounded who might yet arrive from the square and take them back to Waterloo. Later on, I went to Waterloo myself to obtain medications and bandages for dressing, but, again, I was disappointed here also. After searching in vain through all of Waterloo, I turned back to go to the battalion. On the way, I met Brigade Surgeon Doctor Lauprecht and Assistant Surgeon Adler who came from the square to do more dressing [of the wounded]. I returned

* Pflugk-Harttung's footnote: Marginal note by Colonel von Vincke: 'An interrogation of the orderly will be undertaken immediately.'

with them to the first houses of Waterloo, where we started dressing. After having dressed a number of English and Hanoverians, we were not only completely upset by the retiring cavalry but were carried away ourselves.* This might have happened towards 8 o'clock. We soon lost Brigade Surgeon Doctor Lauprecht in the pressing crowds in which we were always forced to move on the way to Brussels. About one hour before Brussels, I met Junior Assistant Surgeon Jecklin and the orderly with the medical supplies. I was kept from returning to the battalion at this point, partly because my horse had lost a horseshoe during the hasty ride and was limping badly. Since there was no farrier to be found in the whole area, nothing was left me but to proceed to Brussels if I wanted to speedily follow the battalion. Then I met Captain von Bertrap of the Peine Battalion, who had been wounded, and he induced me all the more to hurry to Brussels, where I put a dressing on the captain. I was kept from returning from Brussels to the battalion at this late hour by my concern of failing to find it in the darkness. Early on the next morning, on the 19th June, I left Brussels together with Junior Assistant Surgeon Jecklin. After we had put dressings on a number of English and Hanoverian wounded, and had settled the badly wounded Major von Leue, of the Gifhorn Battalion, on one of my stretchers for his further transport, I returned that same morning, on 19 June, to the battalion.†

T. Behrens, Assistant Surgeon Peine Battalion

No. 43 From La Belle Alliance

Pflugk-Harttung's letter no. 101

Report of the Junior Assistant Surgeon Thiele of the Hanoverian Hameln Battalion about his conduct during and after the battle of La Belle Alliance

Saint Denis, 11 July 1815

On the day of the battle, 18 June 1815, I stayed with the brigade, together with the other surgeons of the brigade under the direction of Brigade Surgeon Lauprecht until the moment that the Hameln Battalion formed square, after it had moved from the left flank to the centre of the army. Here, Brigade Surgeon Lauprecht ordered me to go to the dressing station, set up next to a windmill behind the earlier surgeons of the brigade, who were already there, [engaged] in dressing [the wounded]. Before I arrived at that location, I gradually met many [more] fugitives who told me that

* Pflugk-Harttung's footnote: Marginal note: 'The Assistant Surgeon Behrens obviously admits here to his guilt of not having joined the brigade, even though this would have been possible in any case.'

† Pflugk-Harttung's footnote: Marginal note: 'This is correct.' Followed by the signature: St Denis, 19 July 1815. E. Vincke, Colonel and Brigadier.

the allied army was near defeat and dispersed and retiring in haste. These assertions were confirmed when I arrived at the dressing station and found neither surgeons nor wounded, and everybody that I met told me that everything was on the move towards Brussels. Since all of the medical pack horses had been led away and I therefore could not be of any use at this place, and since I could not expect to find either the brigade surgeon or the battalion itself on the battlefield, I considered it my duty to follow as quickly as possible the departed ambulance in the hope there to find my superiors again. When I arrived in Brussels at 11 o'clock (having left the battlefield around 7 o'clock), it was impossible for me to still find the brigade surgeon anywhere. When I went to search for him the next morning, he himself came up to me by accident. I asked for instructions, whereupon he told me that he expected information from Doctor Adler of the Gifhorn Battalion about the location of the brigade; on my part I should still wait on Monday, the 19th, for this information that would allow me to return to the battalion . . .

Thiele, Junior Assistant Surgeon in the Hameln Battalion

Comments by the brigadier:

St Denis, 19 July 1815

If the Junior Assistant Surgeon Thiele had remained on the battlefield until 7 o'clock in the evening, which is not believable, then he still failed in his duty by not showing up at the brigade, thus did not comply with his assignment. Moreover, he does not provide well founded reasons at all for his retiring to Brussels.

E. Vincke, Colonel and Brigadier

No. 44 From La Belle Alliance

Pflugk-Harttung's letter no. 102

Report of the Assistant Surgeon Oppermann of the Hanoverian Hameln Battalion about his conduct during and after the battle of La Belle Alliance

5 July 1815

Only after the cannonade on the left wing had lasted for a while did I go to the windmill located behind the army, in accordance with the order from Brigade Surgeon Lauprecht, and set up a dressing station together with Assistant Surgeon Schröder, in order there to treat our wounded. To better serve the purpose of the facility, I got in touch with Brigade Surgeon Schulze.* As I was about to have a special room filled with straw, etc., for our patients, a Brunswick hussar (if I am not mistaken) arrived

* Of the 4th Hanoverian Brigade.

with an order from a general for a Brunswick surgeon who was also there just then, putting a dressing on the wounded hand of an officer, that he was to go immediately to the rear with his ambulance. Hereupon I went outside the said house to see whether the order I just had heard was indeed in regard to a retreat. Brigade Surgeon Schulze came up to me at once and told me: 'We have to go back, as all appearances seem to demand'. After I had gone back for ten minutes, I met other surgeons, with whom I stayed at one spot for half an hour. The commotion increased all the time, there were military personnel on horseback appearing every minute who most anxiously announced the threatening danger shouting: 'Go back, go back, move on, move on!' I had to make an instant decision; in the absence of any instructions or directions, I chose to join the other surgeons and to go to Brussels. I felt it was my duty to at least secure my medical supplies in order to have them available when our army was again moving forward. Whether the danger was quite that threatening was impossible for me to assess. A half hour before Brussels I lost my medical supplies in the extreme crowding, despite all my careful attention. I made all possible efforts to find them again, but without success. On the following morning, I searched in Brussels for some time in the hope of finding them, but nobody had noticed them. I immediately set off on the march back; but since my horse had a leg injured above the horseshoe and was limping badly, I only arrived at the battlefield in the afternoon. Here I was without any resources and unable to find our brigade at that place. I considered it my foremost duty to follow it without fail, and, upon the advice that I received, went again to the battlefield past Waterloo. After I had moved on for two hours, I was informed differently by a soldier of the Hedemann Brigade,* that, in fact, our brigade had moved off to the right. I followed that direction but was always given incorrect information. On the second day, I met His Excellency Count von Kielmansegge. I asked him for advice, but he assured me that he himself did not know where our brigade might be; I should stay with him, and we would probably find it. This would probably have been the case on 21 June; but once again I was misdirected by an officer of the English [King's German] Legion and others, who claimed that our brigade had marched off at Bavay and now was ahead of the troops that had stayed there. I hurried forward in all haste to reach it; but I found, after having travelled for 4 hours, that I had searched in vain. On the next morning, I learned from a soldier, I do not know from what brigade, that our brigade still had its quarters in the just mentioned town, whereupon I turned back immediately and arrived there on the

* The 4th Hanoverian Brigade (Best's) had been commanded by Colonel Hartwig Hedemann in April 1815.

morning of 22 June at 9 o'clock.
Assistant Surgeon Oppermann of the Hameln Battalion

Comment by the Brigadier:

St Denis, 19 July 1815

The Assistant Surgeon Oppermann is guilty to a greater degree than all the others because he had left the first location designated as a dressing station without an order from me that he would have had to follow. In this way, he probably caused all the other surgeons of the brigade, as well as the horses with the medical containers, to be scattered.
E. Vincke, Colonel and Brigadier

No. 45 From La Belle Alliance

Pflugk-Harttung's letter no. 103

Report of the Assistant Surgeon Oppermann of the Hanoverian Hameln Battalion about his conduct during and after the battle of La Belle Alliance

18 July 1815

On 16 and 17 June, I stayed with the battalion all the time. On the 18th, after the cannonade on the left wing had gone on for some time, I went to the windmill, located behind the army on a hill, in accordance with an order from Brigade Surgeon Lauprecht, to there set up together with Assistant Surgeon Schröder, a dressing station for the wounded. To better serve the purpose of the facility, I got in touch there with Brigade Surgeon Schulze. As I was about to prepare the house at that location to serve as a field hospital, a Brunswick hussar (I believe that I am not mistaken) arrived and brought an order from a general whose name I do not recall to a surgeon, who was also at this house and just then was putting a dressing on the wounded hand of an officer, to immediately go to the rear with his ambulance. I went outside that house to get some men to help me with turning it into a field hospital when Brigade Surgeon Schulze came up and said to me: 'We cannot stay here, we have to go back.' As the commotion was increasing considerably, we went back for a few minutes, but I then halted with my bandages, etc., in the wood on the side of the road. The tumult eventually became so violent and severe that one was torn along. At every other moment, again another military person on horseback would announce the closeness of the threatening danger by loud shouts: 'Go back, go back!' I myself, who had never been exposed to such scenes and having no information nor instruction, had to decide at this moment what to do next. I then believed that my foremost duty would be to secure my medical supplies and horses as best as possible, and therefore to go to Brussels, and have them available if our army would ever go back that far. Half an hour before Brussels, I lost my horses with the medical supplies despite all my efforts and the risk to my life.

The next morning, I searched for them everywhere in Brussels, but one of my colleagues had already taken them. Afterwards, I immediately set out on my return march to the army; however, my horse had suffered an injury above the hoof and was limping severely so that I was only able to arrive at the battlefield in the afternoon. I did not find my brigade there, but followed it immediately, as I considered this to be my foremost duty . . .

Oppermann, Assistant Surgeon of the Hameln Battalion

Comment by the Brigadier:

St Denis, 19 July 1815

The present report exonerates Assistant Surgeon Oppermann just as insufficiently, as did his report of 3 July.

E. Vincke, Colonel and Brigadier

No. 46 From La Belle Alliance

Pflugk-Harttung's letter no. 104

Report of the Junior Assistant Surgeon Jecklin of the Hanoverian Peine Battalion about his conduct during and after the battle of La Belle Alliance

On 18 June, I was on the battlefield near Waterloo, until the square was fired at by the enemy; I then went with Assistant Surgeon Behrens and the medical supplies to the location where the wounded were to be dressed. The assistant surgeon returned from here to the square to inform the battalion where the dressing station was to be set up. But even here, it was impossible to dress [the wounded] because of the many strikes by cannon balls. I therefore went with Brigade Surgeon Schulze and the Assistant Surgeons Bendschneider,* Oppermann, and Schröder, whom I had met there, as far as the windmill. We needed to leave also that place, partly because of the artillery fire, partly because of the information from an English officer that we could not stay there as the enemy was approaching. We then moved into the wood to the right of Waterloo. However, the pressing from the crowds became so great that we were unable to stay there for very long. I lost the medical pack horse because the orderly had left together with the Assistant Surgeons Oppermann and Schröder, who had been torn away by the retreating crowd. During

* I have been unable to identify this doctor nor the unit to which he was attached.

my search for the medical pack horses I found a number of wounded in the first village, whose wounds I then dressed. Afterwards, I hurried off after the pack horses, and after a lengthy search I found the medical pack horses of the Hameln and Gifhorn Battalions. On my continued search, I came to a house where there were a number of wounded that I put dressings on. A short time later, the Assistant Surgeons Adler and Behrens arrived; the latter's horse was limping badly. It was too late for turning back, and we believed that we might fail to find our battalion.

On the way, we met wounded Captain Bertrab and went with him to Brussels, where we remained until daybreak. We then hurried towards the battalion and arrived there the same morning of the 19th. We put dressings on a number of wounded on our way.

J. F. Jecklin, Junior Assistant Surgeon, Peine Battalion

Comment by the Brigadier:

St Denis, 19 July 1815

Although Junior Assistant Surgeon Jecklin has not provided a fully acceptable excuse for his retiring to Brussels, he was, however, the first to return to the brigade on the 19th, at the place, where most of the wounded French had been gathered during the battle and who were without a surgeon and he was most active in providing those men, as well as a number of Englishmen and Prussians, with dressings.

E. Vincke, Colonel and Brigadier

No. 47 From La Belle Alliance

Pflugk-Harttung's letter no. 105

Report of the Assistant Surgeon Schröder of the Hanoverian Hildesheim Battalion about his conduct during and after the Battle of La Belle Alliance

During the battle on the 18th, I, the undersigned, was with the battalion while the artillery fire had lasted for some time and until the brigade had formed square. I was then ordered by Brigade Surgeon Lauprecht to go immediately to the windmill near Waterloo and to set up, together with several surgeons, a dressing station. I went there at once, and, by the time of my arrival, the other surgeons, who were given that assignment earlier, had been forced to leave the originally designated place because of the heavy artillery fire. Because the cannonade became more concentrated towards this spot, and even rendered the second selected place too insecure for our purpose and also being too far removed from our brigade, we were forced to leave this place on the order of an English artillery officer who screamed at the top of his voice: 'Go back, go back!'

At this moment, as a headlong retreat erupted, with everybody falling over each other and shouting 'Go back, go back!' We were torn along by this mass towards Brussels. It was impossible to escape because of the numerous artillery and cavalry, which overran each other. I stayed in Brussels for several hours to await the end of the retreat which still became more immense. Towards evening, I attempted to return to the battalion, although the retreat had not ended yet, but was unable to pass through the retreating crowd which was getting still stronger. I then had to turn around and spend this night in Brussels . . .

Schröder, Assistant Surgeon of the Hildesheim Battalion*

Comment by the Brigadier:

St Denis, 19 July 1815

I cannot accept at all the excuses of Assistant Surgeon Schröder as valid or exonerating for his going back to Brussels and, in particular, for his failure to at least return to the brigade in the early morning of the 19th. It also appears that he did not take care of the medical containers at all. The orderly who has been leading the medical pack horse shall be interrogated immediately.

E. Vincke, Colonel and Brigadier

No. 48 From La Belle Alliance

Pflugk-Harttung's letter no. 106

Court protocol concerning the conduct of Brigade Surgeon Lauprecht on his flight from La Belle Alliance to Brussels

In Session, St Denis, 19 July 1815

At the order of Colonel and Brigadier von Vincke, Captain von Bertrab appeared and deposed as follows: That his name is Herrmann von Bertrab, born at Markoldendorf,† 28 years of age, and has served as a captain in the Peine Battalion for about 15 months.

At about 8 o'clock in the evening of the 18th of last month, as he came back from the battle wounded, he encountered in the wood on the highway to Brussels the Brigade Surgeon Lauprecht, who was walking and leading his limping horse. He then had, of course, complained to this surgeon about his wound, who had answered that he could not help him because he had no equipment on hand. There was no further conversation and they were soon separated by the pressing crowds; in

* Pflugk-Harttung's footnote: A similar Report exists from Junior Assistant Surgeon Bornträger of the Hildesheim Battalion.

† Markoldendorf can be found 3 miles west of Einbeck in Germany.

particular, neither had he told him that the French cavalry was pursuing them, nor had he advised him to go back.

On the highway, there was an intermingling of individual cavalrymen and foot soldiers and artillerymen. Some officers had shouted: 'Stand fast, you fellows!', whereupon a half squadron rode back. Some soldiers had said: 'The French are coming!' others responded, saying that they would defend themselves.

*Praelect[is] et ratih[abitis] dep[ositis]** appeared Brigade Surgeon Lauprecht, as requested.

He was told that Captain von Bertrab unreservedly denies having told him on the 18th of last month on the highway to Brussels that the French cavalry was pursuing them, or having advised him to go back. He [Lauprecht] was requested to explain this matter, whereupon he stated the following:

On the 18th of last month, an officer wearing a grey coat and yellow sash had encountered him and shouted at him: 'I am wounded; for God's sake, save yourself, the French cavalry has cut us off and is pursuing us!' At that time, dusk was about to set in, and that officer was at least 12 paces away from him. Being somewhat short sighted, he had not closely looked at his face, but had believed to have recognised Captain von Bertrab by his voice. He had a very feint recollection, by the way, that he had also told that officer, who was sitting on a wagon, that he had no equipment on hand.

Captain von Bertrab's rejoinder was that on the 18th of last month he had made the entire trip to Brussels on horseback and had worn a grey cape.

Quibus praelect[is] et ratih[abitis] dim[ittitur] ut supra in fidem.†

August von Hartmann Bacmeister Major, Adjutant

No. 49 From La Belle Alliance

Pflugk-Harttung's letter no. 107

Protocol of the interrogation of the Orderlies Hansen, Brandes, and Baymann concerning their conduct on their flight from the battlefield to Brussels

In Session, St Denis, 20 July 1815

Today appeared, as requested, Orderly Hansen of the Peine Battalion and stated, *praevia seria admonitione de veritate dicenda*‡ as follows:

* Latin: After the statements had been read and approved.

† Latin: Having been read to them and approved by them, they were discharged, the above being correct.

‡ Latin: After a serious warning beforehand about being truthful.

That his name is Christian Hansen, born at Schrum,* 23 years of age, and serves since last Easter as orderly in charge of the medical pack horses of the Peine Battalion. He was now interrogated.

Question: Why did he, in the battle of the 18th of last month, leave the place that he had been assigned as his station at the beginning of same?

Answer: On the 18th of last month at about 4 o'clock in the afternoon, the Junior Assistant Surgeon Jecklin of the Peine Battalion, who was with him at the dressing station without Assistant Surgeon Behrens being present, had told him: He should follow him with his horses and stay with him. Thereupon the junior assistant surgeon had walked ahead, and he had followed him with the horses and medical containers. Together with the two surgeons of the Hildesheim Battalion and the orderlies and medical pack horses of the Hameln and Gifhorn Battalions, they had set out on the road to Brussels, where they had arrived at about 9 o'clock in the evening. Moreover, he would be willing to affirm under oath his statement given today.

His praelect[is] et ratih[abitis] dim[ittitur].†

Thereafter, Orderly Brandes was told to step forward, was admonished to tell the truth, whereupon he stated the following:

That his name was Jürgen Heinrich Brandes, born at Rottenbuch, County Möhnesee, 28 years of age, serves for about 15 months now as orderly in charge of the medical pack horses of the Gifhorn Battalion. He was interrogated:

Question: Why, on the 18th of last month, did he leave the place that had been assigned to him as his station at the beginning of the battle?

Answer: Two surgeons, whom he did not know, had ordered him on the 18th of last month to go to the site at the windmill. A surgeon in a red uniform with a yellow collar, whose name he did not know, had ordered him at about 3 o'clock in the afternoon to stay with his horses with the orderlies and medical pack horses of the Hameln and Peine Battalions. As there was no surgeon present of the Gifhorn Battalion, he then followed with his horses the other orderlies as they left the dressing station with their horses. They all of them arrived in Brussels in the evening when it was already dark. He could affirm all of this under oath.

---

* Schrum is in Schleswig Holstein.

† Latin: After this had been read and approved, he was discharged.

NOT AT WATERLOO

Foreign Veteran Battalion

No. 50 Major Georg von Coulon*

From J. Kannicht, All of This Because of Napoleon: From the war diary of George von Coulon, Major in the Royal German Legion, and the letters of his wife Henriette 1806–1815, *Bernard & Graefe Verlag, Koblenz, 1986*

Georg von Coulon on information he received from others on the action at Quatre Bras and the Battle of Waterloo.†

The Brussels coach did not arrive here from Brussels on the 18th because the route between Enghien and Brussels had been blocked by masses of troops, baggage wagons, etc. My host still received the newspaper by way of Mons. According to that newspaper, severe fighting had taken place on the 15th and 17th in the area of Quatre Bras, some 5 lieues‡ distance from Brussels, after which the allies had remained in possession of the battlefield. It is believed that the action will be resumed today. It seems the allies had great losses in dead and wounded, since the commandant at Brussels has issued a proclamation that a General Hospital will be set up in Brussels and that all residents are requested to provide bedding, dressing material, etc.; otherwise the wounded will be lodged in their houses. May God grant that the allies will prevail.

On 19 June until the afternoon, only sad news arrived about the allies, and it was said that the French were only 3 hours away from Brussels. Towards evening, however, it became clear that this information was false;

* George Coulon, Beamish no. 1,175, served with the KGL serving in the Baltic and Mediterranean throughout the wars and in the Netherlands with the Veteran Battalion. He went on half pay on 25 July 1815 and died at Stade in 1827.

† This report, written during and immediately after the campaign is a useful example of the reports prevalent behind the front throughout the campaign, with its evidence of misinformation and false rumours causing extreme consternation within the eagerly anticipating and frightened populace.

‡ About 15 miles.

the ringing of all the church bells announced to the public important and agreeable news and the prevailing consternation changed to transports of joy. We learned from the local governor who had received a despatch from Brussels and from an English engineer officer who had been sent off from the army and had taken part in the battle, that the enemy army under Bonaparte had advanced to Charleroi on the 16th and, after driving back the Prussian advance posts, had taken possession of this city. In response to this news, the Duke of Wellington had our 1st, 2nd, 3rd, and 4th Divisions assemble near Enghien; the Prussian army had moved closer to ours.

On the 17th, the Brunswick Corps was ordered to advance together with the 1st Division and attack the enemy at Charleroi. This was done, but the enemy held on to his position and many men were killed, as was also the Duke of Brunswick. In the meantime, the astute Duke of Wellington had the army move ahead, and on the 18th at 12 o'clock noon, the battle began to rage near Quatre Bras [clearly should be Waterloo] and lasted until 9 o'clock in the evening. The Prussian army arrived at 4 o'clock and took part in deciding the outcome of this day. The enemy was put to flight everywhere. The English officer said that both sides had fought hard, and that the French cuirassiers and lancers had charged our infantry three times, but that they were repulsed each time, also, that the enemy had lost 110 cannon and a large number of dead and wounded. By the time the officer left the army, more than 7,000 prisoners had been taken, etc., etc.

Late this evening, news arrived from Brussels that 150 of the enemy's guns had been captured, and that he was in full flight and was pursued by Wellington. We will learn more about this tomorrow and also about the losses on our side which were said to be quite significant in both officers and soldiers. Two English generals were killed, and Earl Uxbridge, who commanded the cavalry, had lost a leg. The losses of the legion are not yet known. I am afraid that many brave officers and soldiers have lost their lives, as also among the Hanoverians. Thank God this first battle has been a disaster for that scoundrel; the enemy's spirits will be dampened, and ours will be raised all the greater.

If the Russian and the Imperial [Austrian] troops are lucky in a similar way, it is to be hoped that Bonaparte's end will be near, even though many more men will have to die until then.

On 20 June official bulletins from Brussels announced that the enemy army was fleeing and was pursued by both our troops and the Prussians. On their part, the Prussians have captured 60 cannon, and it is estimated that the allies have taken 12,000 prisoners.

At noon today, Lieutenant Weyhe[*] of the 8th Battalion arrived here unexpectedly from the army to visit his wife for a few hours. He confirmed that the French army had been beaten completely, but asserted also that the allies had had heavy losses. He told me that, of the 8th Battalion, Captains Voigt and Westernhagen and Lieutenant Mahrenholz[†] had been killed, and that Lieutenant Colonel Schröder, Captain Rougemont, Lieutenants Brinckman, Sattler and Moreau[‡] had been wounded, and that it had lost many of its non-commissioned officers and soldiers. He had also learned that Colonel Ompteda had been killed and that his Brigade Major Einem[§] had been severely wounded, also that Colonel Du Plat had been seriously wounded. Captain Goeben of the 1st Light Battalion and Major Bösewiel of the 2nd Light Battalion had been killed.[¶] He did not know what had happened at the other battalions since he had been ordered to take wounded men to Brussels immediately after the battle.

---

* Lieutenant Charles Ferdinand von Weyhe, Beamish no. 708.

† Captain Augustus William von Voigt, Beamish no. 982, Captain Thilo von Westernhagen, Beamish no. 992, and Lieutenant William von Marenholz, Beamish no. 998, were all killed at Waterloo.

‡ Lieutenant Colonel Schröder, 2nd Line, KGL, Beamish no. 1018, died of his wounds on 22 June 1815; Captain Charles Emanuel William Rougemont, Beamish no. 702; Lieutenants Julius Brinkmann, Beamish no. 698, Johann Christian Sattler, Beamish no. 711, and Ensign William Moreau, Beamish no. 724.

§ Captain Gotfried von Einem, KGL, Beamish no. 3, was attached to 2nd KGL Infantry Brigade.

¶ Captain Augustus Alexander Von Goeben, Beamish no. 993, and Major Adolphus Bösewiel, Beamish no. 975, were both killed at Waterloo.

APPENDIX 1

Evidence of Halkett's Capture of General Cambronne

Descriptions by witnesses, with explanatory text

By an unknown author

A French general, whose name is Cambronne, I believe, was with the French Guards as they were retiring, and who made strong efforts to bring the battalions to a halt and back to order . . . Our Brigadier, Colonel Halkett, noticed this, and, with unequalled intrepidity, rode through the French tirailleurs, who provided cover to the retiring columns, to this general and brought him along, despite his strong resistance, before the length of the line through the enemy tirailleurs to make him his prisoner.

Ensign Heinrich Bergmann, 2nd Line Battalion, KGL

It was 8 o'clock . . . the Hanoverian Infantry Bataillon Osnabrück, which under the leadership of Colonel Hugh Halkett had assisted the brigade (Adams) by protecting the latter's flank, met, when arriving at the plateau of Belle Alliance, the First Chasseur Regiment of the French Imperial Guard under General Cambronne's command which retreated in good order.

Halkett, at the head of the Osnabrückers, called upon the French to surrender, but as Cambronne, who accompanied the last company of his regiment on foot urged his men to resist, Halkett gave orders to fire. The French there upon accelerated their steps, but General Cambronne, probably too proud to run, was overtaken and made prisoner by Halkett who rode up to him at full speed.

Lieutenant Richers, Osnabrück Landwehr Battalion

An officer of the Osnabrück Battalion, Lieutenant Richers, later colonel and commander of the 2nd Hanoverian Infantry Regiment, reports:

I was now in front, and was able to observe, and the following has vividly been impressed in my memory . . . A high-ranking officer, accompanied by two other mounted officers, was particularly active in his efforts to bring the Old Guard again to a halt. He could be seen encouraging them while riding back and forth and our men had already repeatedly been told to fire at those riders. The horse of the high ranking officer eventually fell down after being struck by a bullet. The rider was lying under the horse and was not immediately able to free himself. We now shouted at Colonel

Halkett who was riding between our front ranks that the particular officer in the distinctive uniform, on whom he had kept his eyes, had fallen. As soon as the colonel had seen this, he drew his sabre, set the spurs to his horse, and rushed at the gallop towards the rider on the ground, leaving fugitives to his right and left, and thus in fact, being in the middle of the enemy. As the colonel approached the fallen rider, he had already freed himself from the horse and stood upright, I believed to have seen how the colonel slashed at him. All our men nearby and I myself ran towards the scene because the colonel was obviously in the greatest peril, as he could be killed from all around by a bullet or the thrust of a bayonet. Still, none of the Frenchmen had any time left to save their general, and the words '*sauve qui peut*' were of the utmost significance here, because even the general's mounted companions had galloped off. At the moment that the general had become the colonel's prisoner, the colonel gripped him by the collar and dragged him alongside his horse in our direction. I and three or four privates were the first to approach them. As we reached them, the colonel halted with his prisoner, turned him loose, and asked him who he was. The general was bleeding copiously from a head wound, blood was flowing all over his face, and after wiping the blood from his mouth with his hands he answered: '*Je suis le général Cambronne*.' I am unable to say whether Cambronne's wound was caused by a slash from Colonel Halkett or by a bullet; we just halted there for a brief moment, and then at the colonel's command, all of us rushed forward. Late in the evening, after the battalion had come to a halt, I heard that Sergeant Führing and three men had escorted General Cambronne to Brussels. Führing had later often told us about this escort episode, and that Cambronne had given him his watch and money pouch; he had also asked that his epaulettes be taken off because he was well known in Brussels and would not want to be recognised there as a prisoner.

Sergeant Führing, Osnabrück Landwehr Battalion

Sergeant Führing of the Osnabrück Battalion, later a janitor at the consistory or church council in Osnabrück, to whom Halkett had handed over his prisoner for transportation, no officer being available, has also recorded his experiences at Waterloo. I pick out the following from his narrative:

Alerted by repeated shouts, I saw at a distance our brave and bold Colonel Halkett, who always stayed near us, engaged in a fight with the enemy general; I hurried there, held the tip of my *Hirschfänger* [short sabre] against the chest of our colonel's adversary, who immediately dropped his sword to the ground, shouting, '*Pardon Monsieur!*' The prisoner had been wounded above one of his eyes, and I heard from our colonel's conversation with the general that the latter said that he was a Brigade General [Major General] of the Imperial Old Guard.

In this way, the general became our prisoner due to the boldness of the brigadier colonel who surveyed everything with his calm and imperturbable determination and personally hurried to the spots of greatest danger. It was obvious that the prisoner could not be freed by his own men if one takes into account that they were heavily pressed in their battle with us and the Scottish infantrymen.*

Being put in charge [of him] by Colonel Halkett, I then took away the prisoner, together with three of our men whom I myself had selected. We might just have left the range of the firing, when the prisoner handed me his watch and money pouch

* The 71st Foot were part of Adams's brigade.

with the words '*Tenez, Monsieur*'; he later gave me his golden epaulettes and his aiguillette. I kept the watch, the money I shared with my comrades and the other objects I returned to the prisoner on the advice of other officers even though he refused to accept them . . .

He follows with a description of how an unauthorised individual, 'an officer with a detachment of 30 men', tried to take the prisoner away from him, how he refused to surrender him and how two Brunswick hussar officers came to his assistance in this critical situation. He then continues:

Towards 11 to 12 o'clock in the evening, I delivered the prisoner to the hussars near Brussels who were in charge of collecting prisoners and, after taking leave from General Cambronne, returned with my three comrades to our brothers-in-arms, whom we met the next morning on the victory exalted battlefield near the farm of Belle Alliance.

Ensign Lyra, Osnabrück Landwehr Battalion

Ensign Lyra was his company's only remaining officer, who led it during the last phase of the battle, and he has commented on, and confirmed, Führing's account. But he believes that he had to insist on his authority as company commander, as he writes:

It may be true that Führing held his *Hirschfänger* against General Cambronne's chest, whose head had been wounded by a grazing bullet, whereas the latter had been arrested by Colonel Halkett and then been turned over to me. Although I will not dispute that Colonel Halkett had chosen the very brave and dependable Sergeant Führing to transport the prisoner, in as much as he had been of help in this bold feat, I nevertheless must object that Führing, without my knowledge and permission as his company commander, had gone off and had selected on his own three men to accompany him. Even a civilian would understand, moreover, a non-commissioned officer and soldiers may leave their company only if this is with the company commander's prior knowledge and permission, of which no exception can be made under any circumstances. I am therefore compelled to amend Führing's relation with respect to the full truth and in regard to this point that Colonel Halkett brought the prisoner to the left flank of our battalion, at whose outermost division I happened to be. It was from there that Sergeant Führing took the prisoner away with the men assigned by me and after he had received my permission.'

In supplementing the above descriptions it will not be without interest to learn more about Cambronne's watch and seal since they are a not unimportant proof regarding the present question. Führing relates as follows:

The watch was later sold to Registrar Lyra upon his repeated requests. Richers says:

I have often seen Cambronne's watch, both while it was in Führing's possession as well as after it was acquired by Ensign Lyra, who was later a chancellery registrar. It was a silver watch with an enamelled clock face, and Cambronne's coat of arms had been engraved on its exterior.

Lyra had been forced by health reasons to retire from military service in 1816 and had been employed as a chancellery registrar in Osnabrück. In his book *Letters in Low German, etc.* (Osnabrück 1845) he writes:

The watch as well as the appended seal of this brave hero of the pyramids are my lawfully and deservedly acquired property, by which I believe to possess one of the most interesting relics of the great day of the Battle of Waterloo. Both are provided with the coat of arms conferred by Napoleon, an upright standing lion surrounded by nine burning grenades in a blue field; in its honorary escutcheon, at the right an honourary sword, a crown at the top of the escutcheon; the casing carrying the decoration of the Légion d'honneur.'

General Freiherr Hugh von Halkett

Editor Dehnel's comments:

Regarding the following relation of the capture of General Cambronne, known worldwide, the editor of these pages has received the special permission of General H. Halkett who gave it with the particular intention 'to respond to the many requests that he received, and to put an end to the doubts and uncertainties that still are raised from time to time about the memorable incident and that primarily have had their origin in France'. The simple and humble relation by the general himself, most of it written here in dictation and then confirmed by his signature, runs as follows:

General Hugh Halkett

The Hanoverian Infantry Brigade under my command on the day of the Battle of Waterloo, consisting of the Osnabrück, Salzgitter, Bremervörde and Quakenbrück Battalions, was employed, besides other troop bodies, in the defence of the orchards surrounding Chateau Hougoumont for a long period of time. We were involved there in some hot engagements.

After the last major, but completely unsuccessful, attack by the Imperial Guards upon the British position, I received orders to have my brigade advance together with the English one of Colonel Adam.

At that moment, I had only the Osnabrück Battalion near me, which stood next to the eastern hedge in an open field, the other battalions were still situated between the hedges in the orchards of Hougoumont. I followed Adam's Brigade, but sent my Aide de camp, Captain August von Saffe* of the 1st Line Battalion of the German Legion, to the other battalions to bring them the order to follow us without delay. During our advance, Captain von Saffe was killed before transmitting the order to the other battalions. These then did not follow.

In the meantime, I had advanced with the Osnabrück Battalion, about in line with Adam's Brigade, against three battalions of Napoleon's Old Guard. These fired at us and we returned the fire while we moved closer to them. They turned about and retired, we followed. They turned around once more and fired another volley that we did not leave unanswered.

In this contest we had approached within 200 paces of the old veterans of the French Emperor. Several times I shouted at them: '*Rendez-vous mes amis!*'

While I could hear that my challenge was answered, I did not understand their words.

* Captain Augustus von Saffe, Beamish no. 985.

The enemy continued to retire. Their commanding officer was at first on horseback and urged them energetically to stand fast, but in vain. I saw him somewhat later with two aides de camp about 150 paces behind the column, but now on foot after the loss of his horse.

Riding in front of the Osnabrück Battalion, I might have been only about 100 paces away from this officer of superior rank when I made the decision to attack him in person. I put the spurs to my horse, galloped at him, and menaced him with my sabre raised high.

He at once threw away his sabre and shouted: *Je me rends!* [I surrender] and let me know that he was General Cambronne. He then walked ahead of me in the direction of our line. After a few steps my horse that had already been wounded was struck again by a ball and collapsed under me. While I quickly tried to free myself from the saddle, the exceptionally strong animal jumped up again with me on it, and I now noticed that my prisoner attempted to escape. I hurried after him, held him by his aiguillette, led him to our troops, and handed him over to a sergeant.

Immediately after this incident, the Osnabrück Battalion captured a French battery located to its left near the Guards, and then followed the long disorderly, tightly pressed enemy masses to the first houses of Genappe. We there let a column of Prussian cavalry pass by, which hurriedly pursued the French, and we then occupied a few houses and spent the night among wounded French soldiers.

A day later, Lord Hill gathered the officer corps of the now reunited brigade at Nivelles and thanked them for their distinguished performance.

APPENDIX 2

Ludwig von Wissel's 'Glorious Feats'

Ludwig von Wissel Glorious Feats of Arms Performed in the Recent Wars by Non-commissioned Officers and Soldiers of the English-German Legion and the Hanoverian Army, *Hanover, 1846*

Compiled from reliable sources by Ludwig von Wissel, Captain of the Royal Hanoverian Artillery.

The following pages have been written only about, and mainly on behalf of, the non-commissioned officers and soldiers.

My source has primarily been the Archive of the Guelphic Medal, access to which has been graciously permitted me, and other detailed and reliable information of which I have availed myself, as needed.

This medal was instituted on 12 August 1815 for non-commissioned officers and soldiers who have distinguished themselves in battle, and provides its bearer with an annual cash stipend of 24 thaler. Entitlement to this medal has been examined by a special commission and has to be be supported by actual facts, which have been authoritatively certified (almost always by officers).

A number of meritorious feats of non-commissioned officers and men have already been reported in Beamish's *History of the Legion*; wherever I diverged from these accounts, it was for reasons that I considered significant. Ranks are those at the time of the feat of arms, to the extent that these could be ascertained.

Of Ludwig von Wissel's brief stories only those have been selected that might add interesting details to existing reports on the Waterloo campaign.

4th Hanoverian Brigade at Quatre Bras, Verden Landwehr Battalion

Privates Christian Wolff and David Hambrock

They are surrounded by the enemy while with a skirmishing detachment of the battalion. Wolff knocked down a French officer in a wrestling match, although wounded by the Frenchman. Hambrock kills three enemies. They are freed with the help of their comrades but hardly free again when they see two of their officers, [Lieutenant] von Horst and [Ensign] Plate, still in the enemy's hands. The two brave men rush boldly in on a stronger enemy, save the first officer, but are wounded again and taken prisoner.

2nd Horse Battery, KGL, at Quatre Bras

Senior Artillery Sergeant Ferdinand Nienburg and Gun Captain John Meyer

This battery arrived at Quatre Bras as part of the English Guards Division. These NCOs were with two guns that were placed in a forward position on the Charleroi highway. Protected by infantry standing to their sides, they repulsed with their cannon a heavy and valiant attack of French cuirassiers, during which the two NCOs distinguished themselves by their sangfroid and [the] good effect of their pieces.

Two cannon of an English battery that had lost many horses and men at the beginning of the battle* had been abandoned in front of and to the right side of this battery. During a lull in the fighting, Nienburg and Meyer went there with some horses and men and returned the guns to safety; meanwhile, several gunners on horseback had to fight off some enemy cavalry skirmishers.

1st Light Battalion, KGL, rearguard, 17 June

Sergeant Philipp Lindenau

This battalion formed the rearguard of a column during the retreat from Quatre Bras to Waterloo on 17 June and had halted at Genappe. Its commander, Lieutenant Colonel L. von dem Bussche, rode off to reconnoitre the area to be able to post pickets at a moment's notice if required. In the meantime, an order came to continue the retreat immediately. Lindenau had to stay back and await and inform the lieutenant colonel accordingly. But the latter had already been notified and had followed a different route to the battalion. Lindenau kept waiting for some time, until enemy cavalry was approaching. Favoured by the terrain, he took off in a hurry; but the enemy cavalry skirmishers moved on just as fast, and as he came out of a sunken roadway he was discovered by the enemy. He ran ahead, crossing hedges, enclosures and cornfields, but two horsemen overtook him; he shot one of them, the other hurried off, perhaps being frightened, or misled by Lindenau's shouts that gave an impression as if more of his comrades were nearby. He quickly reloaded his rifle and continued on his way. He still had three hours of marching to cover, bearing to his right where the enemy advanced in lesser strength. When he emerged into the open, having left a footpath lined by hedges, he saw two enemy mounted chasseurs who had just then wounded and taken prisoner an English hussar officer. He at once shot dead the horse of one of them and attacked the other with fixed sword bayonet; both enemies were taken prisoner. The English officer urged the sergeant to let the prisoners go and use the horse to return quickly to his battalion; but Lindenau killed the horse and made the two enemies march ahead of himself. With his good luck, while having the enemy's vanguard advancing on both sides, he thus arrived at his battalion in the evening.

2nd Brigade, 1st Light Battalion, KGL, at La Haye Sainte

Corporal Henry Müller

He had shown his bravery in many an action and had acquired the reputation of being one of the best shots. While at La Haye Sainte, he asked to be placed in a forward position and had two men with him whose only job was to load rifles for him. He aimed at officers in particular. During an enemy attack he shot the leader off his horse. At another one, he felled a higher ranking officer who had marched on foot in front of his column and, in order to encourage his men, was swinging his sabre and shouting,

* No English batteries were present at Quatre Bras when the battle commenced.

'*Avancez*.' When this officer fell, the entire column retreated in disorder. Müller had to assume command of his company when it had to abandon La Haye Sainte.

1st Hanoverian Brigade

Feldjäger Julius Brinkmann and Wilhelm Brinkmann, Kielmansegge Feldjäger Corps.
With a part of their corps together with Nassauers, they were posted in a small wood at Hougoumont. This was attacked by the enemy with a superior force. The defenders were driven back, and Captain von Reden and several Feldjäger, including these two, were surrounded. Wilhelm escaped, however, and although wounded by shots sent after him, alerted another part of his company. These, together with British Guards, drove the French back and freed the men who had been surrounded.

Julius had stayed with Captain von Reden and was wounded; as soon as he had been freed, he grabbed his rifle and went after the enemy. When his weapon was smashed, he hurried into the building, obtained another one from a wounded comrade, and kept on fighting. Although forced to go to a hospital in the evening, he returned to his company on 20 June as soon as he has heard of the army's advance.

1st Hanoverian Brigade, action at Hougoumont

Sergeant Mann, Grubenhagen Field Battalion
Detachments of General Count Kielmansegge's Hanoverian Brigade had been sent to Hougoumont. Here Mann truly showed the '*Mann*' [man] he was. During the most heavy skirmishing, he made his young men use the terrain most skilfully, while maintaining good order. He had already proven himself a master of this kind of fighting at Quatre Bras where he had served as an outstanding example. His rifle had been shot up and he quickly picked up another that was lying on the battlefield.

2nd Light Battalion, KGL, action at La Haye Sainte

Sergeant George Stöckmann
In advancing ahead of his men a French cuirassier officer came close to La Haye Sainte. Stöckmann shot his horse dead, jumped quickly over the wall and took the officer prisoner while under enemy fire and in front of the officer's men.

When the 8th [Line] Battalion moved in line against enemy infantry and was surprised by cavalry and dispersed, the officer carrying its colours was severely wounded and fell to the ground, close to La Haye Sainte. Disregarding the perils, Stöckmann hurried there and took the colours back to safety.

3rd Line Battalion, KGL, action at Hougoumont

Corporal Christian Brinkmann
He was with the specially formed light battalion. After seizing the Hougoumont orchard, this detachment had been engaged from behind a hedge in vigorous skirmish fire with enemy tirailleurs. An enemy Staff officer was coming close to the hedge. Brinkmann quickly jumped through the hedge into the open and took him prisoner right in front of his men.

4th Line Battalion, KGL, action at Hougoumont

Sergeant Cristoph Brandt
The four light companies of the first four battalions of the legion had been combined into a battalion of its own. It had severe losses; its commander and the four captains

had been killed or wounded within a very short time. The same fate eventually happened to the Adjutant, whose duties Brandt now performed with distinction. In the afternoon, this battalion, supported by the 2nd Line Battalion, had to drive the French from the Hougoumont orchards. As soon as this had been accomplished after fierce fighting, Brandt hurriedly saw to it that several gaps in the hedges were barricaded through which the enemy might have penetrated again.

4th Line Battalion, KGL, action at Hougoumont
Rifleman Henry Rohlfs
An officer attested to the bravery of this man as follows:

'After the combined light companies of the four line battalions (1st, 2nd, 3rd, 4th), together with the 2nd Line Battalion, had driven the enemy out of the orchard of Hougoumont on 18 June 1815, I and Rohlfs happened to be at the left wing of the skirmish line in a ditch behind a hedge. Apparently not noticing us, an enemy captain on horseback came close to us; I jumped up and grabbed the horse's bridle, but had to let go again if Rohlfs had not come to my aid and taken the captain prisoner. That man offered his watch and purse to Rohlfs, but he nobly declined to take them.

During the brief period of our presence in that orchard, Rohlfs managed to shoot down some 12 to 14 enemy tirailleurs and two officers; before he fired he said to me each time: "Sir, now it's that one's turn"and each time the target dropped to the ground. But then he was wounded himself and fell down; he now, in a prone position from behind his knapsack, shot down a few more enemies. Soon thereafter we took part in the advance'.

5th Line Battalion, KGL, in square behind Haye Sainte
Rifleman Johann Milius, 1st Light Battalion
At Waterloo, the 5th Line Battalion stood in square. It was repeatedly attacked by a regiment of French cuirassiers, which, after each unsuccessful charge, retired to lower ground nearby where it was safe and able to reform. Only the commander of the regiment halted alone on an elevation, kept our square under observation, and ordered another charge at what he believed to be at favourable moments. After the fifth unsuccessful charge, Rifleman Milius, whose leg had been struck by a canister ball – he afterwards had to stay for nine months at a hospital –was brought into the square.

Soon thereafter, Colonel von Ompteda mentioned how desirable it would be if the brave colonel of cuirassiers who rode back and forth on the elevation like a vedette and seemed to be invulnerable, could be chased off his observation post. The [5th] Battalion's riflemen were in La Haye Sainte.

Milius heard the colonel's words, and asked to be brought before the front of the square; since he could not walk and was already very weak, this had to be done by several men. The second shot brought the annoying Frenchman down from his horse. Our colonel greatly praised the brave rifleman who so willingly and usefully had overcome his failing powers.

1st Hussar Regiment, KGL, on patrol 17 June
Cavalry Sergeant Schrader
On the evening of 17 June 1815, Schrader and one of the hussars of his squadron

were on patrol. He observed four cavalrymen at a distance of 50 paces and heard them talking in French. His hussar comrade was told to rush at the enemy with loud shouts, while Schrader came from the opposite side. However, the enemy remained unfazed and galloped towards the hussars. As it turned out, they were cuirassiers, and no advantage could be expected from standing up to their greater number and armour.

Schrader therefore shouted at the [other] hussar for them to take to flight, hoping that this would cause the enemies to separate. This ruse succeeded; the French followed them and thus became parted. Schrader now quickly turned around his strong horse, attacked the leading one and felled him with a cut to his face, then went to help the hussar who was engaged with two others. One of those he unhorsed with a cut to the horse's neck; both the third one and the fourth, who had come on in the meantime, threw away their swords and asked for pardon. The four cuirassiers and their mounts were handed over to Schrader's squadron.

3rd Hussar Regiment, KGL
Hussar Frederick Liberty
During the first charge on 18 June 1815, his horse's bridle had been cut into pieces; it could no longer be controlled and took off towards the enemy lines. He galloped past an enemy square, several shots were fired at him but missed their target. He then happened into another infantry formation and was stopped by two lancers and taken to a group of prisoners. Because his horse could not be led off, he was ordered to repair the bridle. He needed no second telling, pulled a cobbler's awl and thread from his tool bag and stitched the bridle back together. As the enemy paid no particular attention, he quickly jumped on his horse and fled. Although the lancers took after him and he was hit by some shots, he was able to escape without serious injury and returned to his regiment. He took an active part in the other charges in which he also saved his fellow hussar Meyer who had been encircled by four French horsemen by shooting dead one enemy and with his sabre putting the others to flight.

3rd Hussar Regiment, KGL
Hussar Henry Bergmann
During an engagement of cavalry pickets at Waterloo, a French corporal cursed the Germans in German, causing General von Arentschild to express his displeasure. Bergmann left the line, charged at the corporal and cut him off his horse in no time at all. Inspired by his own feat, he later on, while his regiment stood opposite a French one and its commander had stopped somewhat in front of its ranks, he galloped at him and quickly sabred him off his horse in front of his men.

3rd Hussar Regiment, KGL
Hussar Scharnhorst
During a melee of his squadron with French cuirassiers he lost his sabre. In this situation he was attacked by a French officer. Scharnhorst managed to quickly turn around his agile horse and grab his opponent by the collar in an effort to drag him off his horse. In this he did not succeed, however, and he received three wounds before he contrived to get hold of the enemy's sabre and wrestled with him for its possession. But now, Hussar Afpello came to his comrade's aid and struck the Frenchman with such a powerful cut that the man's head hung by his side.

3rd Hussar Regiment, KLG
Hussar George Meywerk
An honourable discharge and a pension had been approved for him as a result of wounds he had suffered in an earlier campaign that took nine months to heal. When war broke out anew in 1815, he returned to his unit, however, and bravely fought at Waterloo. It was then that he defeated a captain of the French cuirassiers in a duel during which he himself was wounded.*

1st Horse Battery, KGL (Captain A. Sympher)
Gun Captains Carl Heine and Henry Niemeyer
Before moving into action, this battery stood in the second line for a long time where it suffered some losses from enemy artillery fire. After several batteries had moved out of the first line due to lack of ammunition, it eventually advanced there and came under heavy artillery and skirmish fire. Here it assisted greatly in repelling the last heavy French attacks.

Heine and Niemeyer soon were the only active gun captains; they were kept busy hurrying from one piece to the next, taking care of the effective targeting of each gun. The crews also were taking losses; at Niemeyer's cannon five gunners had been killed or wounded. Niemeyer himself was struck by a canister ball in his lower left leg but remained active. In the evening, he brought back to the battery the ammunition reserve element, which in the general confusion had retired to one hour's distance from the battlefield . . .

When the ammunition, particularly canister shot, was about to become depleted at a critical moment, enemy columns threatened to renew their attack. Heine on his [own] initiative with two gunners quickly searched out nearby abandoned and shot-up limbers and waggons while under heavy fire. Fortune was with him, and his volunteering was crowned with the best of success; the search turned up the desired ammunition which was then hauled to the battery and most effectively used at the very moment that the French Guard launched its attack.

4th Foot Battery, KGL, general action, 18 June
Gun Captain Christian Denecke and Artillery Driver Ludolph Eickmann
In its first charge, the enemy cavalry approached unexpectedly from the left wing. Denecke was in command of the howitzer on the right flank and had not noticed the enemy advancing from the flank, while searching for other targets. However, Eickmann did, and quickly drove up with the limber and shouted at his gun captain

* This episode has apparently been reported in greater detail by Edward Cotton, *A Voice from Waterloo*, Brussels, 1849, p. 256, as follows:

A hussar and a cuirassier had got entangled in the mêlée, and met in the plain, in full view of our line: the hussar was without a cap, and bleeding from a wound in the head, but that did not hinder him from attacking his steel-clad adversary. He soon proved that the strength of cavalry consists in good horsemanship and the skilful use of the sword, and not in being clad in heavy defensive armour. The superiority of the hussar was visible the moments the swords crossed: after a few wheels a tremendous facer made the Frenchman reel in his saddle, and all his attempts to escape his more active foe became unavailing; a second blow stretched him on the ground, amidst the cheers of the light horseman's comrades, the 3rd German hussars, who were ardent spectators of the combat.

that the enemy was already on the left flank of the battery.

But limbering up could not be done fast enough on the soft muddy ground; several gunners jumped on the limber with the loading utensils and hurried towards the squares while Denecke fired the charge already in the gun and threw himself underneath the piece.

During the following cavalry charges, Eickmann promptly came up with the limber so that the gun could be brought back in time. At Quatre Bras, the howitzer became separated from the remainder of the battery, where it lost a number of men. Eickmann dismounted and volunteered to help service the gun now that it was particularly important and by its effective fire, their piece inflicted considerable losses to the enemy cavalry.

When at Waterloo all of the ammunition had been fired off, Denecke at his own initiative helped out with his men at a nearby English battery that was short of manpower.

1st Hanoverian 9-Pounder Foot Battery

Gunnery Cadet Weste

At the beginning of the battle, the 1st Battery stood near Mont St Jean in reserve, where it was already exposed to enemy cannon balls. It was soon ordered to the centre to perform its death-dealing service and suffered considerable losses from enemy musketry and artillery fire. Of its four officers, three were wounded and one of them, Lieutenant von Schulzen mortally. Advancing in column, the battery formed up in a depression before moving to its emplacements. An enemy shell then struck the limber box of the howitzer that was under the cadet's command. The cartridges and bombs ignited and caused a devastating explosion; the limber was demolished, the gun carriage damaged, several horses and men horribly killed or mutilated. Because the cartridges exploded first, throwing the nearest of the crew to the ground, these men were partially protected from the following explosion of the bombs. In the meantime, the other guns could not be allowed to tarry and moved to their battle position. The howitzer was out of service, and only a few of the crew remained uninjured. The young cadet had been felled by the impact and was rendered unconscious, but soon recovered. Although wounded in his face, he hurried to the battery, which was then in action, and from his arrival took over the command of the No.1 gun whose gun captain had been wounded. With his bravery and sangfroid, he not only took care of this duty but also served as a gunner, since very soon this crew had only three unwounded men left.

In the morning of the 19th, only two of the six guns could be moved because of lack of men and horses. Weste asked to be put in command of one of them, which position was granted him.

APPENDIX 3

Officers of the Brunswick Corps in 1815

From Dr Carl Venturini Umfis einer pragmatischen geschichte des kriegswesens im Herzogthum Braunschweig, *Magdeburg, 1837*

General Commanding
Duke Frederick Wilhelm

Aide de Camps of His Highness
Major von Mahrenholz
Captain von Lubeck
Captain Bause

Á la Suite
Colonel von Herzberg
Major von Grone

Corps Commanders
Colonel Olfermann
Captain Morgenstern
Captain von Zweifel

Quartermaster General
Lieutenant Colonel von Heinemann
Major von Wachholz, Chief of Staff
Lieutenant Meineke
Ensign Gille

War Department Office of Customs
Major Steinacker
Aide Paymaster Trott

War Department Commissariat
Major and General Graebe
Kings Commissary Reindel
Kings Commissary Biedt
Kings Surgeon Dr Pockels

War Department Auditor
Auditor General du Roi

War Department Priest
Priest Westphal

Hussar Regiment
Major von Cramm
Lieutenant Adjutant von Unger
Lieutenant Adjutant Floto
Major von Oeynhausen
Major von Hennings
Captain von Holm
Captain Schnelle
Captain Kuster
Captain von Pavel
Lieutenant Lambrecht
Lieutenant Eisener
Lieutenant Rudolphi I
Lieutenant Schrader
Lieutenant August Haberlandt
Lieutenant von Praun
Lieutenant Riemann
Lieutenant Ahlers
Lieutenant Clauditz
Lieutenant Erich
Lieutenant Haberlin
Lieutenant Zerbst
Lieutenant Cuppius
Lieutenant Scheerenberg
Lieutenant Schwenke
Cornet Dormeyer

Cornet Engelbrecht I
Cornet Menz I
Cornet Menz II
Cornet Riemeyer
Cornet August Langenstrassen
Cornet George
Cornet Pohlemann
Cornet Corvinus
Cornet Wilhelm Langenstrassen
Paymaster Aschenborn
Quartermaster Koppe
Surgeon Wagner
Veterinarian Gieseke

Uhlans
Major Pott
Adjutant Lieutenant Matterne
Captain Muller
Captain Topp
Lieutenant Weyrather
Lieutenant Dammann
Lieutenant Fricke
Cornet Fredeking
Cornet Salomon
Cornet Ludersen
Cadet Fritsch
Surgeon Kruger

Avante Garde
Major von Rauschenplatt
Lieutenant Adjutant Leuterding
Lieutenant Adjutant Carl von Buttlar

Jäger Corps
Captain Berner
Captain Mahner
Lieutenant Metzner
Lieutenant Pauly
Ensign Theuerkauf
Ensign Kobus
Ensign Muller
Ensign Friedemann

Light Infantry
Captain von Griesheim
Captain von Ritterholm
Lieutenant Ahrberg
Lieutenant Pockels
Lieutenant Muhe
Ensign Gerlach
Ensign Lerche
Ensign Otto Ahrens II
Paymaster von Amtsberg
Surgeon Meinike

Light Infantry Brigade
Lieutenant Colonel von Buttlar
Captain Brigade Adjutant von Mosqua
Surgeon Dr Drude

Leib Battalion
Major von Prostler
Captain Adjutant von Brombsen
Captain von Thiede
Captain von der Heyde
Captain von Tschischwitz
Captain Telge
Lieutenant von Bredow
Lieutenant Haberland I
Lieutenant Melchior
Lieutenant Eduards
Lieutenant Krober
Ensign Klefert
Ensign Zerling
Ensign von Hollern
Ensign Parey
Ensign Kappel
Ensign Majewsky
Paymaster Horst
Surgeon Heimburg

1st Light Battalion
Major von Hollstein
Major von Steinwehr
Lieutenant Adjutant von Sommer
Captain von Bülow
Captain von Specht
Captain von Meibom
Captain Rover
Lieutenant Wilhelm von Specht
Lieutenant Tiemann
Captain Weidemann
Ensign von Hantelmann
Ensign Wagenknecht
Ensign Wackerhagen
Ensign von der Brinken

Ensign Fricke
Ensign Zeitheck
Ensign Sangerwein
Ensign Crumpf
Ensign Berwig
Paymaster Ribbentrop
Surgeon Dr Drude

2nd Light Battalion
Major von Brandenstein
Major Koch
Captain Adjutant Martini
Captain von Passinsky
Captain von Hullesen
Captain Gose
Captain Ludovici
Lieutenant Mittendorf
Lieutenant Schmidt
Lieutenant Ewald
Ensign Scheffler
Ensign Hinke
Ensign Mannsfeld
Ensign Grabau
Ensign Sensemann
Ensign Ritter
Ensign Tittel
Ensign Wassmuth
Ensign Bruns
Paymaster Koch
Arzt Schmidt

3rd Light Battalion
Major Ebeling
Major von Unruh
Lieutenant Adjutant Kohler
Captain von Braun
Captain von Frankenberg
Captain Hausler
Captain von Rauh
Lieutenant Christian Haberland
Lieutenant Horstel
Lieutenant Franz von Specht
Ensign Louis von Buttlar
Ensign Teichmuller
Ensign Damm
Ensign Hemmerich
Ensign Togel
Ensign Gotthard
Ensign Bieliss
Ensign Louis Seeliger
Ensign Maasberg
Paymaster Captain Degener
Surgeon Willke

Line Infantry Brigade
Lieutenant Colonel von Specht
Captain Adjutant von Aurich

1st Line Battalion
Major Metzner
Major von Gillern
Major von Forster
Captain Adjutant von Lochhauser
Lieutenant Adjutant Drewes
Captain von Schwarzkoppen
Captain von Munchhausen
Captain von Pallandt
Captain Pessler
Lieutenant Wirth
Lieutenant Biermann
Lieutenant Scherff
Lieutenant Pluntz
Lieutenant Mahner
Lieutenant von Schwarzkoppen
Ensign von Meyern
Ensign Franke
Ensign Hersche
Ensign Eisfeld
Ensign von Hanstein
Paymaster Harke
Surgeon Dr Franke

2nd Line Battalion
Major von Strombeck
Major von Wolffradt
Lieutenant Adjutant Hartmann
Captain von Bülow II
Captain von Bohlen
Captain Gruttemann
Captain Rudolphi
Captain Schleiter
Lieutenant Muller
Lieutenant Matterne
Ensign von Bockelmann
Ensign Hauptner
Ensign von Vechelde

Ensign Brauns
Ensign Scholz
Ensign Nolte
Ensign Lindwurm
Ensign Bellieno
Ensign Strube
Paymaster Kuster
Surgeon Dr Reiche

3rd Line Battalion
Major von Normann
Captain Adjutant Wolff
Captain von Ritterholm I
Captain von Breymann
Captain von Waltersdorff
Captain von Pavel
Lieutenant Geyer
Lieutenant Rudolphi
Lieutenant Dedekind
Ensign Deichmann
Ensign Schroter
Ensign Ahrens
Ensign Kubel
Ensign Rathsel
Ensign Kayser
Ensign Gellerich
Ensign Pfeiser
Paymaster Meyer
Surgeon Dr Heuer

Ersatz (Reserve) Battalion (not at Waterloo)
Major von Munchausen
Major Graf von Schonfeld
Battalion Adjutant von Schleinitz
Captain von Rosenberg
Captain Roussel
Captain von Klenke
Captain von Wedel
Lieutenant Siemonis
Ensign Buchling
Ensign Gehrig
Ensign Rudemann
Ensign Stutzer
Ensign Meyer
Ensign Seubert
Ensign Rhamm
Surgeon Wrede

Artillery
Major Mahn
Lieutenant Adjutant Lemme

Horse Battery
Major Moll
1st Lieutenant Lenz
1st Lieutenant Diederichs
2nd Lieutenant Wolf
2nd Lieutenant Bathe
2nd Lieutenant Zuchschwerdt

Foot Battery
Major von Heinemann II
Captain Orges
1st Lieutenant Schulz
1st Lieutenant Bredenscheid
2nd Lieutenant Kortge
2nd Lieutenant Meichsel
Surgeon Osthoff
Dr Bieling

Train
Captain Warnecke

APPENDIX 4

List of King's German Legion Officers Transferred to the Hanoverian Landwehr Battalions on 25 April 1815

From Bernhard Schwertfeger, Geschicht der königlich Deutschen Legion 1803–1816, *Hahn'sche Hofbuchhandlung, Hanover, 1832*

3rd Hanoverian Brigade

Landwehr Battalion Bremervorde

Captain von der Decken	2nd Line Battalion, KGL
Lieutenant Wahrendorff	1st Light Battalion, KGL
Lieutenant Doring	2nd Light Battalion, KGL
Ensign von Suckow	7th Line Battalion, KGL
Ensign Cropp	2nd Line Battalion, KGL
Ensign Luning	2nd Line Battalion, KGL

Landwehr Battalion Osnabrück

Captain Dreves	3rd Line Battalion, KGL
Lieutenant Appuhn	3rd Line Battalion, KGL
Lieutenant von During	1st Line Battalion, KGL
Lieutenant von Weyhe	1st Line Battalion, KGL
Ensign Knop	2nd Light Battalion, KGL
Ensign Neuschafer	7th Line Battalion, KGL

Landwehr Battalion Quackenbruck

Captain Hulsemann	1st Light Battalion, KGL
Lieutenant Poten	8th Line Battalion, KGL
Lieutenant Schadtler	1st Light Battalion, KGL
Lieutenant Hurtzig	2nd Light Battalion, KGL
Ensign Friedrichs	2nd Light Battalion, KGL
Ensign Meyer	2nd Light Battalion, KGL

Landwehr Battalion Salzgitter

Captain Rudorff	1st Light Battalion, KGL
Lieutenant Hotzen	8th Line Battalion, KGL
Lieutenant von Both	1st Light Battalion, KGL

Lieutenant Winckler	5th Line Battalion, KGL
Ensign Rubenz	1st Light Battalion, KGL
Ensign von Welling	1st Light Battalion, KGL

4th Brigade

Landwehr Battalion Luneberg	
Captain von Hohnhorst	3rd Line Battalion, KGL
Lieutenant Tormin	3rd Line Battalion, KGL
Lieutenant Schröder	1st Line Battalion, KGL
Lieutenant von Arentsschildt	1st Line Battalion, KGL
Ensign von Reiche	1st Line Battalion, KGL
Ensign Backhaus	7th Line Battalion, KGL
Landwehr Battalion Verden	
Captain Brauns	8th Line Battalion, KGL
Lieutenant Luderitz	8th Line Battalion, KGL
Lieutenant Billeb	2nd Line Battalion, KGL
Lieutenant Ziel	2nd Line Battalion, KGL
Ensign Best	1st Light Battalion, KGL
Ensign Garvens	2nd Line Battalion, KGL
Landwehr Battalion Osterode	
Captain Curren	3rd Line Battalion, KGL
Lieutenant Kumme	1st Line Battalion, KGL
Lieutenant Best	1st Line Battalion, KGL
Ensign von Beaulieu	1st Line Battalion, KGL
Ensign Martin	7th Line Battalion, KGL
Landwehr Battalion Munden	
Captain Heydenreich	4th Line Battalion, KGL
Lieutenant Kulemann	2nd Line Battalion, KGL
Lieutenant La Roche	2nd Line Battalion, KGL
Ensign Baron le Fort	1st Line Battalion, KGL
Ensign von der Hellen	1st Line Battalion, KGL

5th Brigade

Landwehr Battalion Hameln	
Captain Hartmann	2nd Line Battalion, KGL
Lieutenant Pape	4th Line Battalion, KGL
Lieutenant von Ingersleben	2nd Light Battalion, KGL
Lieutenant Fischer	2nd Line Battalion, KGL
Ensign von Schlutter	3rd Line Battalion, KGL
Ensign Breymann	3rd Line Battalion, KGL

Landwehr Battalion Hildesheim	
Captain George Ludewig	4th Line Battalion, KGL
Lieutenant von Heimburg	3rd Line Battalion, KGL
Lieutenant von Hartwig	1st Light Battalion, KGL
Lieutenant von Geissmann	5th Line Battalion, KGL
Ensign E. Backhaus	7th Line Battalion, KGL
Ensign Wischmann	5th Line Battalion, KGL
Landwehr Battalion Peine	
Captain Lueder	3rd Line Battalion, KGL
Lieutenant von Uslar	3rd Line Battalion, KGL
Lieutenant William Appuhn	3rd Line Battalion, KGL
Lieutenant Kathmann	2nd Line Battalion, KGL
Lieutenant Helmrich	7th Line Battalion, KGL
Ensign E. Rodewald	3rd Line Battalion, KGL
Ensign von Uslar	2nd Line Battalion, KGL
Landwehr Battalion Gifhorn	
Brevet Major Leue	4th Line Battalion, KGL
Lieutenant von Hodenberg	8th Line Battalion, KGL
Lieutenant von Jeinsen	4th Line Battalion, KGL
Lieutenant Grahn	8th Line Battalion, KGL
Ensign Luning	4th Line Battalion, KGL
Ensign Mannsbach	4th Line Battalion, KGL

6th Brigade (Not at Waterloo)

Landwehr Battalion Nienburg	
Captain Brinckmann	8th Line Battalion, KGL
Captain Stolte	2nd Light Battalion, KGL
Lieutenant Kessler	4th Line Battalion, KGL
Lieutenant Rumann	4th Line Battalion, KGL
Lieutenant Poten	7th Line Battalion, KGL
Lieutenant Siebald	4th Line Battalion, KGL
Ensign Friedrich von Brandis	4th Line Battalion, KGL
Ensign Sander	8th Line Battalion, KGL
Landwehr Battalion Hoya	
Captain Rumann	4th Line Battalion, KGL
Lieutenant Otto	4th Line Battalion, KGL
Lieutenant von Einem	1st Line Battalion, KGL
Lieutenant von Witte	4th Line Battalion, KGL
Ensign von Losecke	7th Line Battalion, KGL
Ensign Spiel	8th Line Battalion, KGL
Ensign Seffers	8th Line Battalion, KGL

Landwehr Battalion Bentheim

Brevet Major Kuckuck	3rd Line Battalion, KGL
Lieutenant Breyman	1st Light Battalion, KGL
Ensign Weiss	3rd Line Battalion, KGL
Ensign von Reinbold	3rd Line Battalion, KGL
Ensign Baring	3rd Line Battalion, KGL

APPENDIX 5

List of Officers of the Hanoverian Army in the Netherlands in 1815

A. und R. von Sichart, Geschichte der königlich-hannoverschen Armee, *vol. 5. Hannover und Leipzig Hahn'sche Hofbuchlandlung, 1898*

Lieutenant General Carl von Alten
Adjutant General Colonel von Berger
Assistant Adjutant General Major von Schlutter
Chief Adjutant 1st Lieutenant Wichmann, 1st Lieutenant A. von Kielmansegge
Quartermaster General Major Kuntze
Assistant Quartermaster General Captain von Schubert
Quartermaster Ensign Schultze
Assistant Provost Marshal Ensign von Winkelmann
Engineer Officer Lieutenant Dammert
Staff Surgeon Dr Spangenberg
Assistant Surgeon Bothe
Post Master Captain Muldener
Commissary Diedrichs
Chief Auditor Cumme
Brigade Auditors Lieutenants Meyer, Wagemann, Selig, Nanne, Backmeister, Köster
Brigade Surgeon Dr Schulze, Sander, Lauprecht
Assistant Surgeon Degering
Priests Biermann, Block, Ungewitter, Bodemann, Cruse

Artillery
Major Heise
Captains von Rettberg and Braun
First Lieutenants d'Huvele and W. Muller (adjutant)
Second Lieutenants Stünkel and C. Muller
Assistant Surgeons Ruge and Schumacher
Veterinarian Haspelmath

Cavalry
Colonel von Estorff

Adjutant Cornet Schultz

Hussar Regiment Prince Regent

Colonel von Kielmansegge
Majors von dem Bussche and von Estorff
Captains von Schlepegrell, Heckert, von Lübbe, Lindemann, von Spörken, and von Dachenhausen
Lieutenants Sander, Frank, Heus, Meyer, von der Wense, Fromhagen (adjutant), von Schulte, Ritter, von Hedemann and Reinecke
Cornets von Bülow, von Laffert, Heldberg, Nöbling and Wettern
Surgeon Ulrich
Assistant Surgeon Karstens
Veterinary Kuhne

Hussar Regiment Bremen–Verden

Colonel von dem Bussche
Lieutenant Colonel H. von der Decken
Majors von der Beck, von Gadenstedt
Captains von Zesterfleth, von der Wisch, Pralle, von Arentsschildt and F. von der Decken (aide de camp to General Decken)
Lieutenants Claus von Plate, von der Decken, Cohrs, von Klencke, Dallmann, Jaeger, von der Wisch (adjutant) and George von Plate
Cornets Wilmans, von Munchhausen, von der Decken, von der Wisch, Marcard, von Stemshorn and von dem Bussche
Surgeon Wilmans
Assistant Surgeon Owen
Veterinary Hilmer

Hussar Regiment Duke of Cumberland

Lieutenant Colonel von Hake
Majors von Meltzing and von Uslar
Captains Count Munster, Schenk von Winterstedt, von Landesberg, Bremer, von Hodenberg
Lieutenants von Reden, von der Decken, von Dachenhausen (adjutant), von Adelebsen, von Arenstorff, von Scheele, von Offen and von Drechsel
Cornets von Klenck, von Schachten, von Plate, von Berlepsch, von Schwanewede and von Bock
Surgeon Jacobi
Assistant Surgeon Fiorillo
Quartermaster Herzog
Veterinary Stahl

Infantry

1st Brigade

Major General von Kielmansegge
Adjutant Lieutenant Hanbury

Field Jägers

Lieutenant Colonel von Spörken

Captains von During, von Reden, von Steinberg (adjutant) and von Haxthausen (on the Staff)
First Lieutenants Grote, von Meding and von Seebach
Second Lieutenants von Münchausen, von Plato and Schulze
Assistant Surgeon Völger
Quartermaster Schorkopf

Field Battalion Bremen

Lieutenant Colonel von Langrehr
Major Müller
Captains von Lepel, von Scriba, von Bazoldo and Von Elern
Lieutenants Gustav von Duistorp, Theodor von Quistorp, Frederick von Bülow, Tschirschniz, Büttner, Lührmann, Krüger and von Schlepegrell
Ensigns Bruel, Althauss, Bösch, Meyer, Hartmann, Kleinhanns and Wehner (adjutant)
Surgeon Dr Bacmeister
Assistant Surgeon Hegar
Quartermaster Scriba

Field Battalion Verden

Major von Schkopp
Captain G. von Bothmer, von Bandemer, von Achen and C. Jacobi,
Lieutenants Selig, Wilhelm von Brandis, Ernst von Brandis, Suffenplan, Wilkens and von Martels
Ensigns Buck, Pluns, Becker, Spindler, Gerhard (adjutant), von Plessen, von der Lanken and von Gentzkow
Surgeon Dr Hein
Assistant Surgeons Franckenberg and Lange
Quartermaster Nedden

Field Battalion Osnabrück (Duke of York)

Major F. von Bülow
Captains von Lösecke, von Pavel, von Graevemeyer and C. von Arentsschildt,
Lieutenants von Wrede, Mehlis, Cleve, Petersen, Beste, Moll, Müldener, Renneberg (adjutant), von Marenholz, von Maydell and Wyneken
Ensigns Müller, Fromme, Cleve, Hamelberg, Georg Jacobi and Rabius,
Surgeon Dr Thielen
Assistant Surgeon Dorsch and Probst
Quartermaster Cleeves

Field Battalion Lüneburg

Lieutenant Colonel A. von Klencke
Major von Dachenhausen
Captains von Bobardt, Korfes, Rall and Carl Jacobi
Lieutenants Stegmann, Börries, Brandt, Creydt, Collmann, von Plato, von Duve, Ritter and Volger
Ensigns von Plato, von Hamelberg, Schaumann, von Weyhe, von Pentz (adjutant) and Sachse
Surgeon Dr Karsten
Assistant Surgeons Schmeisser and Koch
Quartermaster Kuckuck

Field Battalion Grubenhagen
Lieutenant Colonel von Wurmb
Major von Stockhausen
Captains von Heimburg, von Bauer and Elderhorst
Lieutenants von Hugo, Lütgen, Westphal, von Tallard, Marwedel, von Grote, von Lütken and Heinsius
Ensigns von Oldershausen, Horn, Neimke, Ernst, von Bülow, Stiepel, Rasch and Woltag
Surgeon Dr Volger
Surgeon Zimmermann
Quartermaster Mahlstedt

3rd Brigade
Colonel Hugh Halkett
Adjutant Lieutenant Wahrendorff
Landwehr Battalion Bremervörde
Lieutenant Colonel Schulenburg
Major W. von der Decken
Captains Scheuch, Rüter, Mansbendel and Guillmar
Lieutenants Bertram, Müller, Vögemann, von Windheim (adjutant), Meyer, Loeper, Ehlers and Warnecke
Ensigns von Holt, Dreyer, Lemke, von Hassell, Holthusen, Wilken and Lamprecht
Assistant Surgeon Hagemann
Quartermaster Ensign Alex
Landwehr Battalion Osnabrück
Lieutenant Colonel von Münster
Major von Drewes
Captains Gotthard von Quernheim, Quentin and Appuhn
Lieutenants Uffel, Witte (assigned to headquarters), Schramm, Körner, Richers, Schmedes (adjutant and Beermann
Ensigns Lyra, Mannes, Niehenke, Klöntrup,Berghoff, Meyer and Koch
Surgeon Dr Sander
Assistant Surgeon Clacius
Quartermaster Breusing
Landwehr Battalion Quackenbrück
Lieutenant Colonel von dem Bussche and Hünefeld,
Major Hulsemann
Captains von Tornay, von Böselager, von Wrede and C. Poten,
Lieutenants Mackeprang (adjutant), Meyer, Schimpf, von Morsay, Schorcht, Lüllemann, Kloevekorn and Klingenberg
Ensigns Lange, Buddenberg, Dyckhoff, Reese, Buck and Ahlhausen
Assistant Surgeon Rühe
Quartermaster Blume
Landwehr Battalion Salzgitter
Majors F. von Hammerstein and G. Rudorff
Captains C. von Hammerstein, Wiedemann, Dietrichs and Hotzen
Lieutenants Michaëlis (Adjutant), Wipking, Jentsch, Giesecke, von Spangenberg, Siemens, Praël

Ensigns Mull, Richter, Schwarze, Borkenstein, Grovermann, Zacharias, Röttiger and Schrader
Surgeon Topken
Assistant Surgeon Homeyer

4th Brigade
Colonel Best
Adjutant Captain von Heimburg
Landwehr Battalion Verden
Majors C. von der Decken and Brauns
Captains von Witzendorff, Siegener, Osterwald and Lüderitz
Lieutenants Wagener, von Hinüber, von der Horst, Koch (adjutant), Hurtzig, Witte, Reibsch and Wynecken
Ensigns Clüver, Henkel, Siegener, Plate, Strandes, Nordmeyer and Kotzebue
Assistant Surgeon Fröhlich
Quartermaster Blöte
Landwehr Battalion Lüneburg
Lieutenant Colonel von Ramdohr
Major von Hohnhorst
Captains C. Tormin, von Reiche, von Kamptz and T. Tormin
Lieutenant Koch, Menge, Schneider, Ernst Becker, Carl Becker, Heymann (adjutant), Glahn and von Dassel
Ensigns Böhmer, Wilh, Meyer, Dornauer, von Bülow, Ernst Meyer and Siegener
Assistant Surgeon Scartmann
Quartermaster Gast
Landwehr Battalion Osterode
Major F. von Reden and Curren
Captains von Papet, von Ingersleben, Beermann and von Rauschenplatt
Lieutenants Probst, Kettler (adjutant), Creve, Jenisch, Deppe, Lamprecht and Behrens
Ensigns Freytag, Bachmann, Beermann, Schanz, Hanebuth and von Garmissen
Assistant Surgeon Preer
Quartermaster Schwabe
Landwehr Battalion Münden
Major F. von Schmidt and Heydenreich
Captains von Voigt, le Bachelle and von Hanstein
Lieutenants von Berckefeldt (adjutant), Schrader, von Spitznas, Wrisberg, Brenning, von Seebach, Schwenke and Firnhaber
Ensign Murray, Oppermann, Schweppe, Meder, Domeyer and Habenicht
Assistant Surgeon Bentschneider
Quartermaster Reichmann

5th Brigade
Colonel von Vincke
Adjutant Captain von Ludewig
Landwehr Battalion Hameln
Majors von Strube and Hartmann
Captains Blanckart, Lütgen and Pape

Lieutenants Kistner, Hotzen (adjutant), Meyer, Avenarius, Kemmer, Boening, Hampe and Kahle
Ensigns Schramme, Marquard, Wenzel,Rocca, Lackemann, Lauenstein and Giesselmann
Assistant Surgeon Oppermann
Junior Assistant Surgeon Thiele

Landwehr Battalion Gifhorn
Major G. von Hammerstein and Leue
Captains Wiedenfeld, von Unger, von Wick and von Hodenberg
Lieutenants Pflugmacher, Schwacke (adjutants), Schmidt, Preiser, Meyer, Ludewig and Hemmelmann
Ensigns Kneese, Brüggemann, Kellner, Rotermund and Wiede
Assistant Surgeon Adler
Quartermaster Riehl

Landwehr Battalion Hildesheim
Lieutenant Colonel Count G. von Rheden
Major Ludewieg
Captains von der Groeben, Raeben, August Brandis and von Heimburg
Lieutenants Wundenberg, Nonne (adjutant), Carl Brandis, von Ilten, Mertens, Hartwieg, Kaufmann and Römer
Ensigns Wilke, Deppen, Muller, Hansen, Rust, Büsching, Werner and Wöhler
Assistant Surgeon Schröder
Junior Assistant Surgeon Bornträger
Quartermaster Schrage

Landwehr Battalion Peine
Lieutenant Colonel Count von Westphalen
Major Lueder
Captains von Horn, von Bertrab, Krumhoff and von Uslar
Lieutenants Serges, Blume, Wilcke, Courgelon (adjutant) Gericke and Klöpper
Ensigns Schulze, Köhler, Elkann, Duvel, Wiedemann, Meyer, Kaufmann and Bodenstedt
Assistant Surgeon Behrens and Jecklin
Quartermaster Höbet

6th Brigade

Major General Lyon
Adjutant Lieutenant Richard

Field Battalion Lauenburg
Lieutenant Colonel von Benoit
Major von Holleufer
Captains Völger, Hildebrand, von Witzendorff and von Reiche
Lieutenants Cumme, Klencke, Voigt (adjutant), Flügge, von Berger, Schneider, Spall, von Hennings, Langreuter, Sontag and von Wickede
Ensigns von Bülow, von Hantelmann, and Dammert
Surgeon Dr Friedrichs
Assistant Surgeon Waack and Basse
Quartermaster Cumme

Field Battalion Calenberg

Lieutenant Colonel C. von Bock
Captains von Sothen, von Linsingen and von Helmoldt
Lieutenants Neubauer, Rupstein, Köring (adjutant), von Meding, Wedemeyer, von Krummes, von Bothmer and von Hedemann
Ensigns Crome, von Bock, Müller, Tellkampf, von Goeben, Hartmann, Eggers and Sprengel
Surgeon Dr Thomas
Assistant Surgeon Spangenberg and Kellner
Quartermaster Basse

Landwehr Battalion Hoya
Lieutenant Colonel von Grote
Major Rumann
Captains Clüver, Boden, Stolz and Otto
Lieutenants von Alten, Starke, Cordes, von Grote (adjutant), Clüver, von Köhler and Raven
Ensigns Brauns, Wehrhan, Drechsler, Augspurg, Rodewald, Narjes, Tiensch and Schorcht
Assistant Surgeons Hempel and Leszell
Quartermaster Siebke

Landwehr Battalion Bentheim
Majors Croupp and Kuckuk
Captains von Bülow, Nolte, Reichard and von Beesten
Lieutenants Thorbeck (adjutant), Conrad, Schmidt, Woempner, Blickwedel, Reichard, Meyering and Goldschmidt
Ensigns Keun, Koenig, Criegée, Lindemann, Lammering, Wedekind and Weber
Assistant Surgeon Markwordt
Quartermaster Zeeman

Landwehr Battalion Nienburg
Major Brinckmann and Stolte
Captains Luhmann, von Strube, von Dassel and Kessler
Lieutenants Meyer, Erythropel, Koster, Kirchhoff (adjutant), Reiche, von Grote and von Könemann
Ensigns Wesemann, von Lösecke, Meyer, Mirow, Meyrose, Luhmann, Surhoff and Schramm
Assistant Surgeon Aschendorf
Quartermaster Griffel

Reserve Corps
Lieutenant General von der Decken
Chief of General Staff Colonel Martin
Adjutant General Captain Meyer
Aide de Camp Captain F. von der Decken
Lieutenant Quartermaster Captain Schaedtler
Commander of the Artillery colonel Röttiger
Staff Surgeon Dr Wedemeyer
Auditors Campe, Tuckermann, Conrades and Wehner
Priests Grupe, Keidel, Sprengel and Kropp
Post Master Ensign Kestner

Appendix 5: List of Officers of the Hanoverian Army in the Netherlands in 1815

1st Brigade

Lieutenant Colonel A, von Bennigsen
Adjutant Lieutenant von Bennigsen

Field Battalion Hoya

Lieutenant Colonel E. von Bothmer
Major A. von Bothmer
Captains Steidl, von Werthmüller, von Frankenberg and von Bissing
Lieutenants Eckendahl, Warnecke (adjutant), von Treplin, Roel, Eulhard, Rust, Westphal, Schreibel and Breymann
Ensigns Giefe, Evers, Böhme, Kraut, Thornton, Schiffel and Brunken
Assistant Surgeon Schulenburg
Quartermaster Möller

Landwehr Battalion Bremerlehe

Major A. von der Decken
Captains von Stahl, von Horn and Vogelsang
Lieutenants von Wersebe, Helmke, von Hanffstengel (adjutant), Georg August von der Decken, Ludwig von der Decken, Ahrens, Tröbener, Griebel, Georg Conrad von Hanffstengel, Biedenweg, von Heimburg, Kestner and Dassel
Ensigns von Pufendorf and Christian Tröbener
Sergeant Major Wille and Brandt
Assistant Surgeon Tasche
Quartermaster Seyler

Landwehr Battalion Melle

Major von Donop (on leave)
Captains Terheyden, Bünger, Hahn and Tilée (Commandant of the Depot in Antwerp)
Lieutenants Krukenbaum (adjutant), Lacroix, Engelke, Kramer, Jobusch, Meyer, Heilmann and Basse
Ensigns Brüning, Staffhorst, Schröder, Kramer, Staeger, Horst, Meyer and Schröder
Sergeant Major Grafflage
Assistant Surgeon Bussmann
Quartermaster Schöpper

2nd Brigade

Colonel von Beaulieu

Landwehr Battalion Northeim

Majors von Harling (on leave) and Delius
Captains Hartmann, Becker, Tieling and von Hugo
Lieutenants Alberti, Basson, Heinsius, von Martens (adjutant), Lassal, Soltenborn, Reinhard, Kolle and Heldt
Ensigns Gödecke, Friese, Bergmann, Dreyer, Niemann, Klingsoehr, Bartels and Dürr
Assistant Surgeon Kaiser
Quartermaster Schuster

Landwehr Battalion Alfeld

Major Dammers
Captains Hahn, Basson, and von Holle

Lieutenants Koch, Feussner, Müller(adjutant), Allershausen, Hennigs, Falkenhagen, Franke, Mehliss and Leeser
Ensigns von Alten, Röhrsen, Müller, Ulrich, Höbel, Meyer, Mühlhan and Schmidt
Surgeon Thorrmann
Assistant Surgeon Wallroth
Quartermaster Merkel

Landwehr Battalion Springe
Major von Münchhausen (on leave)
Captains Lüderitz, Reinhard, Weniger and Mayer
Lieutenants von Heimburg, Schaaf, Henze, Laurentius, Grimsehl (adjutant), Schlüter, Kohlmann, Steinecke, Küppel, Neussel, Lüderitz, Rehren and Garms
Ensigns Blume, Hornemann and Grimsehl
Quartermaster Sergeant Kohlmeyer
Assistant Surgeon Koch
Quartermaster Westphal

3rd Brigade
Lieutenant Colonel C. von Bülow
Adjutant Lieutenant Bernstorf
Surgeon Dr Medel

Landwehr Battalion Lüchow
Major Purgold
Captains von Bennigsen, Walter, Schilling and Hartmann
Lieutenants Schulz, Redlich, von der Horst, von Schulzen, Pflug, Mackeprang and Blumenthal (adjutant)
Ensigns Oberfeld, Block, Meyer, Wentz, Fischer, Kramer, Sammann, Müller and Erdmann
Sergeant Major von Plato
Assistant Surgeon Krebs
Quartermaster Wiesen

Landwehr Battalion Celle
Lieutenant Colonel von dem Knesebeck
Major von Witzleben
Captains von Mandelsloh, von Werlhof and Schneider
Lieutenants Rupstein, Könemann, von Ilten, Schmersahl, Schlüter, Drevesen, Schmidt (adjutant), Schäfer and von Bothmer
Ensigns Schlüter, Hurtzig, Anton Berber, Lampe, Joseph Berber, Zum Berge, Grass and Grube
Sergeant Major Thies
Quartermaster Sergeant Wilcken
Assistant Surgeon Eichhorn
Quartermaster Köhler

Landwehr Battalion Ratzeburg
Major Ch. Von Hammerstein
Captains Fr. Von Bothmer, Meyer, Illing and von Heimbruch
Lieutenants Cappe, Diederichs, Wille, Meine (adjutant), Bethe, Schubert and Vicke
Ensigns Mecke, Halfeld and Hesse
Quartermaster Sergeant Strebel

Sergeant Majors Bethe and Willers
Assistant Surgeon Ruhstradt
Quartermaster Drechsler

Landwehr Battalion Ottendorf
Major H. von der Decken
Captains von Schlütter, Berson and Wilken
Lieutenants Leschen, Abel, Rickweg, von Lütcken, Koller, Schlichting (adjutant), Thumann, Richters and Fritscher
Ensigns von Windheim, Buhr, Segelte, Matthaei, von der Osten and Lübbern
Sergeant Major Callenius
Assistant Surgeon Andrée
Quartermaster Beauché

4th Brigade
Colonel Bodecker
Adjutant Lieutenant W. Appuhn
Surgeon Meyer

Landwehr Battalion Hanover
Major von Weyhe
Captains Bornemann, von Heimburg, von Jeinsen and von der Lüde
Lieutenants Bansen, von dem Bussche (on the Staff), Toppius, Schaaf, von Heimburg, Steinwedel, Schmid (adjutant), von Lüde and Bünning
Ensigns Rohde, Bode, Ludewig, Böhme, Lampe, Meyer senior, Meyer junior, Schötler and Barth
Cadets von Westernhagen and Eichhorn
Assistant Surgeon Dr Buchhorst
Quartermaster Ernst Ahlborn

Landwehr Battalion Neustadt
Major von Hodenberg
Captains von Linsingen, Behr, Barth and Ruperti
Lieutenants Pfotenhauer (adjutant), Möllenbeck, Schuster, Müller, Dittmer, Biener, von Uslar, Förster (on the Staff) and Nolte
Ensigns August Mensching, Förster, Dierking, Vieth, Lodemann, Heinrich Mensching, Meyer, Wenzel, and Crusius
Assistant Surgeon Langenbeck
Quartermaster Stolze

Landwehr Battalion Uelzen
Major Soest (on leave)
Captains Kuntze, Strube and von Diebitsch
Lieutenants Dempwolff, Becker, Knoche senior, Schilling (adjutant), Meyer, Richers, Hölty and Knoche junior
Ensigns Leporin, Bilfinger, Schulze, Stein, Heitmüller, Blauel, Sievers and Reiche
Assistant Surgeons Ohle and Schulz
Quartermaster Heinrich August Ahlborn

Landwehr Battalion Diepholz
Major von Bar
Captains Naumann and Schumann
Lieutenants Gaffky, Behre, Hartmann, Soltenborn (adjutant), Lorenz, Gersting,

von Voss and Lucée
Ensigns Ocker, Wiethoff, Pieper, von Roques, Holsch, von Reiche, Arendt and von Hinüber
Quartermaster Sergeant Dettmer
Assistant Surgeon Jütting
Quartermaster Ridderhoff

Harzer Schutzenkorps
(only arrived with the army after 18 June)
Major C. von der Decken
Captains von Mansberg and von Marenholtz
1st Lieutenants Schröder, von Grote, Schönian, von Wickede and Schwencke (adjutant)
2nd Lieutenants von Adelebsen, Hüpeden and Meyer
Assistant Surgeon Dreyer

APPENDIX 6

List of Officers of the Nassau Regiments on 1 June 1815

From R. Kolb, Unter Nassaus Fahnen: Geschichte des Herzoglich Nassauischen Officiercorps 1803–1866, *Bechtold, Wiesbaden 1903*

1st Nassau Regiment

Colonel Ernst Steuben

Lieutenant Colonel Ferdinand von Hagen

Divisional Surgeons Pammert and Sendler

Quartermaster Linz

Auditeur Wilhelm Petsch

1st Battalion

Major Wilhelm von Weyhers

Adjutant Captain Gottfried Schnabel

Grenadier Company

Captain Peter Schüler, 1st Lieutenant Peter Bickel, 2nd Lieutenant Ludwig Wollmerscheid

1 Jäger Company

Captain Joseph Rohm, 1st Lieutenant Wilhelm Nies, Lieutenant Ernst Menzler

3 Jäger Company

Captain George Gerau, 1st Lieutenant Ludwig Dormann, 2nd Lieutenants George Zander and Waima Remy

5 Jäger Company

Captain Friedrich Weiz, 1st Lieutenant Theodor Kochler, Lieutenant Carl Macco

7 Jäger Company

Captain Ludwig von Preen, 1st Lieutenant Friedrich Giese, 2nd Lieutenant Joseph von Bonhorst

Flanker Company

Captain Carl von Waldschmidt, 1st Lieutenant Franz von Truschess, 2nd Lieutenant Wilhelm Best

2nd Battalion

Major Adolph von Nauendorf

Adjutant Captain Ludwig Schmidt

Grenadier Company

Captain Georg Theodor Alefeld, 1st Lieutenant Johann Braun, 2nd Lieutenant Ludwig Stahl

2 Jäger Company

Captain Carl Ebhard, 1st Lieutenant Heinrich Merten, 2nd Lieutenants Gustav Neuhof and Carl Emmel

4 Jäger Company

Captain Friedrich Schnelle, 1st Lieutenant Friedrich Rückert, 2nd Lieutenant Carl Trombetta

6 Jäger Company

Captain Peter Becker, 1st Lieutenant Heinrich Heusener, Lieutenant Christian Finkler

8 Jäger Company

Captain Heinrich von Normann, 1st Lieutenant Gustav Nies, Lieutenant Rudolf Braubach

Flanker Company

Captain Carl von Weitershausen, 1st Lieutenant Carl Rau, 2nd Lieutenants Heinrich von Gagern and Carl Zollman

Landwehr Battalion

Major Friedrich von Preen

Adjutant A. Franz Stamm

Grenadier Company

Captain Caspar Dern, 1st Lieutenant Peter Moureau, 2nd Lieutenant Wilhelm Franz

1 Jäger Company

Captain Philipp Heidt, 1st Lieutenant Carl Caesar, 2nd Lieutenant Heinrich Schirmer

2 Jäger Company

Captain Philipp Rohm, 1st Lieutenant Christian Gemmer, 2nd Lieutenants Carl von Eyss and Valentin Frank

3 Jäger Company

Captain Johann Oswald, 1st Lieutenant August Wagner, 2nd Lieutenant Carl Schweikart

4 Jäger Company

Captain Friedrich Rückert, 1st Lieutenant Adolph Rath, 2nd Lieutenant Georg Hammes

Flanker Company

Captain Carl des Barres, 1st Lieutenant Jacob Graf, 2nd Lieutenants Friedrich von Bock and Carl von Esch

2nd Nassau Regiment

Colonel Friedrich Wilhelm von Goedecke

Lieutenant Colonel Fr. Ernst Umbusch (at the depot in Mastricht)
Commanders of Battalions
1 Major Friedrich Sattler
2 Major Philipp von Normann
3 Major Gottfried Hegmann
Adjutant Majors: Captains Fr. Carl von Mülmann and Fr. August von Steprodt
Regimental Surgeon: Carl Friedrich Seebach
Regimental Quartermaster: Captain Franz Joseph Schreiner
Regimental Auditor: Captain Wilhelm Petsch
Battalion Doctors: Georg Meyer, Hermann Calmano and J. B. Cöls
Battalion Surgeons: Philipp Jamin, Edmund Coels, Albert Hoepfling, Dr Friedrich Hehner
Captains: Alexander Coustol, August Frensdorf, Friedrich Philipp Goedecke, Jacob Lissignolo (at the depot), Moritz Büsgen, Carl von Rettberg, Christian Wernecke, Johann Schmitt, Martin Theodor Kathreiner, Ernst Ebel, Ernst von Reichenau, Fr. Wilhelm Schlosser, Carl Keim, Franz Joseph Müller, Joseph Weilburg, Peter Trittler, Julius von Malapert, Joseph von Trapp and Ludwig Wirths
1st Lieutenants: Werner Wittig, Heinrich Ludwig Wilhelm, Carl M. Robert von Neufville, Carl L. Magnus von Holleben, Johann Müller, Johann Christian Harz, Wilhelm von Steprodt, Carl August Foudel, Wilhelm Eyring, Carl Vollrath Weber, Carl Hergenhahn, Johann Wiersberg, Peter Quint, Carl Dümmler, Andreas Harth, Heinrich Fuchs, Johann Georg Hoelzgen and Anton Hundhausen
2nd Lieutenants: Mathäus Müller, Georg Fries, Carl Goetz, Carl Jos. Bach, Heinrich von Schmiedern, Wilhelm Schumann, Johann Sossy, Wilhelm Nadouceur, Johann Rosenbaum, Mathias Leiter, Christian Pflug, H. Wilhelm Wagner, Nicolas Elsen, Wilhelm Goedecke, Franz Goedecke, W. Heinrich Jung, Friedrich von Trott, Heinrich Wenzel, Franz Ferdinand Cramer, Carl Fischer, Wilhelm Medicus, Carl Schmidtborn, Wilhelm Meder, Carl Reinhard Haeuser, Heinrich Krell, Philipp Hief, Wilhelm Humbel, Johann Geibel, Ludwig Volmar, Johann Christian Gehra, Wilhelm Weth, Franz Carl Stammel and Johann Heinrich Perzgen

No. 28 Regiment Orange Nassau

Colonel Prince Bernhard Carl von Saxe- Weimar
Quartermaster: Lieutenant Colonel August Wilhelm Oppermann
Assistant Quartermaster: 2nd Lieutenant Friedrich Adolph Winter
Weapons Officer: Philipp Christian Sartor
Clothing Officer: Franz Ludwig Seigneux
Regimental Surgeon: Friedrich Huthsteiner

1st Battalion

Lieutenant Colonel W. Ferdinand von Dressel

Major Carl Ludwig Sartor
Adjutant Major: Lieutenant Colonel Wilhelm Ludwig Clamberg
Battalion Surgeon: Albert Fritze
Captains: Wilhelm Bartmann, Philipp Friedrich Herborn, Abraham Carl Kaempher, Friedrich Christian Jeckeln and Eberhard Götz
1st Lieutenants: Wilhelm von Brender, Friedrich Schlarbaum, Heinrich Richter, Friedrich Müller, Friedrich Rath and Eberhard Engel (fell 16 June).
2nd Lieutenants: Ferdinand Conradi, Florus Stift, Johann Carl Raht, Fr. Jacob Chelius, Heinrich Schneider, Ludwig Vollpracht, C. August Friedrich Rubach and Friedrich Wenkebach

2nd Battalion

Lieutenant Colonel Ph. Schleyer
Major Wilhelm Vigelius
Adjutant Major Heinrich Wald
Battalion Surgeon : Albert Jacob Gustav Doering
Division Surgeon Eberhard Neuendorff and Franz Mauer
Captains: Johann Pfaff, Jacob von Bierbrauer, Gustav Wilhelm Reusch, Amoenus Rommershausen and Carl Hartmann
1st Lieutenants: Balthasar von Rühle, Friedrich Ernst Ebhard, Johannes Post and Johann Erfurt
2nd Lieutenants: Friedrich Hauesler, Robert von Canstein, Andreas Benedict, Adolph Keller, Christian Eberhard, Wilhelm Heussler and Heinrich Carl Georg

Orange Nassau Volunteer Jägers

Captain Emilius Bergmann
I have been unable to trace the names of any other officers with this unit.

Depot at Dillenburg

Majors von Reichenau and Jacob Ludwig
Auditors Friedrich Stahl and Franz Eikstein
Titular Captain W. Scheurer
1st Lieutenants Wilhelm von Reichenau and Alexander Byrenheid
2nd Lieutenants Valentin Carl Becker, Friedrich Pagenstecher and Adolph Seebach

Depot at Duisburg

Captain von Kergefroy

BIBLIOGRAPHY

In any work of this kind, a great number of books have been used for reference, but a few have been particularly helpful and I list these here. The date of publication shown shows the version seen by me. The source and references for original unpublished material has been inserted at the relevant points for greater ease.

Adkin, Mark *The Waterloo Companion*, Aurum Press Ltd, London, 2001

Anon. *The Army List,* War Office, various edns

Anon. *The Waterloo Medal Roll*, ed. C. J. Buckland, Naval and Military Press, Dallington, 1992

Anon. *The Battle of Waterloo by a Near Observer*, 10th edn (2 vols), London, 1817

Beamish Ludlow, N. *History of The King's German Legion*, London, 1832–7

Boulger, D. *The Belgians at Waterloo,* London, 1901

Dalton, Charles *The Waterloo Roll Call*, Eyre & Spottiswoode, London, 1904

Dellevoet, André *The Dutch-Belgian Cavalry at Waterloo*, De Cavalerie, The Hague, 2008

Franklin, John *Waterloo Hanoverian Correspondence*, vol. 1, 1815 Ltd, Dorchester, 2010

Glover, Gareth *Letters From the Battle of Waterloo*, Greenhill Books, London, 2004

Glover, Gareth *The Waterloo Archive*, vol. II, Frontline Books, London, 2010

Miller, David *The Duchess of Richmond's Ball, 15 June 1815*, Spellmount, Staplehurst, 2005

Mullen, A. L. T. *The Military General Service Roll 1793–1814*, London Stamp Exchange, London, 1990

Ompteda, Baron Louis *In the King's German Legion*, H. Grevel & Co., London, 1894

Siborne, H. T. *The Waterloo Letters*, Arms & Armour Press, London, 1983

Siborne, W. *History of the Waterloo Campaign*, Greenhill Books, London, 1990

INDEX

of correspondents

INDEX

of officers and places mentioned in the letters